P9-DIG-961

# Civil Rights
## and
# Social Wrongs

Published in Association with
The Balch Institute for Ethnic Studies

THE BALCH
INSTITUTE
FOR ETHNIC STUDIES

# Civil Rights
# and
# Social Wrongs

## Black-White Relations Since
## World War II

EDITED BY
JOHN HIGHAM

The Pennsylvania State University Press
University Park, Pennsylvania

Library of Congress Cataloging-in-Publication Data

Civil rights and social wrongs : Black-white relations since World War II /
edited by John Higham.

    p.      cm.
Revised papers of a symposium presented at the Balch Institute for
Ethnic Studies, Philadelphia, Pa., during Oct., 1994.
"Published in association with the Balch Institute for Ethnic Studies."
Includes bibliographical references and index.
ISBN 0-271-01709-0
    1. United States—Race relations—Congresses.  2. Afro-Americans—Civil
rights—History—20th century—Congresses.  3. Pluralism (Social sciences)—
United States—History—20th century—Congresses.  4. United States—Social
conditions—1945–  —Congresses.  I. Higham, John.  II. Balch Institute
for Ethnic Studies.
E185.615.C584   1997
327.73—dc21
                                                97-8568
                                                  CIP

Copyright © 1997 The Pennsylvania State University
All rights reserved
Printed in the United States of America
Published by The Pennsylvania State University Press,
University Park, PA 16802-1003

It is the policy of The Pennsylvania State University Press to use acid-free paper
for the first printing of all clothbound books. Publications on uncoated stock satisfy
the minimum requirements of American National Standard for Information Sciences—Permanence of Paper for Printed Library Materials, ANSI Z39.48—1992.

# Contents

# PART FOUR: TOWARD THE FUTURE

# Preface and Acknowledgments

For a quarter of a century, The Balch Institute has dedicated itself to the mission of promoting greater intergroup understanding through the following unique perspectives: nationally significant museum, library, and archive collections representing more than eighty ethnic groups; more than seventy museum exhibitions; and educational programming for all ages, including symposiums and publications.

The Institute's work bridges diverse audiences and academic disciplines and promotes recognition of commonalities as a means of learning to respect differences.

This assessment of the present state of black-white relations in the United States looks backward and forward: backward to the changes the twentieth century has wrought in the old and troubled connections between Africans and Europeans in this western world, and forward to the further initiatives that still must come. The civil rights movement of the 1960s provides our point of departure.

The resulting symposium, which The Balch Institute for Ethnic Studies convened in Philadelphia in October 1994, was part of a two-day program marking the thirtieth anniversary of the Civil Rights Act. The first day featured a celebratory luncheon at the Down Town Club. There Barbara Jordan received the 1994 Balch Award for outstanding contributions to intergroup understanding and human rights. In closing, a combined choir from two African American churches brought a tear to the eye and a lump in the throat of many in that great company.

The second day was for the symposium. From both races it assembled the most thoughtful authorities we could enlist to consider the gains and failures in race relations since 1964. Most especially, the participants were asked, in the title of the event, "Is There a Dream for Today?" How can the basic spirit of the civil rights movement be revitalized and redefined?

With that as our goal, we sought a range of opinion—not an unlimited range to be sure, but a relevant diversity. To stimulate communication we needed moderate voices rather than confrontational ones, voices that could be heard in churches, classrooms, and civic agencies as well as in corporate boardrooms and private foundations. In the interest of a fully founded colloquy, the editor has supplemented five of the presentations that were made that day with an equal number prepared by observers and outside authorities.

As a deliberation among scholars who are addressing a wide, unspecialized audience, a project of this kind connects the Balch Institute's mission to teach with its obligation to learn. In a period of increased intolerance, we need to continue the discussion about our multicultural society, identifying commonalities before we list differences. We are especially grateful to the William Penn Foundation for underwriting the event and for its ongoing support of the Institute's work. We all owe a special note of thanks to both John Haas and John Higham for the energy, commitment, and inspiration that made the symposium and this book possible.

John Tenhula<br>
President and CEO<br>
The Balch Institute

As editor, I must add my thanks to Werner Sollors and Kenneth Kusmer for their friendship and advice; to Hugh Davis Graham for a searching and immensely helpful critique of the entire manuscript; to an anonymous reviewer at the University of North Carolina for teaching me the inadvisability of neutrality when great issues are at stake; to Balch staffers Cindy Ferguson and Eric Pumroy for unstinting support; and to the National Humanities Center for a time of reflection and research during which the African American experience rose before me as the crucial challenge in understanding modern America.

John Higham

PART ONE

Trends in Race Relations

# CHAPTER ONE

# Introduction

## A Historical Perspective

## JOHN HIGHAM

No one can say for sure when the modern civil rights movement began. Like all deep changes in human affairs, it had numerous antecedents and a long gestation.

Conventional wisdom has often singled out a historic decision of the U.S. Supreme Court as the catalyst of a mass movement. In 1954 the Court in *Brown v. Board of Education of Topeka* declared unanimously that the South's customary separation of black from white systems of education was unconstitutional. This sweeping order, calling for the desegregation of American public schools, marked the culmination of twenty years of litigation by the largest and most prestigious black organization, the National Association for the Advancement of Colored People.

Founded in 1909 by a small, predominantly white band of upper-class reformers, the NAACP concentrated from the outset on investigating and contesting infringements of the rights of black people.[1] Its patient building of the legal foundations of modern civil rights required the continuous collaboration of black lawyers and white judges. The career of the NAACP's chief advocate, Thurgood Marshall, suggests how closely the two elites could work together. After successfully arguing twenty-nine cases before the Supreme Court, Marshall was himself elevated to that august bench as the nation's first black Supreme Court justice. He was "Mr. Civil Rights."

Although the *Brown* decision was a great victory, its aftermath makes clear how insufficient an agreement between elites can be in changing a social order. *Brown* did not by itself desegregate many schools, nor did it call forth a triumphant crusade. Instead, it provoked overwhelming resistance in the South and only tepid interest in the North. The number of northern and western congressmen willing to sponsor civil rights legislation actually declined steadily from a peak in 1952 to a new low in 1960. In the South the decision released a tidal wave of racial hysteria that swept moderates out of office or turned them into demagogues. State and local officials declined to obstruct a revival of the Ku Klux Klan. Instead, they employed every conceivable device to maintain segregation, including harassment and dissolution of NAACP chapters. The atmosphere of those post-*Brown* years was best summed up in Governor George Wallace's inaugural address in 1963. Speaking at a time when the system of segregation was beginning to crumble, Wallace announced that he would "draw the line in the dust and . . . say, Segregation now! Segregation tomorrow! Segregation forever!"

It was by provoking this confrontation that *Brown* contributed greatly to a civil rights mobilization. The Court's order galvanized white southerners to a resistance so furious that an equivalent energy and dedication inflamed the opposing demand for racial justice. From a merely sectional issue, civil rights was transformed in the early 1960s into an absolute national priority.[2] The Supreme Court had spoken, and the integrity of the nation was now at stake.

Before the awakening of the 1960s and the *Brown* decision that preceded it, a chain of causation points to earlier origins. Tracing the chain, we are led back to the period between the two world wars, when friends of civil rights often despaired of even incremental gains. Major changes seemed dreamlike in their remoteness. Still, the interwar years reveal the first noteworthy stirrings of racial democracy since the collapse of Radical Reconstruction.

Perhaps the beginning of it all was in a migration that awakened new expectations among the most downtrodden black people in the nation. In the early twentieth century the largely rural black population of the South existed in a state of subjugation, many of them at the margin of subsistence. Trapped on the land by debt and ignorance, ravaged by disease and malnutrition, and subject to extremely punitive social controls, they had fallen in some ways below the condition of their forebears.[3]

Nevertheless, they had one great freedom that the slaves had lacked. They could move away. Many did just that when World War I abruptly cut off the European immigration on which America's industrial heartland had relied. As word of labor shortages in northern cities spread, an answering thrill of hope for freedom and personal dignity ran through the rural South.[4] The southern migrants soon learned, in the words of Langston Hughes, that the road north was "no crystal stair." But it affected everything that followed. It shifted the center of black America from a somnolent country-side to dynamic cities, and it imbued the migrants with a new independence and even militancy. From the "Great Migration" (1916–30) onward, the descendants of the slaves were truly a people on the march.

In the forefront of the march were musicians, bringing an African American cultural heritage from New Orleans and other southern locales to the nightclubs, ballrooms, and recording studios of Chicago and New York. Early on, the new music and uninhibited dance steps made an ecstatic appeal to semi-liberated white youths who joined Harlemites in "stompin' at the Savoy." Before long the big swing bands of the 1930s commercialized jazz and the blues. Their music gave blacks a commanding role in shaping the popular culture of the nation.[5] Never before in the United States had blacks and whites worked together as co-equals.

This is a small but telling example of the interracial synergies that drove the cause of civil rights during the next three decades. In the 1920s the first efforts that had anything like a grassroots base started in the South with a Commission on Interracial Cooperation, which a white Methodist minister, Will Alexander, organized in 1920. Renamed the Southern Regional Council, it brought together black and white church people, teachers, and journalists in hundreds of local groups. They met simply to oppose violence and abuse of law-abiding blacks and to promote mutual respect. As yet very few southerners dared to criticize segregation.[6]

That came in the 1930s with the Fellowship of Southern Churchmen, the Southern Tenant Farmers Union, and a major growth in the membership and initiatives of the NAACP, which was due in no small measure to the enthusiasm of black women.[7] For virtually all whites, north and south, racial reform was a low priority. But black determination was growing, and in certain fields commonalities formed. Not only in popular music but also in organized labor and among an intellectual elite, the 1930s encouraged hopes for racial democracy.

Difficulties abounded, of course, especially in labor relations. Having gained a significant foothold in heavy industry through the protection and encouragement of antiunion employers, blacks viewed trade unions with understandable suspicion. White workers, for their part, despised blacks as pawns of the bosses, rivals in the job market, and threats to their own social status. At the same time, however, the Depression was so indiscriminately devastating that it fostered in the nation at large a sense of sharing a common burden and perhaps also a common destiny. Both class and national consciousness resisted racial and ethnic separateness. The large numbers of black workers in the mass-production industries made unionization imperative; the radical idealism of many labor leaders made an egalitarian perspective morally compelling. By using African Americans as organizers, electing them to prestigious offices, and including them in parties and dances, industrial unions such as the Steel Workers Organizing Committee gave some substance to a declared policy of "absolute racial equality in Union membership." Once the new unions became well established, many of them reverted to a covert defense of white supremacy, but the doors they had opened for blacks would not easily be shut.[8]

The literature of the 1930s also promoted a celebration of the "common man," although ambivalence blurred the identity of that mythic figure. On one hand, a passionate sympathy for the disinherited characterized the predominantly naturalistic fiction of the decade. On the other hand, it is hard to say how much of that sympathy applied to blacks. White novelists scarcely wrote at all about African American life, very likely because they knew so little about it and had not yet learned to value it. Whatever the reason, no one plumbed the mind and spirit of a helpless, victimized black man until a young black author, Richard Wright, produced *Native Son* at the very end of the decade. This solitary masterpiece suddenly illuminates what the widening social sympathies of the 1930s made possible. Wright found a readership that no African American writer before him had reached. When the Book-of-the-Month Club in early 1940 selected *Native Son* for its members, the literature of racial protest burst into mainstream discourse with unforgettable power.[9]

Less dramatically but more decisively, social scientists in the universities of the 1930s made a civil rights crusade all but inevitable. White sociologists and psychologists joined their black counterparts—those few who had gained admission—in research that totally discredited the racist assumptions of traditional scholarship. Gunnar Myrdal's *An American Dilemma*, commissioned in 1938 and published in 1944, capped a veritable revolution in thought.[10] Myrdal argued confidently that racism would gradually give way because it contradicted a higher morality, an "American Creed" of liberty, equality, and opportunity to which all Americans in some degree subscribe. Massively documented, the two-volume work seemed to confer the authority of science on the liberal nationalism that undergirded Myrdal's paradigm. In the late 1960s that paradigm would break down as its confidence in the triumph of national idealism shattered. But for twenty years or more it sustained all the advances of public policy on racial issues. It sealed the interracial alliance for civil rights.[11]

The fact that *An American Dilemma* was conceived in the 1930s and published in the 1940s aptly symbolizes the relationship of the depression decade to the racial progress of the war years. The era before Pearl Harbor, and especially the Great Depression of the 1930s, was crucial in shaping the spirit in which the war was fought. More than any previous war, World War II drew Americans together. But their wartime sense of a national community and a common purpose was built on earlier struggles and gains. By the time of World War II, democracy was slowly regaining an interracial dimension it had largely lost in the late nineteenth century.

To appreciate the significance of the interwar period, one need only compare the frame of mind in which Americans fought the two world wars. In the first war, fears of disloyalty and racial subversion prevailed. Democracy was implicitly for white men only. In the second, the nation was more ready for an egalitarian construction of the American Creed. Theoretically at least, democracy was for all peoples. The nation was a human multitude, but it could not yet be concretely visualized as multiracial. American soldiers were no longer "Yanks." They had become "G.I.s"—a pan-ethnic symbol of uniformity—rather than a gathering of races. Nevertheless, the invisibility of race in the popular culture of the 1940s was both a sign of significant improvement and a symptom of the guilt that hid its face in a war against a flagrantly racist enemy.[12]

The great buildup of defense production in 1940 had hardly begun when an avalanche of criticism from black organizations descended on the White House for tolerating racial discrimination in war industries. A. Philip Randolph, a prominent African American union leader, took brilliant advantage of the contradiction between discrimination and a democratic war effort. Going beyond the usual tactics of protest, Randolph in 1941 organized a huge nationwide march on Washington designed to publicize racial discrimination and possibly disrupt war production. The prospect of 100,000 black people descending on the Capitol, their banners declaring "We Loyal Col-

ored Americans Demand the Right to Work and Fight for Our Country,"
unnerved the administration. After resisting for weeks, Franklin D. Roosevelt signed a precedent-setting executive order banning discriminatory hiring within the federal government and by its suppliers. For African
Americans, Randolph's unyielding stance was an inspiring model. According to a leading historian of this period, it "catalyzed the supporters
of civil rights into a mass movement that could not be ignored."[13] Further
giant demonstrations during the war would undoubtedly have backfired.
But membership in the NAACP jumped nearly ninefold, and protests
against segregated public facilities in various southern cities displayed the
increasing restlessness of African Americans.

After World War II, as attention turned to domestic problems, the growing civil rights movement still had little access to the political system. That
is what it got from Harry Truman. A border-state president, Truman had
never before shown a special interest in race relations. Now he moved
decisively to solidify a coalition between liberal Democrats and black voters.

Truman's first step in 1946 was to create a solidly liberal panel of influential dignitaries, whom he called the President's Committee on Civil Rights.
Its stinging report, "To Secure These Rights," excoriated discrimination
and prejudice because they violated fundamental American ideals and dam-
aged not only blacks but other minorities as well, including Jews, Catholics,
American Indians, Mexican Americans, and Japanese Americans. Although
Congress was unmoved, Truman pressed ahead. In 1948, on his own authority as commander-in-chief, he ordered an end to racial segregation and
discrimination throughout the armed forces of the United States. He then
ran for reelection on a civil rights plank, which split the Democratic party.
By a very narrow margin Truman carried the election, in spite of losing
four southern states.

In making civil rights a major national issue, Truman gave voice to a
significant growth of moral awareness among the nation's elites. As a politician, he was also counting on the exploding population of blacks in northern
cities to offset the votes he would surely lose in the then "Solid South."
Blacks did indeed rally to Truman in 1948 in much greater numbers than
they had ever turned out for Franklin Roosevelt. In this evenly balanced
contest, black voters in three big swing states—California, Illinois, and
Ohio—produced an electoral college majority for "the man from
Missouri."[14]

Overall, the civil rights movement of the twentieth century rose like a multistage rocket on the Fourth of July—each phase setting off a more impressive one. Just as the Great Migration awakened and then disillusioned the mass of southern blacks, the Depression gave their discontent a fresh ideological thrust, World War II expanded it and added mainstream leadership, and in 1954 massive resistance to the *Brown* decision ignited an explosion. National elites played an essential role in all but the first of these phases. In the final, culminating stage, elites and masses merged.

This fourth stage began a year after the *Brown* decision, when a dignified, law-abiding seamstress named Rosa Parks, going home from work in Montgomery, Alabama, was arrested because she declined to give up her seat—just behind the white section—to a white man who was standing. Mrs. Parks was a Methodist and a person of unimpeachable integrity. Hardly a day after her arrest, the local black churches organized a boycott of Montgomery buses.

During an epochal year-long struggle, ordinary black people found in their churches a fortress that could shelter and inspire a militant movement. At the cost of unemployment and the risk of violence, the boycott demonstrated the power of collective action. It also brought to national attention the twenty-seven-year-old Martin Luther King Jr.[15]

No one else could match King's ability to inspire even the humblest of his people. Yet support from national elites remained indispensable. Under the pressure of bombings, injunctions, and sheer exhaustion, the Montgomery boycott was on the verge of failure when a Supreme Court ruling saved it by declaring the city's segregation ordinances unconstitutional.

Still, the victory was dazzling, and the fame it brought to King drew him outward to teach the ethics and tactics of nonviolence wherever people would listen. Here was a means by which courageous blacks in southern towns and cities could challenge the white power structure with their bodies, their loyalty to one another, and their communal institutions. The rank and file of southern blacks took heart. Hesitantly at first, but armed with a sense of invincible righteousness, young people—some mere high school students—risked their lives by moving into the front lines of protest and resistance. From boycotts the movement spread to drives for registering black voters, then to relentless sit-ins by courteous, well-dressed college students at department-store lunch counters reserved for whites only. Throughout these campaigns a small but vital minority of young southern whites shared the dangers and the brotherhood of an interracial crusade.[16]

Confrontations, accompanied by favorable court decisions, brought dramatic victories for desegregation in some southern or near-southern cities. In other places nothing changed. Every public school in three Lower South states remained completely segregated in 1960.[17] About the same time, a visit to Manteo, North Carolina, which I had never seen before, brought home to me the stunning extravagance of southern segregation. As my six-year-old daughter and I made our way down the main street to a doctor's office, the black people we passed stepped humbly into the gutter in order to ensure us a lordly, untouched passage on the ample sidewalk. On reaching the office, we found that African Americans were waiting patiently until all the whites were seen.

In still other places during those mid-century years, change came unheralded, almost invisibly, in little alterations of speech, behavior, and attitude, as if the old ways simply began to seem unreasonable and demeaning. As early as 1947, the Brooklyn Dodgers recruited Jackie Robinson, the first African American to play major league baseball. (Since the turn of the century, husky blacks had battled whites in the widely stigmatized sport of prize-fighting, but brawlers had never been admitted to the higher level of the "nation's pastime.") Among blacks Robinson's breakthrough converted an ingrained disdain for the major leagues into jubilation. Other white baseball club owners were reluctant to follow Branch Rickey's profitable disregard of the old taboo. Nevertheless, without quite knowing what they were doing, the owners and the fans together turned major league baseball into a great civic festival at which blacks and whites mingled and rooted for the home team. Few worried or even noticed that this ongoing integration of mass culture brought about a swift disintegration of Negro leagues and all-black movies, and that the same process would in time undermine African American newspapers. Meanwhile, leading urban newspapers paid their own quiet deference to a more egalitarian popular culture by dropping from news stories any gratuitous labeling of individuals by race.[18]

Looking back later at this atmospheric and largely invisible side of the civil rights movement, former segregationists sometimes wondered how it all came about. A Louisianan, talking to Robert Coles in the 1970s, pondered this question only a few years after a white reign of terror had peaked in Mississippi:

I never would have dreamed . . . that we'd come to this—the black people holding their heads up as high as ours everywhere you go in this town. It's been a revolution. Now that it's over, I can't figure out when it began and when it ended, how it all came to take place. All I know is that it *did* happen. . . . My wife too. We couldn't think of going back to the old days. We've forgotten how it was then. I'll not say that we're 100 percent for all the minorities. But we're living in a different time, and we have to go along with it, you see.[19]

Before this sense of an extraordinary transformation touched large parts of the South, the region underwent a climax of turmoil in the early 1960s. Occurring simultaneously in dozens of cities, sit-ins, picket lines, street demonstrations, and mass arrests displayed the dangers of civil disobedience. The most daring militants ventured beyond sit-ins. Their "Freedom Rides" on interstate buses, sponsored by James Farmer's Congress of Racial Equality, deliberately provoked mobs intent on upholding segregation. By defying local mores and paying the price in beatings and imprisonment, the freedom-riders riveted national attention. Meanwhile, in the North, other chapters of CORE took a lead in increasingly militant picketing and boycotts of companies that discriminated against black applicants for employment.

As the movement grew, what was primarily a middle-class protest attracted lower-class blacks as well. Always more unruly than the smaller middle class, lower-class blacks in the larger towns and cities of the late nineteenth century had fairly often clashed with the police, particularly over the arrest of other blacks.[20] The civil rights movement gave this largely suppressed anger a coherent focus and outlet.

At the same time, the strongly Christian ethos that Martin Luther King Jr. infused into the freedom struggle elevated it above a simple racial collision. "This is not a war between the white and the Negro," he insisted, "but a conflict between justice and injustice." A recent historian has noted that King's nonracial charity—his willingness to forgive the sins of the past—left open an opportunity for reconciliation between fellow southerners once the battle was won.[21]

One further factor gave a finally decisive push to the civil rights movement in the 1960s. This was the unstinting support it received from every branch of the federal government—executive, legislative, and judicial. Until 1963, Truman's successors in the White House took little initiative on civil rights; Congress took less. In the late spring of that year, however, John F. Kennedy abandoned equivocation. For five successive days television images of police brutality had traumatized public opinion throughout the nation: images of police with snarling dogs attacking throngs of screaming black children in the streets of Birmingham, Alabama. The Department of Justice, together with local business leaders, intervened to settle the immediate crisis, and Kennedy stepped forth as a belated but finally vigorous civil rights spokesman. Over the following months, Congress worked out an omnibus law designed to enforce virtually all the aspects of civil rights that were in contention. In both houses of Congress the measure received overwhelming bipartisan majorities. In the Senate the Republican leader, Everett Dirksen, bestowed a sententious blessing. Civil rights were, declared this pillar of northern conservatism, "an idea whose time has come." On the crucial vote in the Senate, all the non-Southern Democrats voted in favor and only three Republicans from states outside the South and Southwest joined in opposition. Beyond that extended South, the principles of civil rights commanded something like a national consensus.[22]

The Civil Rights Act of 1964 shattered the legal defenses of segregation by greatly enlarging the authority of the federal government to take action in behalf of minority rights. New agencies such as the Equal Employment Opportunity Commission were created to root out discrimination in employment based on race, color, sex, religion, or national origin. The Justice Department was authorized to initiate suits against discrimination in public accommodations and in public schools. The U.S. Office of Education was charged with helping school boards to carry out desegregation plans. Especially forceful was Title VI, which empowered the Justice Department to cut off federal funds to any organization, state or private, that engaged in discriminatory practices.

What the new law left unbreached was the South's traditional battery of restrictions on voting rights. Into that direction Martin Luther King quickly turned the mounting strength of the civil rights movement. At Selma, Alabama, in March 1965, a bloody confrontation over racial disenfranchisement erupted between a choleric sheriff and marchers gathering from all over the United States. A detachment of Alabama state troopers, wielding bullwhips and shrieking Confederate yells, drove into the defenseless marchers. The new president, Lyndon Baines Johnson, called up 1,800 National Guardsmen to protect the procession, which swelled into an enormous, triumphant march on the state capitol. In national opinion the legitimacy of the southern resistance to equal rights was broken.

Johnson's attorney general was already preparing what became the Voting Rights Act of 1965, designed to override local and state obstacles to voting. The act prohibited local registrars from using literacy tests or other devices to keep citizens away from the polls. Under certain conditions the new law authorized federal examiners to compel the registration of qualified applicants. This measure, and subsequent extensions of its provisions, wrought a dramatic increase in voting and office-holding by African Americans. The number of black elected officials in the South rose from about 70 in 1965 to 1,600 ten years later.[23]

This was still a very small fraction of the total number of elected officials in those states. But after the mid-1960s the South tired of strife. Its self-inflicted wounds even underwent a partial healing. The idea of integrated education gained wide acceptance, especially after the Supreme Court in 1971 ordered a large-scale program of busing throughout the countywide school district for Charlotte, North Carolina. With a surprising degree of white cooperation, the South had become the nation's most integrated region. Before long, repentant racist demagogues like George Wallace were angling for African American votes and sometimes gaining reelection that way. Meanwhile, the huge migration of southern blacks to the North and West reversed itself. In the second half of the 1970s a return migration to the South outnumbered departures by two to one. Many of the back-trackers said they were drawn southward not only by cheaper living but also by greater friendliness and personal security in the region they had earlier fled.[24]

After 1965 the ongoing struggle for school desegregation spread rapidly across the North and West, where injustice was less blatantly formalized and legal remedies therefore less available and efficacious. Expansion literally exploded the civil rights movement, turning what had been a loosely organized crusade into something more like an upheaval or an earthquake. The breakup began during the euphoria of the great victories of 1964–65. With the assassination of Martin Luther King in 1968 it became irrevocable. Lawrence Fuchs, in Chapter 3, tells the story of this splintering and of the emergence of new black spokesmen "who did not talk the language of civil rights." To Fuchs's account it may be helpful to add that the breakup of a more-or-less unified movement into a more volatile, hydra-headed rebellion was due at least in part to the widening of its social base.

Although the classic goals of the civil rights crusade were universal, they paid off most directly in status and dignity for the black middle class. Already rising in material terms, the middle class chiefly demanded the respect and protections due to every individual regardless of origins or group identities. In realizing those foundational principles, the extraordinary gains the civil rights movement was making—at least through 1965—raised expectations of accelerating social integration in the foreseeable future. One of the leading authorities on race relations, for example, predicted in 1962 that over the next three decades racial enmity would decline to the minor level of Catholic-Protestant prejudice. Astonishingly, whites as well as blacks in the 1960s anticipated rapidly continuing racial progress. Asked to designate the most important national problems, respondents in a 1963 survey of public opinion named civil rights and race relations more often than any other problem, and in contrast to previous surveys a substantial majority of white respondents endorsed integration of public schools.[25] That was where the next step would be taken.

In the midst of these glowing visions of equal rights and opportunities, however, lower-class blacks in the cities of the North and West felt an overwhelming deprivation. They knew that job discrimination was pervasive, that the great faraway victories for civil rights were making no difference in their own daily lives, and that their better-off neighbors were joining the exodus from choking cities to green, segregated suburbs, leaving the black masses penned in decaying ghettos. In truth, the black population of major northern cities had become more isolated from whites in every decade after 1910, and undoubtedly more hostile to external authority. Martin Luther King's eloquent March on Washington address in 1963 summed up the problem of relative deprivation in an ever more affluent society: "The Negro lives on a lonely island of poverty in the midst of a vast ocean of material prosperity and finds himself an exile in his own land."[26]

Two further factors made northern ghettos more explosive in the mid-1960s than ever before. One was the extraordinarily vivid and pervasive impact of a new medium. Along with horrendous scenes of racial conflict in the South, television brought into every living room what one commentator has called "the voluptuous festival of American excess."[27] Paradoxically, the electronic revolution bombarded black youths daily with fantasies of hedonistic self-indulgence among whites just when actual contact between the two races in northern cities was reaching its lowest point.

The anger and envy that a crass culture of affluence provoked was supercharged by a second factor that intensified all of the constrictions of ghetto life. From 1940 to 1970 a second great migration from the rural South—far larger than the Great Migration of the World War I era—swelled to bursting the black ghettos of the urban North and West. More concentrated than any other internal migration in American history, the southern exodus now was less a quest for opportunity than an uprooting: a ruthless displacement from the countryside by agricultural mechanization.[28] The resulting inundation of inner cities forced a huge expansion of black neighborhoods. While panic spread in the white ethnic communities adjoining them, the migrants found themselves locked into the "hypersegregation" that Douglas Massey describes in Chapter 5 below. This drastic isolation fueled an alienation and a sense of powerlessness that erupted in the appalling ghetto riots of 1964–68.[29]

The outbreaks in northern cities in the mid-1960s marked a new stage in black-white relations. Summer after summer, from coast to coast, a cumulative total of more than one hundred major riots and innumerable smaller ones inflicted incalculable devastation in black neighborhoods, largely through fire and looting. In addition, the fierce hostility that rooftop snipers and rock-throwing youths displayed toward firefighters and undermanned police units brought home to white America the depth of this civic crisis— the most traumatic since the Civil War era. What the crisis might portend was difficult to grasp, however, and its long-term significance has never been carefully studied.

There was, of course, an inescapable continuity with the civil rights struggle in the South. The glowing examples of heroism and success set by southern civil rights activists spurred northern blacks to demonstrate that they too could defy white authorities and get away with it. Actually, for several years before the riots, strident forms of social action, partly borrowed from the South and partly devised by a growing black nationalist movement, had broken out in northern cities.[30]

Also, southern experience weakened the initial responses of northern officials to provocative incidents. The general public outrage at repressive police tactics in the South made northern authorities hesitant to intervene decisively at an early stage before disturbances got out of hand. When the police did respond forcefully, their long-standing reputation for brutality further inflamed the mobs. Loss of life was heavy. The racial disorders recorded from 1965 to 1969 left about 250 persons dead and 83,000 under arrest.[31] In contrast, the largely nonviolent character of the southern protests had kept casualties and destruction of property at a relatively low level.

Perhaps the greatest difference between the southern crusade and the northern disorders was in the programmatic character of one and the aimlessness of the other. The riots had no visible leadership, no positive or articulated goals. They were even less purposeful than the characteristic race riot of the past, in which a crowd would gather to kill or drive away people of a different origin, or to protest violently a government policy. In the northern riots of the 1960s blacks never marched on civic centers or other symbols of authority, nor did whites and blacks battle in the streets or invade each other's territory. Not once, the Ford Foundation reported, did blacks rise up spontaneously to beat and kill whites, as they would in Miami in 1981 and in later outbreaks.[32]

During the northern riots, whites shrank from the areas of disturbance—except for young thrill-seekers, who sometimes joined exuberantly in looting and shooting. Typically, an incident of alleged police misconduct would spark a rampage by underemployed young blacks hanging out in the neighborhood, who felt little identification with any local community, little hope of improving themselves, and a great deal of hostility to white police and merchants. This could quickly escalate into attacks on white-owned stores, then into a massively indiscriminate destruction of entire blocks and neighborhoods. In Detroit, for example, 2,509 stores were looted, burned, or destroyed, including 611 supermarkets and food stores, without much discrimination between black and white businesses.[33] The riots could therefore be seen partly as criminal carnivals—and all the more plausibly because they coincided with an unprecedented increase of violent crime, which in turn was connected with a raging heroin epidemic that was ravaging black ghettos. From then on, in the culture of the street, guns were a luring symbol of manhood.[34]

The press did not help. It spread groundless rumors of great revolutionary conspiracies. It persistently played down the involvement of white teenagers in the looting. It largely ignored the middle-class blacks who came out in the streets to guard property, to protect firefighters from the mobs, and to help people who were lost or homeless. One study has estimated that 11 percent of the population in riot areas took part in the disturbances, while 16 percent opposed them.[35]

Whatever the role of crime, drugs, and alienation, they cannot account for an immense irrationality: the self-destruction of housing in terribly congested neighborhoods. Here, perhaps, we come back to the tragedy of the Second Great Migration. A revolution in agriculture was driving literally millions of southern blacks into urban enclosures that were far more confining and dangerous than the familiar world they had left. Although the newcomers may not themselves have figured largely in the riots, their destabilizing invasion exacerbated all the other problems of the ghetto. The fires of the mid-1960s were acts of orgiastic release on the part of young men who needed to do something for themselves but did not know how.

Early public reactions to this enormous urban convulsion were aston-ishingly muted. Among whites no overt backlash materialized, perhaps in part because the riots never touched a major civic institution or a visible group outside the afflicted areas. Instead of public anger, one remembers shock, sympathy for the rioters' desperation, and much anxiety about the future. The anxiety was immediately evident in a scramble on the part of business leaders and foundations to listen to black nationalists and to fund their projects.[36] Articulate opinion carefully refrained from censoring the ghetto-dwellers for destroying their own neighborhoods.

No extraordinary measures followed. A bipartisan commission appointed by Lyndon Johnson painted a gloomy prospect of "extreme polarization" between a white society located outside of large central cities and "a Negro society" concentrated within those cities. To prevent that polarization, the commission proposed sweeping enlargements of federal programs to create jobs, provide housing, improve schools, and sweeten welfare. Chimerical in their scope and never given official endorsement, the recommendations were largely ignored.[37] Nevertheless, executive agencies and the federal courts moved forward for nearly a decade with the racial remedies they had in hand before the upheaval. Racial liberalism was still ascendant, and at least until the mid-1970s economic and educational equality between the races advanced.

On young blacks the riots left a far deeper mark. Shoot-outs with police, and the ensuing unwillingness or inability of authorities to offer dramatic new ways of reversing the deterioration of life in the ghettos, stoked African American anger. Even before the riots started, the attitudes that crystallized in 1966 in the slogan "Black Power" were gathering force in the fiery speeches of Malcolm X and the radicalization of young black activists in the civil rights movement.

The meaning of the slogan was never precise. For some it meant rebellion, separation, or exodus from white America. For others it stood for little more than a sharply heightened ethnic solidarity. Essentially, Black Power was a call for racial self-determination. It repudiated integration as an unde-sirable goal and cooperation with liberal whites as an enfeebling tactic. Demanding "real" power for more autonomous black communities, the Black Power movement concentrated on building racial pride, strength, and a distinctive culture.[38] This was a frontal attack on the spirit, methods, and aims of the civil rights movement. It involved a rhetoric of deliberate provocation against white allies, as when the most aggressive black activists attacked Jewish support for Israel and demanded from liberal white churches $500 million in reparations under pain of "long years of sustained guerrilla warfare."[39] Many young blacks in northern cities, amid the ruins of their communities, heard these cries as a vivifying declaration of war.

While the attitudes associated with Black Power flourished, the programs it promoted shriveled. Concrete projects—political, military, and economic—went nowhere. They lasted hardly more than a year or two. By 1973, as an identifiable, organized movement, Black Power was just about dead. However, it had launched a wider, generational rebellion, for which it was both a model and the first major expression. The youthful vigor, confrontational style, and cultural assertiveness that Black Power popularized among young blacks was speedily taken up by feminists, college students, other ethnic minorities, and gay rights advocates. In their different ways, all these oppositional groups combined two underlying principles of the Black Power movement: a rejection of external authority and an overriding allegiance to an exclusive community.[40]

The ego strength that could come from believing that "black is beautiful" and from a corresponding sense of racial brotherhood can scarcely be doubted. Nevertheless, these benefits were won at a terrible price. For one thing, the demand for autonomy reopened and deepened a long-standing conflict in black America. Insistence on racial solidarity inevitably clashed with an ongoing yearning for integration. The new black culture was divided against itself. A second great cost was the damage that racial separateness, as it stiffened, would do to the larger civic culture. In all the liberation movements of the 1960s, hatred of external authority entailed a profound disillusion with an America that was now perceived as despicably repressive. In none of those movements, however, was the support of the people and the state so indispensable as in the cause of racial justice.

Although the growing disarray of the late 1960s ravaged the civil rights movement, it lived on as an institution entrenched in law and government, pressing where it could for further reforms, and enjoying substantial public support or at least acquiescence. As Lawrence Bobo reports in Chapter 2, public opinion polls showed a rising acceptance of desegregation until the mid-1970s.[41] The white liberals and radicals who lost their place in predominantly black organizations remained for the most part staunch sympathizers. They found plenty to do in the parallel movements for empowering other groups that were suffering from collective disadvantages of origin or inheritance. Instead of taking offense, New Left students theorized that coalitions and alliances could be preferable to a single, unifying movement.

While these roiling crosscurrents were hitting the universities, civil rights supporters pressed on to desegregate the public schools in northern cities. There the struggle focused on "de facto" segregation, which arose basically from the real-estate market—not from laws as in the South. As Douglas Massey shows so tellingly in Chapter 5, residential segregation was the most formidable and damaging of all the inequities that constricted the life chances of African Americans. A final, major civil rights law in 1968, banning racial discrimination in the sale or rental of housing, led to incremental improvements, but not to a massive demand from either blacks or whites for thoroughgoing enforcement.[42] Many who wanted a more integrated society preferred an indirect approach through education: perhaps residential segregation could be eased and offset by desegregating the public schools. That was the crucial civil rights project in the late 1960s and early 1970s.

Federal courts had begun to rule that segregating public schools by neighborhood was unconstitutional. Judges reasoned that official policies in locating those schools, and assigning pupils and teachers, had reinforced racial boundaries. The remedy was to redistribute the students by busing or other means and thereby achieve a better racial balance. When such transfers were compulsory, they aroused fierce opposition from neighborhood associations, racists, libertarians, and anxious parents, all intensely resentful about the interference of "limousine liberals" who sent their own children to private schools. In ghettoized areas such as Harlem, where white children were simply not available for any kind of desegregation, black parents found themselves fighting not for integration but for local control of schools. These early struggles, pitting champions of "community control" against integrationists who wanted uniform standards in education, dramatized the new, disturbing cleavage between blacks and white (often Jewish) liberals.[43]

Nevertheless, the desegregation of schools lurched forward, driven in some places by lawsuits and court orders and in many other places by voluntary initiatives of educational leaders. In spite of intense resistance to busing, it brought a substantial long-term increase in integration outside of the largest metropolitan areas. Moreover, this classroom mixing has apparently had no ill effect on the achievement of whites and has had distinctly desirable effects on delinquency, dropout rates, and achievement-test scores of blacks. According to a study by the Rand Corporation, the average math and reading scores of black secondary school students increased 19 percentile points between the mid-1970s and 1990. Since the scores of whites rose much less, the gap between black and white students shrank substantially.[44]

Initially, the undesirable outcomes of busing were felt not within the educational process but outside of the schools in the surrounding turmoil that busing created. White ethnic neighborhoods fought federal court orders not just as racially undesirable but also as assaults by remote judges on the autonomy of the local community. Out of anger, residents either voted down school taxes and sent their children to parochial schools, or moved away.[45] In both cases public schools suffered. Then an exasperated and increasingly conservative Supreme Court in 1974 called a halt to the pursuit of integration through further enlargement of the scope of busing. In *Milliken v. Bradley* the Court ruled out any large-scale, compulsory transfer of students across the enormous divide of class and race between tough inner cities and genteel suburbs. The advance of school desegregation seemed stymied.

Yet it continued to grow—slowly—on a voluntary basis. Nearly all of the largest school systems have developed "choice" programs that now attract more than a million students to strategically located "magnet schools." Through their special offerings, these schools induce parents to send their children by bus to racially mixed schools that are not perceived as a threat to segregated neighborhoods.[46] Residential segregation of blacks in large American cities remains nearly as high as it was when the Fair Housing Law of 1968 was passed. But the mingling of schoolchildren on neutral terrain has become widely acceptable.

Aside from busing, the other remedy for racial discrimination that emerged in the 1960s and made headway in the 1970s was "affirmative action." Although indirectly and rhetorically about rights, affirmative action was more directly an exercise of administrative preferences—first in behalf of racial minorities, and then in favor of other historically disadvantaged groups as well. There was nothing novel or constitutionally irregular about governments or private bureaucracies favoring a class of citizens who need special help. Consider, for example, the Freedmen's Bureau, which Congress created in 1866 to assist the newly freed former slaves in the conquered South, or the long history of federal water policy, tax laws, and veterans legislation—all of which singled out a particular group for government benefits.

What was new about affirmative action as a governmental policy in the 1960s was the extension of judicial power that it entailed. Traditionally, federal judges had defended constitutional rights against legislative intrusion. Now they handed down results that legislatures were not delivering. In some of its earliest efforts to enforce the Civil Rights Act of 1964, the U.S. Department of Justice turned to the courts for remedies that the laws left obscure. To make a lily-white craft union in New Orleans admit non-whites, the Justice Department secured a court order requiring the union's hiring hall to refer jobs to whites and blacks on an equal basis. From that small beginning, thousands of plans, orders, and decisions flowed in the ensuing years. In effect, judges and litigants pursued equal rights not just for individuals but for an increasing variety of aggrieved groups.[47]

In Chapter 3, Lawrence Fuchs sketches the opposition to affirmative action that became ever more vocal in the 1980s and early 1990s. Assertions of a *right* to preference by one group after another, Fuchs argues, have gradually entangled the courts in what he sees as a morass of conflicting legal claims. Rights should be universal, not preferential or group-specific. Those who take this view believe that a growing sense of entitlement to such "rights" on the part of many aggrieved groups is becoming too divisive for the good of society as a whole. Disputes over affirmative action are driving blacks and whites apart instead of bringing them together.

Erwin Chemerinsky, in Chapter 4, offers a different approach. He contends that the affirmative action argument, though divisive as presently constructed, is thoroughly wrongheaded. It counterposes rhetorical abstractions instead of analyzing actual social conditions. It does not recognize that policies called "affirmative action" employ very different means in addressing different situations. The crux of the matter, Chemerinsky suggests, is not rigid rights but rather a massive, complex heritage of inequality that government is obliged to deal with. In discussions about affirmative action, he concludes, "the conversation must be about specific practices under particular circumstances."

Whether one leans toward Fuchs's or Chemerinsky's position, it is significant that both take pains to avoid simplistic, categorical judgments. Neither embraces the unqualified affirmations of affirmative action that were prevalent among liberal intellectuals and politicians twenty years ago.[48] Writing several months after the other papers in this volume were presented at the Balch Symposium, Chemerinsky takes aim not at Fuchs's moderate position but at the more sweeping antipathy to bureaucratic racial preferences that has spread far and wide since the symposium met.

Finally, in the only chapter in this book that has already been published separately, a leading demographer, Douglas Massey, makes a powerful argument for massive, multi-pronged governmental efforts to destroy the desperate poverty in racial ghettos. Massey might be construed to suggest that governmental affirmative action has suffered chiefly from a scattershot approach that awards small advantages to too many claimants and fails to address the common problems of American urban society.

It seems clear that various sorts of affirmative action contributed to hopeful advances in racial equality in the 1960s and 1970s because the public at large was mostly either acquiescent or supportive. The entire structure of affirmative action policies came about during an era when the life chances of African Americans were improving on many fronts and government was commonly seen as an appropriate vehicle for carrying that improvement forward.

The widening access of African Americans to better primary and secondary school education contributed in important ways to other gains they were making in the 1970s. Improved schooling enlarged dramatically the pool of young blacks who were eligible for recruitment by colleges and universities, which now vied with one another to increase the presence of nonwhite students on their campuses. As a result, between 1965 and 1977 the number of blacks attending college quadrupled, rising from 274,000 to 1,100,000. Federal grants went to colleges with a high proportion of minority students, while corporations developed an increasingly serious interest in recruiting African American graduates.[49] Aided by these educational stimuli and by more direct forms of affirmative action designed to counterbalance discrimination in employment, an expanding black middle class established itself securely in nonsegregated professions, in government bureaucracies, and in business. Reliable studies indicate, for example, that a middle class expanded from one-tenth of the black population in 1965 to one-third in 1990.[50]

Next to education, politics was the arena in which blacks made the most significant advances during the decade after the riots, and cities were the terrain on which those victories were won. The huge tide of black migration from the rural South to the urban North peaked in the 1960s. By the end of that decade, blacks in many cities were for the first time winning election to municipal councils and even the mayor's office. Concentrated by residential segregation, black voters prevailed in more and more precincts as whites retreated from the expanding perimeter of the urban ghetto. In spite of this social separation, the pragmatism of American municipal politics frequently enabled black candidates for mayor to gain office through alliances with white liberals and other groups that were dissatisfied with the political establishment.

Although the change that the new black politicos could bring about was limited, it was far from inconsequential. By 1990 most major cities had black mayors, and blacks had won congressional seats in all districts where they formed a voting majority. Inevitably, the officeholders shifted the political style of African Americans from unalloyed protest or apathy to the exercise of power as a legitimate interest group, and a new sense of civic participation kept hopes for change alive. In a 1984 opinion survey, 62 percent of blacks *disagreed* with the statement "People like me don't have any say about what the government does."[51]

This heightened civic involvement brought not only psychological rewards but also substantial material gains. In major cities the patronage systems that whites had long controlled now worked for blacks as well. Even as cities were laying off workers, thousands of public jobs—from department heads to sanitation workers—passed into the hands of African Americans. Affirmative action plans, authorized in Washington, nourished minority businesses through contract set-asides; and in the early 1970s federal subsidies for construction of public housing provided an additional windfall.[52]

What African Americans accomplished in the late 1960s and the early 1970s in education, social standing, and political clout came at a significant cost. It contributed to the breakup of the original civil rights movement, based on collaboration between whites and a largely unified black community. The benefits of these later years went so disproportionately to a thriving middle class that escaping from the ghettos took precedence over organizing them. Simultaneously, the gains that middle-class blacks were making on some levels made all the more painful the tenacity of discrimination in housing and prejudice in everyday life. In short, the revolution of rising expectations was once more, in the mid-1970s, heightening racial antagonism.

But blacks as a people, for all of their gains, no longer held the particular advantages that had energized them a decade before. Now there was a paucity of charismatic leaders, a shrinking company of allies, and no agreement on what to do. One result was a hatred of whites, which spilled out initially in the rhetoric of black power and then spread as the pace of racial advancement slowed. Truculence on one side and irritation on the other—together with crime in the streets and disorder in the public schools—aggravated a massive flight of whites from big cities. The twenty largest cities of the Northeast and the Midwest lost 24 percent of their white population in the 1970s. Even on college campuses, whites and blacks were disengaging, turning inward to their own familiar communities. As early as 1967, black college students were declining invitations to join established fraternities and instead insulating themselves in their own societies. By 1972 the quest for racial solidarity had produced at many major colleges and universities a near-total segregation between white and black students outside of classrooms.[53]

The general sense of a retreat in race relations gained credence from larger changes in American culture and institutions, the most important of which was surely economic. Between the beginning of World War II and the mid-1970s the American economy enjoyed a sustained growth unequaled before or since in the twentieth century. Wages rose steadily for whites and blacks, for skilled and unskilled alike. The proportion of blacks living in poverty fell from 92 to 31 percent.[54] Federal and state support flowed to public housing and inner-city schools in what seems generous measure compared with today. Social Security benefits were repeatedly liberalized. Between 1965 and 1973, federal expenditures on public aid more than doubled.[55]

About the time of the oil embargo in 1973 the boom ended. Ambitious social programs in many cities fell under the axe of retrenchment. Both the real hardships and the blocked aspirations of the ensuing years revealed the fragility of the racial progress that abounding prosperity had sustained. The rapid growth of a black middle class slowed; its access to higher education declined. A federal task force investigating working conditions reported in 1974 the startling discovery that the most dissatisfied group of American workers were young blacks in white-collar jobs. Meanwhile, unemployment surged, conditions in urban ghettos deteriorated, and the proportion of poor black families headed by women jumped from 56 percent in 1970 to 70 percent in 1982.[56]

Of these unfavorable changes, the most serious was the rise of unemployment, especially among young black males in the inner city. Their crushing disadvantage inflamed, if it did not induce, nearly all the other racial maladies. Beyond the immediate effects of the business cycle, a fundamental shift in the urban labor market was placing these new claimants for work at an extraordinary disadvantage. American cities were losing the heavy industry that had employed masses of semi-skilled workers. Instead, a post-industrial economy based on the exchange of information and the provision of specialized services was emerging. For such work the black middle class was generally well suited, but a large part of the lower class was unqualified.

Crowded into isolated, inner-city ghettos with inferior schools, surrendering to hopelessness and crime, many dropped out of the labor force altogether. Many more worked intermittently, but proving to be unreliable, lost their jobs to immigrants whose eager availability was an ironic consequence of a major success of the civil rights movement: removing racial discrimination from the nation's immigration laws. It is little wonder that a summit meeting of fifteen black leaders in 1977 agreed that increasing job opportunities should be their top priority. That would have to take precedence over traditional civil rights goals.[57]

Lower-class blacks trapped in decaying urban slums were not the only segment of American society to feel the sting of economic change in the 1970s and after. Large sections of the white working class, together with its middle-class friends in modest Italian, Polish, and Irish neighborhoods, could see their jobs draining away also—sometimes to cheaper locations in the United States, often out of the country entirely. According to recent studies by the U.S. Census Bureau, the gap in median income between fully employed black men and fully employed white men has remained fairly constant since the early 1970s. Proportionately, however, white male incomes have fallen more than black male incomes.[58] Instead of sensing a common fate, each race blamed the other.

In the cities of the North, antipathy toward blacks among working-class whites and European immigrants went back a long way. It was deeply rooted in competition for jobs and housing and in fears of racial and moral pollution. But the hostility waxed and waned according to changing circumstances. Ignited by the Great Migration, it flared around the time of World War I. Under the egalitarian influences of the New Deal it receded, then rose again in the 1940s when migration from the South resumed on a massive scale. Once more in the mid-1960s, working-class racism lessened, this time in the face of a powerful national taboo. But it was never much below the surface. As the huge black migration to northern cities pressed relentlessly into adjoining white ethnic neighborhoods, panic at the prospect of dispossession was reinforced by the shrinkage of industrial employment.[59] Under these circumstances the political coalition that Harry Truman created—the coalition that made the victories for civil rights possible—came apart.

An early sign that white support for civil rights issues was weakening appeared in the election of 1968. George Wallace, running now as a third-party candidate for president, campaigned strenuously against the new civil rights agenda of preferences and quotas. Through such devices, he charged, government bureaucrats and arrogant liberal elites were pushing plain working people around. "They have looked down their noses at the average man on the street too long," Wallace thundered.

Four years later the Democratic National Convention did just what Wallace complained about. Meeting under a new set of rules that favored women, African Americans, liberal reformers, and young activists, the convention removed from the nominating process the congressmen, mayors, and party wheelhorses who represented the rank and file of white Democrats. The result was a catastrophic defeat in the 1972 elections, a defeat from which the Democratic party has never fully recovered. The special relevance of that campaign in the history of race relations was the opportunity it gave Republicans to put themselves forward as the true friends of individual rights for all—the party not of racism but of laissez-faire buttressed by decently conservative values.[60]

These are some of the events behind the swings in public opinion that Lawrence Bobo in Chapter 2 scrutinizes in detail, often on the basis of his own careful research. By closely examining sample surveys of racial attitudes gathered since World War II, Bobo has constructed an intriguing interpretation of continuity and change in white racism. Recognizing that people have become steadily more open-minded and egalitarian in the general principles they aver on issues of segregation and discrimination, Bobo finds a large and persistent gap between theory and practice. On implementing liberal principles through governmental action, most whites oppose the vigorous action that blacks consider essential. Bobo concludes that this growing unwillingness of whites to use government to reduce racial inequality masks a new, covert racism that may be driving blacks and whites further apart.

Bobo's thesis leaves some scholars unpersuaded. In contrast to the deeply pessimistic view of the strength of racism that became almost de rigeur twenty years ago, present-day social scientists argue about what constitutes racism and how much group interaction it explains. Without denying either the evil or the persistence of prejudice and discrimination, some doubt that a new racist ideology has emerged. Recognizing a growing public resistance to using strong government in behalf of disadvantaged groups, these writers see the abandonment of liberal reform not as evidence of a resurgent white racism but as symptomatic of a worldwide disillusion with the state. A belief in the capacity of governments to make a better world has faded everywhere, not just in American race relations.[61] Perhaps competition for scarce resources, an overwhelming revival of Americans' attachment to the ideal of personal autonomy, and a breakdown of trust and cooperation on both sides of the racial divide bedevil us at least as much as racism. What is undeniable in Bobo's account is his stress on the differences between black and white views of racial discrimination. Blacks habitually (though not universally) see discrimination as widespread, tenacious, deeply imbedded, and the root cause of their disadvantage and pain. It is always with them.[62] Whites, if well disposed toward blacks, are further from the experience. Most of the time they view race as one problem among many, or as too complex a problem to subsume under the single pejorative label, racism, and in any case as a problem that can continue to diminish. How these contrasting perspectives can dominate the reading of a single body of evidence was dramatically revealed in the nearly total racial division over the jury's verdict in the first trial of O.J. Simpson: exuberant rejoicing among blacks, incredulous dismay among whites.

After the great breakthrough of the 1960s and the conservative reaction of the 1970s, a kind of deadlock has ensued. By most measures the 1980s produced little or no overall improvement. The earnings of black men relative to those of whites stopped growing, and only in the 1990s has the horrendous rate of violent crime fallen appreciably. Female-headed households multiplied, but no more proportionately among blacks than among whites. The rate of unemployment for blacks stayed stuck at more than twice that of whites.[63] What did increase significantly for both races and for the nation as a whole was a disparity of income between the wealthy and the poor.[64] While the discussion of race raged on, this yawning economic inequality, now becoming greater than in any other industrial country, attracted little notice.

In spite of widespread public disapproval, affirmative action policies remained largely in place. Their tenacity can be attributed to ambivalent decisions by the U.S. Supreme Court and even more to support from two powerful interest groups. One effective champion has been a coalition of beneficiaries, the Leadership Conference on Civil Rights. During the 1970s inclusion of new immigrant groups, women, American Indians, and the disabled as legitimate claimants for affirmative action brought together more than 170 organizations within the Leadership Conference. Their vigorous lobbying has resonated with very substantial support from big business, delivered by the National Association of Manufacturers, the heads of many great corporations, and the *Wall Street Journal*. For business leaders, affirmative action means access to diverse markets and a larger pool of highly motivated employees, avoidance of expensive lawsuits, and preservation of social stability. The *Journal,* for example, has argued that national unity would be at risk in a caste society, with whites everywhere at the top of the pyramid and minorities down below. These pressures persuaded both Republican presidents in the 1980s—Ronald Reagan and George Bush—to abandon efforts to reverse affirmative action.[65] Thus, the racial deadlock persisted into the early 1990s in just about all areas save one. That was education.

What came to be called "multiculturalism" in the late 1980s is an educational program that requires pervasive respect for minorities and women and official validation of their distinctive sensitivities and heritages. Its touchstone is the promotion of "diversity," although it endorses only certain kinds of group identities. Under the milder label of "pluralism," multicultural sensibilities had been quietly spreading at all levels of the American school system since the 1960s. Not until the mid-1980s, however, did multiculturalism blossom into a passionate crusade, regarded by advocates as a message of redemption and by opponents as a formula for disaster. Why it erupted at a time of diminishing expectations has been puzzling. In Chapter 6, Nathan Glazer gives a persuasive explanation, grounded in his extensive knowledge of America's public schools.

Most of the argument over multiculturalism, Glazer points out, has focused on colleges and universities. There the concerns of women, nonwhite races in general, and academic entrepreneurs have shaped new curriculums and accompanying changes in research priorities and recruitment policies. By training his sights on primary and secondary schools, Glazer finds a root cause for the moral fervor that invested multicultural reforms. Those reforms were a desperate effort to overcome the continuing failure of education and affirmative action to bring the social and cultural gains that African Americans had expected from the civil rights movement. The reforms were also, I should add, an instance of a characteristically American resort to education when all else fails.

The stagnation of black progress in the 1980s was clearly evident in the poor performance of black children in urban school systems, which in spite of continuing efforts to the contrary were becoming more and more segregated. Other developments heightened the alarm that was rising among educators and foundation officials. The supply of teachers who could be effective role models for nonwhite children was threatened by statewide competency tests that most black applicants failed. At the same time, a new generation of white youth was entering high schools and colleges. Generally, these youngest teenagers knew nothing about the struggle for civil rights and were markedly less tolerant of black attitudes and behavior than their immediate predecessors had been.[66]

A simultaneous revival of immigration brought into American schools for the first time huge numbers of nonwhite children from Latin America and many from Asia. Some of them, especially the Hispanic contingent, needed recognition and motivation no less than native blacks.[67] Surely, thought many white liberals and black activists, a multicultural slant can engage and animate all the minorities.

Glazer writes as a realist, bowing to the inevitable. His emphasis is on human needs and why, in this instance, they cannot be denied. Diane Ravitch, who is also a notable authority on American schools, responds in Chapter 7 as an idealist, grounding her dissent from Glazer in the fundamental principles on which American institutions rest. One of those principles is the fluidity of groups and the importance of individual choice. Multiculturalism, as generally understood, teaches the fixity, separateness, and special value of minority cultures. It therefore misinterprets the common civic culture that unites all Americans. Glazer is impressed by needs that multiculturalism seems to meet at the moment; Ravitch looks ahead to a future in which, she believes, the common culture must and will prevail.

The last part of this book, titled "Toward the Future," widens the argument between Glazer and Ravitch. Ranging outward from the specific issues and the historical particularity of the preceding chapters, all three authors take a long-term view. All ground their reflections in persistent or recurrent features of American life. All seek to prepare us for what may come. Jean Bethke Elshtain, a social and political philosopher, joined the Balch Symposium as a silent observer, charged with writing a supplementary essay that would put our discussions in a larger context. How, we asked her, does the problem of race bear on the future of democracy? Gerald Early, an interdisciplinary literary critic and American Studies specialist, gave the keynote address. His task was simply to consider the issues and dilemmas our project was confronting and generally to speak his mind.

Writing in collaboration with her colleague Christopher Beem, Elshtain looks toward a refocusing of civic consciousness. Neither the cynicism and resentment that infest so many of today's opinion-makers nor the homogenizing triumphalism of the traditional melting-pot idea can arrest an erosion of civic spirit and trust, an unraveling of civil society. Americans can find guidance, however, in Alexis de Tocqueville's recognition long ago that autonomous communities are the strength of American democracy and in Randolph Bourne's depiction of a future America in which innumerable public and private groups freely weave a cosmopolitan nation. Here and in the teachings of Martin Luther King Jr. is a middle way between unity and diversity.

Our other generalist, Gerald Early, also has the whole span of American experience in view, but he is far more of a participant than a philosopher. His location is inside the racial maelstrom; his approach is interior. The issues that all the other speakers would treat as social, institutional, and theoretical problems—affirmative action and multiculturalism especially—Early confronts as inner conflicts within the hearts of a struggling people and within the soul of a nation burdened with a tragic history. Concentrating on paradox, irony, and insoluble contradictions, Early probes the "cunning" of a history that masks the dilemmas of race and nationality in ever-changing appearances. While Elshtain and Beem present a set of choices for Americans, Early sees an underlying continuity in American culture. Elshtain and Beem strike a note of troubled hope, Early sounds a chord of sorrow.

A third and last assessment of the big picture deals with how change takes place in American race relations. It extends the implicit argument of this introduction—namely, that the stagnation of today can be seen in a longer perspective as one phase of a spiraling history. Each major advance loops backward before another spiral arises. Yet the backward turn never returns us to the starting point of the previous phase. Both the surging gains and the bitter disappointments of race relations in the twentieth century have occurred before, and each time some advance toward racial equality has survived. Whether the spiral can recur in the twenty-first century, as it has from the eighteenth to the twentieth, is for each reader to judge.

CHAPTER TWO

# The Color Line, the Dilemma, and the Dream

## Race Relations in America at the Close of the Twentieth Century

LAWRENCE D. BOBO

At the dawning of the twentieth century W. E. B. Du Bois forecast that the defining problem of the twentieth century would be "the color line."[1] His analysis was penetrating. He wrote at a time when most African Americans lived as disenfranchised, purposely miseducated, and brutally oppressed second-class citizens. He wrote at a time when popular conceptions of African Americans were overtly racist, even among the well-educated white elite.[2] As we stand near the dawning of the twenty-first century, the problem to which Du Bois so presciently drew our attention appears no closer to a fundamental resolution in the United States or in much of the rest of the world than it did a century ago.[3] The color line endures.

Four decades after Du Bois's forecast, Swedish economist Gunnar Myrdal completed his monumental work, *An American Dilemma: The Negro Problem and American Democracy*.[4] He identified the conditions and status occupied by blacks and the conceptions of them held by their fellow white

The author wants to thank Mia Tuan and Susan A. Suh for their assistance in the preparation of this chapter.

citizens as a sharp value contradiction in the American polity. Yet Myrdal found grounds for optimism that "the American Dilemma" would be resolved in favor of equality and integration. The premium that the American value system places on individual freedom, equality of treatment, and justice, when coupled with the force of other social trends (for example, war-time mobilization, modernization of the southern economy, expanding educational opportunities), Myrdal reasoned, would gradually lead to the realization of true membership in the American polity for blacks. He did not conclude that the color line was an insurmountable divide in the American experience. Such pessimism Myrdal might readily have embraced, given its distinguished history in the writings of Thomas Jefferson, Alexis de Tocqueville, and Abraham Lincoln.[5] To Myrdal, however, the American Dilemma could and would be resolved.

Perhaps the most resonant voices of the American promise of freedom and equality, ironically, have come from mainstream black leadership and the day-to-day contributions and adaptations of the mass of black Americans. Although bearing the burden of the "color line" and of Myrdal's dilemma, African Americans have largely remained attached to American institutions and culture. To be sure, blacks do so out of necessity, but also it would seem with a good measure of hope. This hope was powerfully articulated in perhaps the single most important American oration of the twentieth century in Dr. Martin Luther King's "I have a dream" speech, delivered on the steps of the Lincoln Monument. Despite signs of growing pessimism, strife, and militancy in the post-1965 period, King continued to espouse his faith in this dream.[6]

My purpose in this chapter is to ask how racial attitudes and relations have changed in the United States. Does the pattern of change in the attitudes of white and black Americans suggest that a resolution of the problem of the color line is at hand? Do we have grounds to believe that the American Dilemma of race is no longer the great fissure in the American polity that it was five decades ago? How do black and white Americans view each other and relations between the groups? Or, to put it in more metaphorical terms, does the color line still divide us, does the dilemma still persist, and is the dream ever to be realized?

There are no simple answers to these urgent questions about American culture and institutions. But in some respects an important change in the tenor of the discussion about these issues has taken place. As the twentieth century draws to a close, we have entered a period of intensified reexamination of the problem of black-white relations and of racial and ethnic diversity in general for American society. The great anxiety and doubt emerging is evident from the titles of a number of prominent books, including Cornel West's *Race Matters*, Douglas Massey and Nancy Denton's *American Apartheid*, Lani Guinier's *The Tyranny of the Majority*, Arthur M. Schlesinger's *The Disuniting of America*, and Haynes Johnson's *Divided We Fall*.[7] By and large, however, these works still occupy a sort of mainstream American dialogue on race. Most of this work espouses, or at least implicitly adopts, an abiding faith in American values and institutions to eventually rise above the divisions of the color line.

More remarkable is the emergence in the mainstream of powerful voices of utter pessimism about race relations. Two such voices stand out. Andrew Hacker, in his provocative book *Two Nations: Black and White, Separate, Hostile, Unequal*, concluded that the United States confronts "a huge racial chasm . . . and there are few signs that the coming century will see it closed."[8] Civil rights activist and legal scholar Derrick Bell, in his book *Faces at the Bottom of the Well: The Permanence of Racism*, is a good deal more blunt. According to Bell, "racism is an integral, permanent, and indestructible component of this society."[9]

Neither book is insensitive to the enormous changes in the post–civil rights era in the status, conditions, and popular conceptions facing African Americans. Apparently momentous changes notwithstanding, Bell argues:

> But the fact of slavery refuses to fade, along with the deeply embedded personal attitudes and public policy assumptions that supported it for so long. Indeed, the racism that made slavery feasible is far from dead in the last decade of twentieth-century America; and the civil rights gains, so hard won, are being steadily eroded. Despite undeniable progress for many, no African Americans are insulated from incidents of racial discrimination. Our careers, even our lives, are threatened because of our color. Even the most successful of us are haunted by the plight of our less fortunate brethren who struggle for existence in what some social scientists call the "underclass." Burdened with life-long poverty and soul-devastating despair, they live beyond the pale of the American Dream. What we designate as "racial progress" is not a solution to that problem. It is a regeneration of the problem in a particularly perverse form.[10]

For both Hacker and Bell, the trends heralded as gains and progress by many analysts fall well short of genuine improvement in race relations.

Indeed, for them each apparent phase and form of racial change merely reconstitutes black oppression on new and more complex ground. When serious, committed, and unabashedly mainstream students of race relations begin to conclude that racial inequality and racism are essentially permanent features of American society, we should all attend very closely.

The review of information on changing racial attitudes discussed below will support three conclusions. These conclusions partly contradict, partly confirm, and of necessity reformulate the pessimism about race relations advocated by Hacker and by Bell. First, the available data suggest that the United States has experienced a genuine and tremendous positive transformation in racial attitudes.[11] A once predominant ideology of Jim Crow racism has, over the past five decades, steadily receded from view. Nonetheless, both Hacker and Bell are correct to talk of a modern problem of racism. The collapse of Jim Crow racism has not been followed by a full embrace of African Americans as true co-equals with whites, deserving of a complete measure of all the fruits of membership in the polity. Instead, a new configuration of negative racial attitudes has recently crystallized. This new cultural pattern of understanding the actual and normative position of blacks in American society is appropriately labeled "laissez-faire racism."[12]

Second, racial discrimination remains a barrier to blacks' full economic, political, and social participation in American institutions. The problem of racial discrimination today is less extreme, absolute, and all-encompassing.[13] Hence, I reject claims that only superficial change in the position of blacks has taken place. However, direct discrimination in jobs, in housing, and in myriad forms of interpersonal interaction continue to face African Americans almost irrespective of the social class background and achievements of the individual black person. In short, the significance of race in social life goes on.

This is an extremely nettlesome issue. Black and white Americans, the surveys show, could not be further apart in their thinking about the problem of discrimination.[14] Blacks perceive it, experience it, and feel it acutely.[15] They become frustrated when whites do not see the problem in the same way. Many whites see tremendous positive gains, cannot understand the steady litany of complaints, and have grown resentful and impatient.[16] Miscommunication and mounting resentments accumulate on both sides as a result.

Third, the problem of social breakdown occurring in poor urban communities has a strong racial overlay and increasing political potence as a device to mobilize voters at the local, state, and national levels.[17] The linkage in the minds of many white Americans between black culture and the problems of family dissolution, welfare dependency, crime, failing schools, and drug use may be setting the stage for a new period of deep retrenchment in civil rights and social welfare provision. All too often, a major subtext of campaigns about reducing welfare and fighting crime is a narrative about generally retaining white status privilege over blacks, and specifically about controlling and punishing poor black communities. This thinly veiled racial subtext of American politics is not lost on the black community. It feeds a growing suspicion and distrust among African Americans that white-dominated institutions may be moving toward overt hostility to the aspirations of African American communities.

# Patterns of Change in Racial Attitudes

The longest trend data from national sample surveys may be found for racial attitude questions that deal with matters of racial principles and the implementation of those principles. Principle questions ask whether American society should be integrated or segregated, and whether we should be a society that treats individuals equally without regard to race. Such questions do not raise issues of the practical steps that might be necessary to accomplish greater integration or to ensure equal treatment. Implementation questions ask what actions—usually by government, especially at the federal level—ought to be taken to bring about integration, to prevent discrimination, and to achieve greater equality.

## *The Decline of Jim Crow Racism*

The available survey data suggest that antiblack attitudes associated with Jim Crow racism were once widely accepted. The Jim Crow social order called for a society based on deliberate segregation by race.[18] It gave positive sanction to antiblack discrimination in economics, education, and politics. It prohibited race-mixing, especially in the form of miscegenation or racial intermarriage. It involved an etiquette of interaction designed to reinforce the inferior status imposed on African Americans. All of this was expressly premised on the notion that blacks were the innate intellectual, cultural, and temperamental inferiors to whites.

Survey-based questions dealing with racial principles essentially asked about the degree of popular endorsement of these tenets of Jim Crow racism. The evidence from national sample surveys of the white population show that at one time the Jim Crow ideology was widely accepted, especially among residents of southern states but outside the South as well.[19] Over the ensuing five decades since the first baseline surveys were conducted in the early 1940s, however, support for Jim Crow has steadily declined. It has been replaced by popular support for integration and equal treatment as principles that should guide relations between blacks and whites.

For example, whereas a solid majority, 68 percent, of white Americans in 1942 favored racially segregated schools, only 7 percent took such a position as early as 1985. Similarly, 55 percent of whites surveyed in 1944 believed whites should receive preference over blacks in access to jobs, as compared with only 3 percent who offered such an opinion as early as 1972. Indeed, so few people are willing to endorse a discriminatory response to either question that both have been dropped from ongoing social surveys. On both of these issues, once-pivotal features of the Jim Crow racist ideology—majority endorsements of the principles of segregation and discrimination—have given way to overwhelming support for the principles of integration and equal treatment.

This pattern of movement away from support for Jim Crow toward apparent support for racial egalitarianism holds with equal force for those questions dealing with issues of residential integration, access to public transportation and public accommodations, choice among qualified candidates for political office, and even racial intermarriage. It is important to note that the high absolute levels of support seen for the principles of school integration and equal access to jobs (both better than 90 percent nationwide) is not achieved for all racial principle–type questions. Despite improvement from extraordinarily low levels of support in the 1950s and 1960s, survey data continue to show substantial levels of white discomfort with the prospect of interracial dating and marriage.

Opinions among whites have never been uniform or monolithic. Both historical and sociological research have pointed to lines of cleavage and debate in the thinking of whites about the place of African Americans.[20] The survey-based literature has shown that views on issues of racial principle vary greatly by region (at least along the traditional South versus non-South divide), level of education, age or generation, and other ideological factors. As might be expected, opinions in the South more lopsidedly favored segregation and discrimination at the time baseline surveys were conducted than was true outside the South. Patterns of change, save for a period of unusually rapid change in the South, have usually been parallel. Level of education matters for racial attitudes. The highly educated are also typically found to express greater support for principles of racial equality and integration. Indeed, one can envision separating the white population into a multitiered reaction to issues of racial justice based on the interaction of level of education and region. At the more progressive and liberal end, one finds college-educated whites who live outside the South. At the bottom, one finds Southern whites with the least amount of schooling.

The degree of expressed support for racial integration and equality is also responsive to a person's age. Younger people are usually more racially tolerant than older people, where issues of principle are concerned. A small but meaningful part of the apparent generational differences in racial attitudes is attributable to the increasing levels of education obtained by younger cohorts.[21] As the average level of education has risen, so too has the level of support for racial equality and integration.

Howard Schuman, Charlotte Steeh, and myself argued that the forces underlying change might also be undergoing change,[22]—that is, they sought to decompose the changing attitudes into that portion of change that can be attributed to cohort replacement effects, or the impact of younger and more liberal generations increasingly replacing older, more conservative generations, versus the portion of change that reflected individual changes in opinion. They found that both processes contributed to the overall positive shift in racial principles. However, the pace of change slowed in the late 1970s and, they argued, was increasingly dependent on cohort replacement effects alone. Such a pattern suggested that the great positive changes associated with the civil rights movement and Black Power protest eras were diminishing.

More recent analyses continue to reveal individual level change and cohort replacement effects. Glenn Firebaugh and Kenneth Davis found that, between 1972 and 1984, changes in racial principles continued in a positive direction.[23] A slightly greater fraction of the change was due to cohort replacement effects, especially in the South. On some issues, such as racial intermarriage, they found only cohort replacement effects and a sharp slowing of positive change. In response to growing signs of racial tension and conflict on college campuses, Steeh and Schuman recently sought to determine whether younger age cohorts had shown any unique pattern of negative change.[24] They found that on most racial issues younger cohorts were still more liberal than their immediate predecessors and continued to change in a positive direction. The only evidence of negative trends occurred across the generations and reflected growing opposition to racial preferences, not to any of the general principle issues.

In short, the transformation of attitudes regarding the rules that should guide interaction between blacks and whites in public and impersonal spheres of life has been large, steady, and sweeping. Individuals living outside the South, the highly educated, and younger-age cohorts led the way to these changes. However, positive changes usually occurred across regions, age-groups, and education levels. At least with regard to racial principles, this change was so sweeping that Schuman, Steeh, and myself characterized it as a fundamental transformation of social norms with regard to race.[25] Analysts of in-depth interview material reached similar conclusions. Bob Blauner's discussions with a small group of blacks and whites living in the San Francisco Bay area led him to conclude:

> The belief in a right to dignity and fair treatment is now so widespread and deeply rooted, so self-evident, that people of all colors would vigorously resist any effort to reinstate formalized discrimination. This consensus may be the most profound legacy of black militancy, one that has brought a truly radical transformation in relations between the races.[26]

Some read this change as having far-reaching implications for transcending the color line and overcoming the American Dilemma. Based on their assessment of the available trend data, one group of survey researchers concluded: "Without ignoring real signs of enduring racism, it is still fair to conclude that America has been successfully struggling to resolve its Dilemma and that equality has been gaining ascendancy over racism."[27]

## The Emergence of Laissez-Faire Racism

The sanguine picture of change, however, changes substantially when attention shifts from principle to policy. Where issues of implementing the social changes needed to bring about greater integration of communities, schools, and workplaces are concerned, we find evidence of an important qualification on the extent of change in racial attitudes. Likewise, where issues of enforcing antidiscrimination laws and taking steps to improve the economic standing of African Americans are concerned, the survey data again point to significant bounds on the scope of positive change in racial attitudes.

At one level, it is not surprising that there are sharp differences in level of support between racial principles and policy implementation. Principles, when viewed in isolation, need not conflict with other principles, interests, or needs. At another, more concrete level, however, choices must often be made and priorities set. Particularly in the domain of racial attitudes and relations, there are large gaps between the principles most white Americans advocate and the practical steps they are willing to undertake to pursue those ends. For example, a 1964 survey showed that 64 percent of whites nationwide supported the principle of integrated schooling, but that only 38 percent believed that the federal government had a role to play in bringing about greater integration. The gap had actually grown larger by 1986. At that time, 93 percent of whites supported the principle of integrated schooling, but only 26 percent endorsed government efforts to increase the level of school integration. Analysis suggests that little of this disjuncture can be accounted for by distrust of government.[28]

Similar patterns emerge in the areas of jobs and housing. Support for the principle of equal access to jobs stood at 97 percent in 1972, while support for federal efforts to prevent discrimination in jobs had only reached 39 percent. A 1976 national survey showed that 88 percent of whites supported the idea that blacks have a right to live wherever they can afford, that only 35 percent would vote in favor of a law prohibiting homeowners from discriminating on the basis of race when selling a home.[29] While the sort of near-exact pairing of principle and implementation items that Schuman, Steeh, and myself were able to compare for the 1942–85 period is no longer possible with the available data, it seems likely that this disjuncture continues.

Implementation items not only typically exhibit lower absolute levels of support than principle items do, and less evidence of positive change, they also are less responsive to a number of other factors. There are smaller differences by age, education level, and region on questions of implementation. The lack of strong age-group differences, education effects, and regional differences implies that policy change in the area of race is not likely to witness the sort of great positive transformation seen for broad issues of principle.

Furthermore, the black-white divide on implementation questions is also sharp. Most of the implementation questions Schuman, Steeh, and myself analyzed showed majority—sometimes overwhelming majority—black

support for government action to bring about integration, to fight discrimination, or to improve the economic conditions of the black community.
Responses of whites were often a mirror opposite, with a clear majority
opposing such a role for government.

The black-white division of opinion is often sharpest on questions of
affirmative action. Bobo and Smith reported that 69 percent of white respondents in a major 1990 national survey opposed affirmative action in
higher education for blacks, while only 26 percent of blacks opposed it.[30]
An equally large gap between black and white views emerged for the question of affirmative action in employment. Whereas 82 percent of whites
opposed giving preference to blacks in hiring and promotion, only 37 percent of blacks adopted a similar position.

Bobo and Smith also attempted to determine whether the black-white
gap in opinions could be explained by differences in social class background,
political ideology and values, and racial attitudes.[31] Their analyses of opinions on several race-specific social policies showed that virtually none of
the black-white gap in opinion could be explained by social class background factors, that a small part reflected differences in political ideology
and basic beliefs about economic inequality, and that a somewhat larger
fraction was attributable to different racial outlooks. However, a substantial
difference in views persisted, despite controls for a wide range of factors.
This suggests, as myself and James Kluegel argue, that there is a set of
collective interests that divide blacks and whites on policy questions of
race.[32]

Part of the reason for the opposition of whites to policy changes favorable
to blacks may be found in the persistence of antiblack stereotypes. A 1990
national survey found evidence of widespread negative stereotypes of
blacks, Hispanics, and Asian Americans.[33] The study showed that whites
tend to perceive blacks as more likely than whites to be unpatriotic, violence
prone, unintelligent, lazy, and to prefer to live off of welfare rather than
being self-supporting. Fully 78 percent of whites in this national survey
adopted this position. Such high levels of negative stereotyping were found
because of a measurement procedure that did not force people to make
categorical judgments, but rather allowed the expression of differing magni-
tudes of group difference. Whereas an overall 78 percent of whites saw
blacks as more likely than white people to prefer to live off welfare, only
a small number understood this to be a stark difference. Most whites expressed only a small difference between the races in tendencies on this and
the other trait dimensions examined. The evidence of persistent negative

stereotyping is not at odds with evidence of positive change in racial principles. These data merely qualify the scope and meaning of those positive changes.

Negative stereotypes help explain the gap between principle and implementation described above and shed light on current racial tensions. The more negative stereotypes a person holds about blacks, the less likely he or she is to support affirmative action policies.[34] In addition, those with the highest negative stereotypes are strongly predisposed to maintain social distance between themselves and blacks. In sum, while Jim Crow racism has fallen into disrepute, images of blacks appear to have remained sufficiently negative to prompt many whites to reject affirmative action and to resist close association with blacks.[35]

Another factor contributing to black-white polarization on the policy solutions to racial inequality is a substantial difference in their thinking about the problem of racial discrimination. The available survey data suggest that most blacks see racial discrimination as a more prevalent problem than do most whites, as having a stronger institutional base than do most whites, and as carrying responsibility for the generally disadvantaged position blacks occupy in American society than do most whites. The black-white gap in thinking about discrimination may be the core factor underlying modern misunderstanding and miscommunication across the color line.

In their 1992 study of the Detroit housing market, Farley and colleagues asked a general question about how much discrimination blacks faced in finding housing wherever they want.[36] They found that 85 percent of blacks perceived "a lot" or at least "some" discrimination, compared with 80 percent of whites. While this difference is not large, they also found that blacks perceived discrimination as having changed little or gotten worse, whereas whites saw discrimination as declining. In addition, they wrote: "Blacks see much more institutionalized discrimination than do whites. . . . While 86 percent of blacks believe that blacks miss out on good housing because real estate agents discriminate, only 61 percent of whites believe this. When it comes to banks and lenders, 89 percent of blacks see discrimination, in contrast, to 56 percent of whites."[37]

Thus, although many whites acknowledge the existence of discrimination, especially in the housing market, they are much less likely than blacks to think of discrimination as having a systematic, institutionalized social basis.

A similar pattern emerges for data from a Los Angeles survey regarding the Rodney King beating and beliefs about the criminal justice system.

Immediately following the 1992 trial in Simi Valley that acquitted the four police officers charged in the beating of Rodney King, a survey conducted by UCLA asked residents of Los Angeles County whether they agreed with the verdicts. Some 96 percent of black respondents said they "disagreed" or "strongly disagreed" with the verdict, compared with only 65 percent of white respondents—a difference of 31 percentage points. When subsequently asked whether blacks usually fail to receive fair treatment in the courts, the difference grew even larger. Some 80 percent of blacks "agreed" or "strongly agreed" that blacks usually do not get fair treatment in the courts, compared with 40 percent of whites.[38]

Other studies have asked respondents to explain the general pattern of socioeconomic inequality between blacks and whites.[39] These studies indicate that blacks are far more likely to see racial discrimination as a major factor explaining black-white socioeconomic inequality than do whites. Whites lean heavily in the direction of attributing racial inequality to the individualistic shortcomings of blacks—that is, to assert that blacks simply do not exert sufficient effort or willpower to "make it" on their own.

According to Bobo and Smith, laissez-faire racism is a new form of racist ideology that has emerged in the post–Jim Crow, post–civil rights era.[40] Although the full argument about laissez-faire racism cannot be developed here, its emergence reflects crucial changes in the economy and polity that at once undermined the structural basis for the Jim Crow social order of the American South and yet left in place the patterns of residential segregation, economic inequality, racialized identities, and antiblack outlooks that existed on a national basis. This new pattern of belief involves staunch rejection of an active role for government in undoing racial segregation and inequality, an acceptance of negative stereotypes of African Americans, a denial of discrimination as a current societal problem, and attribution of primary responsibility for black disadvantage to blacks themselves.

## Ongoing Racial Discrimination

Much of the survey data reviewed above suggests that many whites believe that the playing field has been leveled—that blacks and whites now compete on largely equal footing. Indeed, a nontrivial fraction of whites are convinced that blacks benefit from considerable favoritism.[41] Given the magnitude of black-white economic inequality and the number of domains across which inequalities persist,[42] this state of public perception is, at a minimum, deeply ironic. Popular perceptions notwithstanding, studies of the housing market, the labor market, and other informal spheres of interaction point to the modern-day potency of antiblack racial discrimination.

## The Housing Market

In the housing market, racial residential segregation has long been widespread. Studies in the 1960s found that, irrespective of region, city size, economic base, local laws, and other forms of discrimination, there were high levels of residential segregation by race.[43] Subsequent work showed that little change took place between 1960 and 1970.[44] Furthermore, racial integration was not only more extensive in absolute terms than segregation by social class, but also occurred regardless of social class.[45] Between 1970 and 1980 there was some growth in black suburbanization, a trend that has continued into the 1990s.[46] However, the rate of change remains slow, and the absolute level of black-white residential segregation remains extremely high.

Indeed, black residential segregation from whites is distinctively extreme. Massey and Denton analyzed five different indicators of residential segregation for metropolitan areas.[47] The situation of blacks was so extraordinary that they coined the term "hypersegregation." They defined hypersegregation as high levels of segregation on at least four of the five measures of segregation. They found that blacks in six Standard Metropolitan Statistical Areas (SMSAs) were highly segregated on all five dimensions of segregation. In another four SMSAs blacks were highly segregated on four dimensions. In no SMSAs were Hispanics highly segregated from whites on four or more dimensions. As they explained:

> Blacks are thus unique in experiencing multidimensional hypersegregation. The contrast between them and Hispanics is not easily explained by different socioeconomic characteristics, varying population sizes, different regional locations, contrasting metropolitan conditions. Although our models cannot eliminate the view that some unmeasured objective factor accounts for the discrepancy between blacks and Hispanics, the model lends credence to the view that blacks remain the object of significantly higher levels of Anglo prejudice than Hispanics. Two decades after the 1968 Civil Rights Act blacks still have not achieved the freedom to live where they want.[48]

Data for segregation of Asian Americans and whites suggest even less evidence of isolation by race than is observed for Hispanic-white data.

Careful studies have increasingly ruled out a number of race-neutral explanations of racial residential segregation. For example, intensive studies of the Detroit area have shown that issues of affordability and knowledge about housing costs cannot explain the high rates of black-white residential segregation.[49] Some have argued that mutual ethnocentrism is a major factor in patterns of residential segregation, with blacks and whites preferring to live with substantial numbers of same-race neighbors, thus making meaningful integration impossible.[50] This claim is contradicted by the powerful impact of antiblack stereotypes on the level of whites' willingness to live in integrated areas[51] and by evidence of both negative stereotypes and other measures of prejudice influencing the feelings whites have about social distance.[52]

It is increasingly evident that direct racial discrimination—while not the only cause—is directly implicated in the persistently high levels of racial residential segregation. A number of auditing studies involving matched pairs of white and black home-seekers have found high rates of antiblack bias.[53]

## The Labor Market

It has often been assumed that because of intense competitive pressures there would be little racial discrimination at the low-skill level of employment, the so-called "entry level."[54] Such seemingly reasonable expectations notwithstanding, a growing body of research finds that discrimination constrains black opportunity even at the entry level. In addition, many commentators and analysts point to the growth and size of the new black middle class as evidence of a greatly transformed labor market position for blacks. Yet, there are many indicators that discrimination faced by blacks working in the professional and managerial ranks persists.

In terms of entry-level, low-skill work one major hypothesis for the higher rates of black joblessness is the skills-mismatch hypothesis.[55] Accordingly, many of the jobs available in inner-city communities have education, training, and skill requirements that exceed the actual skills of many inner-city black men, especially young black males. If this is the source of the joblessness for black males, then we might expect to find that black youths living closer to suburban areas would have higher rates of employment than those living in central city areas. But Richard Freeman and Harry

Holzer found no such effect.[56] They studied employment rates among Southside Chicago black youths and black youths on the west side, closer to white suburban communities. Despite the greater proximity to jobs, there was no difference in the level of joblessness. In short, the employment problem black youths faced appeared to be one of "race" not one of "space."

Another hypothesis for high rates of black unemployment and poverty is an overall decline in the availability of low-skill entry-level positions. This claim, however, is contradicted by evidence of blocked access for blacks to the low-skill positions that are available. For example, recent in-depth interviews with employers seeking to fill low-skill positions suggest that they often hold very negative stereotypical images of blacks, especially of young black men. Joleen Kirschenman and Kathryn Neckerman conducted interviews with 185 employers representative of firms in Chicago and the surrounding Cook County area.[57] Although intermixed with ideas about the inner city versus the suburbs, and about class differences in values and behavior, there was powerful evidence of racial stereotyping that informed employer preferences and decisions: "Chicago's employers did not hesitate to generalize about race or ethnic differences in the quality of the labor force. Most associated negative images with inner-city workers, and particularly with black men. 'Black' and 'inner city' were inextricably linked, and both were linked with 'lower class.'"[58] But negative racial stereotypes were not the only problem. Their research showed that employers utilized selective recruitment and other screening mechanisms that had the effect of sorting out many potential black job applicants.[59]

One of the areas of job growth in many metropolitan areas has been the construction industry. Despite job growth and the presence of relatively well-paying low-skill employment opportunities, there is little evidence that blacks were able to make significant inroads into construction employment. Intensive analysis of historical and interview data on the New York construction industry by Roger Waldinger and Tom Bailey shows that race was a crucial factor blocking opportunities for blacks.[60] The structure of much construction work, which varies by season, economic cycle, and other short-term forces, puts a premium on flexible work forces. Therefore, much recruiting is done not through large personnel departments but through interpersonal and kinship networks. Efforts to move toward more universal procedures for access to training and apprenticeships have been effectively thwarted by white-dominated unions, and sometimes white-ethnic-dominated unions, which have preferred to reserve access to their own brothers, sons, cousins, and immediate friends. As a result, Waldinger and

Bailey suggested: "If the employment problems of blacks result from a mismatch of their skills with the job requirements of urban employers, then construction should be the one industry where there should be black workers aplenty. . . . Jobs requiring little schooling there may be in construction, but few of them go to black workers."[61] Thus, even though blacks were in no sense a "wage threat" to white workers, they were effectively excluded from this avenue of well-paying low-skill work.

A recent carefully designed auditing study conducted by the Urban Institute found clear-cut evidence of discrimination in access to low-skill, entry-level positions.[62] Auditing studies, it should be emphasized, come as close to tightly controlled laboratory experiments as real-world field studies can accomplish. They involve sending well-trained white and black job applicants, with identical credentials, to apply for the same positions. Overall, Urban Institute researchers found that in one out of five audits the white candidate advanced further than the black applicant, even though each possessed identical credentials except for race. Differential behavior could include not being allowed to submit an application, no offer of an interview, and finally not being offered a job. They did find some occasions of favorable treatment of blacks relative to whites, but the general pattern was that "if equally qualified black and white candidates are competing for a job, differential treatment, when it occurs, is three times more likely to favor the white applicant than the black."[63]

The black middle class, likewise, continues to face discrimination. Research suggests that black managers face heightened scrutiny and attention from co-workers and supervisors.[64] The black middle class is often locked into organizationally marginal positions that often lack job authority and may even pay less than the pay received by otherwise comparable whites.[65] Many black inroads into the middle class have come in the area of personnel and equal employment opportunity compliance positions.[66] Interview studies with black managers increasingly paint a picture of glass ceilings and artificial barriers to advancement into core managerial ranks.[67] A number of commentators concur that the growth of the black middle class is relatively recent, fragile, and dependent on an unusual era of economic growth and governmental antidiscrimination efforts.[68] It is therefore seriously premature to read the development of a large black middle class as a sign of the end of meaningful racial discrimination in the labor market.

## Other Spheres of Life

Given the data on generally negative stereotypes reviewed above, it is less surprising that blacks run the risk of discriminatory treatment in many different social settings. Journalistic accounts point to a great variety of places and forms of discrimination encountered by blacks, including black middle-class individuals.[69] Urban ethnographers point to the tension-filled dilemma of being "a black male in public."[70] Likewise, one wide-ranging review of social-psychological studies found numerous instances of documented differential treatment of blacks,[71] though the behaviors were often extremely subtle—for example, how far away white persons might seat themselves from a black as opposed to another white person.

Blacks commonly report discrimination in their treatment at public accommodations. One of the more careful investigations involved a replication of a study of how New York City restaurants treated black and white patrons. Both studies employed the "auditing" methodology, where similar couples were trained to enter a restaurant, order similar meals, and even try as best they could to observe how the other pair was being treated. The earlier study had been done in the 1950s and found discriminatory treatment of blacks in about 43 percent of the restaurants examined. Although none of the instances involved a refusal of service, the discrimination involved plainly poor seating or such behaviors as unusually rushed or unusually slow service.[72]

The 1981 replication found a slightly lower rate of discrimination at about 30 percent, though the sample sizes really were not large enough for formal statistical tests. Again, the behavior stopped short of refused service but did include various forms of poor treatment, such as adding on a service charge to the bill in one case.[73] This study is instructive not merely as a carefully designed effort that carried out a replication in order to obtain a measure of behavioral social change; it also draws attention to the complexities of the discrimination situation and the wide discrepancy in frames of reference that blacks and whites typically bring to almost any public setting. As Schuman and colleagues explained:

> Thus black customers are often faced with attempting to evaluate problematic behavior in a way that is incomprehensible to many white customers. The latter may become impatient about poor service, but in most cases they can comfortably attribute this to failures of restaurant staff. Blacks must usually add racial motivation as a possible explanation. Even where careful comparison with customers can help resolve the issue, this demands a social alertness and sensitivity not required of whites. And often no comparison is available (e.g., on a gratuity added to a bill), or if available cannot resolve the issue. Because of this extra dimension to black-white relations, the discovery of *any* signifi-

cant amount of clear discrimination in restaurants has implications beyond its own limited proportion: from the standpoint of black customers—and from the standpoint of our investigation—it renders suspect *all* instances of differential treatment by race.[74]

Such discrimination is a possibility that constantly confronts blacks, whereas among whites it is unseen and difficult to accept as fact when blacks assert that it has occurred.

One of the more innovative and suggestive efforts to understand modern discrimination has come from in-depth interviews with middle-class blacks carried out by Joe Feagin.[75] Based on his interviews, Feagin points to five forms of discrimination typically reported by middle-class blacks: (1) avoidance behavior, where a white person may, for instance, cross the street rather than walk past a black male; (2) rejection or other poor service at various establishments; (3) verbal epithets and name-calling; (4) police threats and harassment; and (5) threats and harassment from others, such as members of white supremacist groups. He analyzes how the frequency of discrimination varied by situation (that is, occured in a public facility or establishment versus on the street) and by the type of behavioral response blacks adopted. For example, 37 percent of Feagin's respondents had encountered some form of poor service or rejection at a public establishment. With regard to discriminatory encounters on the street, 46 percent of those reports involved police harassment and 25 percent involved anonymous whites shouting racial epithets. The most common behavioral response to both public accommodation and street-level encounters with discrimination was some sort of verbal retort or sanctioning, 69 percent for the former and 59 percent for the latter. Resigned acceptance was a more common response in public accommodation sites (23 percent) whereas efforts to withdraw from or get out of the situation were more common in street-level encounters (22 percent).

Like the earlier work by Schuman and colleagues, Feagin's research draws attention to the fundamental difference in perspective between blacks and whites when discrimination is involved. For blacks, such experiences accumulate over the life course for any given individual, and through historical space and time for the group collectively. Feagin argued:

Particular instances of discrimination may seem minor to outside white observers when considered in isolation. But when blatant acts of avoidance, verbal harassment, and physical attack combine with subtle and covert slights, and these accumulate over months, years, and life times, the impact on a black person is far more than the sum of individual instances. . . . The microlevel events of public accommodations and public streets are not just rare and isolated encounters by individuals; they are recurring events reflecting an invasion of the microworld by the macroworld of historical racial subordination.[76]

In sum, racial discrimination continues to influence where blacks live, where they work (and indeed whether they work at all), and innumerable day-to-day encounters as they move through the routines of social living. That this discrimination no longer assumes the blanket form of complete exclusion, coarse insults, and uniform expectations of deferential and subordinate behavior does indeed indicate change, and positive change at that. But in light of the accumulating social science research, it simply is not tenable to assert that racial discrimination is a small or a nuisance issue in modern America. Antiblack racial discrimination is pervasive. It shapes the quality of life experiences and outlooks of African Americans quite profoundly.

# Ghetto Poverty and Racial Politics

Race has long been an issue near the heart of national affairs and politics in the United States. From the drafting of the Constitution to the Civil War, the Fourteenth Amendment to the Constitution, the emergence of the New Deal coalition and more, conceptions of African Americans and ideas about their place in the American social order have played a fundamental role in shaping American national character, values, and institutions.[77] A new politics of race appears to have emerged in the post–civil rights age, a politics that reflects the crystallization of resentments over affirmative action, minority business set-asides, electoral redistricting, and many of the civil rights accomplishments of the "second reconstruction." A major factor in the emergence and coalescence of this new politics of racial resentment can be traced to entrenched ghetto poverty and the social ills of single-parent female-headed households, welfare dependency, delinquency, and crime, which flow from unemployment and poverty. This new political climate has the potential to transform the current prevalent but latent pattern of laissez-faire racism into a more manifest and actively antiblack social force.

## The New Ghetto Poverty

Perhaps ironically, it was Gunnar Myrdal who first seriously applied the term "underclass" to characterize the impact of economic changes on subgroups of the population. He coined the term in his 1963 book, *Challenge to Affluence*, which examined how the "post-industrial economy" was increasingly marginalizing some segments of the population.[78] The next significant use of the term "underclass" came in 1981 with Ken Auletta's series of articles for the *New Yorker.*[79] However, it was William Julius Wilson's *The Truly Disadvantaged* that deliberately used the term "ghetto underclass" in a cogent and pathbreaking analysis of the modern urban crisis.[80]

Wilson used the term "underclass" to draw attention to patterns of behavior and conditions that were increasingly common in inner-city areas that were at odds with "mainstream" standards of conduct. He defined the underclass as including "individuals who lack training and skills and either experience long-term unemployment or are not members of the labor force, individuals who are engaged in street crime and other forms of aberrant behavior, and families that experience long-term spells of poverty and/or welfare dependency."[81] Wilson characterized underclass neighborhoods as "populated almost exclusively by the most disadvantaged segments of the black urban community, that heterogeneous group of families and individuals who are outside the mainstream of the American occupational system."[82]

Wilson developed a compelling portrait of the social pathologies in urban ghetto communities. First, he pointed to high rates of black involvement, both as victims and as perpetrators, in violent crime. Using Chicago as an example, he showed that more than half of the murders in the city occurred in a handful of largely poor and minority neighborhoods. Thus, much of the city's violent crime was tied to the underclass.

Second, Wilson drew attention to the rapid increase in female-headed families among blacks. For example, only 25 percent of black households were headed by single-parent females in 1965. That number had jumped to 42 percent by 1980 and is still rising. To be sure, there is a general secular trend toward later age of marriage and marital dissolution, so this trend is not restricted to the black population. But the absolute levels and pace of change are acutely high for blacks.

The crucial problem is that female-headed households are more likely to be trapped in poverty. This contributes to a third set of problems—namely, an increasing proportion of out-of-wedlock births and welfare dependency. According to Wilson, "The poverty rate of female-headed families was 36.3

percent in 1982, while the rate for married couple families was only 7.6 percent. For black and Spanish-origin female-headed families in 1982, poverty rates were 56.2 percent and 55.4 percent respectively."[83]

The character of urban poverty also changed according to Wilson. Poverty became more concentrated, with a large fraction of urban blacks and Latinos living in "concentrated" poverty communities. By "concentrated" poverty Wilson meant census tracts where 40 percent or more of residents had incomes below the poverty line. Such concentrated poverty, according to Wilson, has led to a new level of isolation from mainstream institutions, patterns of behavior, and expectations.

The root cause of the emergence of the new ghetto poverty in Wilson's analysis is black male joblessness. Transformations in the economy that led to the suburbanization of much manufacturing activity, the shift toward a service-oriented economy, and the increasingly high-technology character and high-skill demands of much inner-city employment created sparse employment opportunities for low-skill black men.

Without accepting Wilson's spatial-mismatch hypothesis, it is clear that urban black male unemployment has reached crisis levels. The rates of black male unemployment and underemployment in urban areas have skyrocketed. Lichter has analyzed several different types of underemployment ranging from non–labor-force participation (labeled "subunemployment") to involuntarily working less than full time or working full time but earning a subpoverty-level wage.[84]

Three patterns stand out. First, since the mid-1970s there has been a steady increase in the ratio of black to white unemployment, rising from 1.9 in 1970–75 to 2.4 by 1982. Second, and far more telling, is a steady rise in the black-white gap in non–labor-force participation, in which the ratio rises from 2.3 in 1970 to 4.8 by 1982. That is, by 1982 central city black men were almost five times as likely as comparable whites to have fallen completely out of the labor force. As Lichter argues, "The nation's urban centers are now undergoing a process of accelerated racial polarization rather than convergence."[85] Third, the absolute gap in total unemployment between white men and black men in central city areas has widened as well. The gap increased from 8.2 percent in favor of whites in 1970 to more than an 18-percentage-point gap in 1982.

## The Racial Subtext of the Politics of Crime and Welfare

These developments, while surely not appreciated with any degree of sociological complexity, have not gone unnoticed by the larger society. As discussed above, the stereotypes of African Americans are negative. Most whites tend to see blacks as lazy, less intelligent, desiring to live off of welfare, and prone to violence.[86] This set of images is lent a "kernel of truth" by the emergence of the new ghetto poverty. As a result, espousing such views of blacks, though intrinsically inaccurate, may increasingly be viewed by some as "reasonable" rather than extreme, categorical, and stereotyped.

In this context, welfare has become a racial issue. It is a particularly effective political tool in a cultural environment where explicit Jim Crow racism is disreputable. The racial component remains hidden behind debate over an ostensibly race-neutral social policy. Racial antagonisms and resentments that may be costly for a politician to appeal to directly can instead be mobilized by a putatively race-neutral assault on welfare waste and fraud.

There are several grounds for assuming that the current politics of welfare reform has a large racial component. First, historical research indicates that the very development and comparatively ungenerous character of the American welfare state can be traced to struggles over the amount and type of financial resources that should be flowing to black individuals and communities.[87] New Deal policies, especially the Great Society reforms of the 1960s, took shape amid explicit concern about the status, conditions, and resources to be placed in the hands of African Americans. Second, research on stereotypes shows that many whites perceive blacks as largely poor, as constituting the bulk of welfare recipients, and as preferring to live off of welfare.[88]

Third, and perhaps most important, antiblack attitudes are significant correlates of opposition to social-welfare-type policies.[89] Iyengar has shown, for instance, that the race of the welfare recipient depicted in media discussions of welfare profoundly affects the way many whites think about welfare.[90] He found that when media coverage of welfare issues depicted single black females with babies, a powerful response was elicited. These mothers were viewed as particularly culpable for their own circumstances and as much less deserving of government assistance than otherwise comparable whites.

The issue of crime also has a strong racial subtext. Like the issue of welfare, politicians can mobilize a segment of the voting public who harbor racial antagonisms and resentments without risking explicitly racist appeals by demanding a more punitive response to crime. As Thomas and Mary Edsall put it, "'Crime' became a shorthand signal, to a crucial group of white voters, for broader issues of social disorder, evoking powerful ideas about authority, status, morality, self-control, and race."[91]

In sum, major economic transformations, coupled with historical racial subordination and potent modern discrimination in housing, jobs, and most spheres of public interaction, have led to the emergence of a new ghetto poverty. This new ghetto poverty has contributed to the solidification of contemporary antiblack stereotypes revolving around welfare dependency, laziness, crime, and a breakdown of social values. Issues of welfare reform and dealing with crime have influenced recent political contests across all levels of government. There is a heavy and unavoidable racial subtext to these political debates and contests. The sophisticated way that the racial subtext escapes denunciation as racist appeals and yet works effectively as a tool to mobilize significant segments of the white voting public is a new turn in American politics. This development is fraught with potential to deepen the feelings of hurt and division that separate black and white Americans.

Does the color line still divide us? Does the dilemma still persist? Is the dream ever to be realized? There is little question that the United States is still sharply divided by race, that the struggle to fulfill national democratic ideals goes on, and that the dream remains far, very far, from realization. As pessimistic as these answers sound, they do not, however, amount to an acceptance of the idea that no meaningful change in American racism has or can take place. The "racial chasm" and "permanence of racism" to which Hacker and Bell, respectively, have written are seriously overstated.

We have witnessed the substantial disappearance of one epochal form of racist ideology. Jim Crow racism once dominated the views white Americans had of black people. This ideology is no longer widely accepted or publicly espoused by any significant number of people. While segregationist notions, including explicitly biological racist ideas, have not completely vanished, they show no sign of making a quick or easy return to popular acceptance.

Nonetheless, a new epochal form of racism has emerged. Bobo and Smith label it "laissez-faire racism."[92] It is a cultural pattern of belief that connects opposition to substantial policy change and activism with regard to improving the status of blacks with negative stereotyping of African Americans, a tendency to deny the potency of modern discrimination, and a view of blacks as largely responsible for their own disadvantaged circumstances.

The emergence of this new form of American racism can be traced, in the
first instance, to the historical erosion of the structural basis for the Jim
Crow economic, political, and social institutions.[93] In the second instance,
it can be traced to the important but partial victories of the civil rights
movement. The 1954 *Brown v. Board of Education* decision, the Civil
Rights Act of 1964, and the Voting Rights Act of 1965 secured the basic
citizenship rights of African Americans. As fundamental as these gains
were, these accomplishments did not directly undo racial residential segregation or the individual and institutional actors that sustain it; these accomplishments did not directly undo tremendous disparities in earnings,
prospects for employment, and wealth-holding that constituted the core
structural bases of racial economic inequality; and these accomplishments
did not wipe away racial identities and a long cultural heritage of disparaging
views of African Americans. Thus, a new antiblack ideology has crystallized, an ideology that is appropriate to a historical epoch in which we have
a formally race-neutral state and economy but a still racially divided social
order and quality of life experience.

Laissez-faire racism has crystallized despite mounting evidence of discrimination against blacks with regard to housing, jobs, and access to many
public spaces. The political climate makes the challenge of improving race
relations that much greater. The very center of American politics is now
infused with thinly veiled racial appeals that call for rolling back the welfare
state, erecting more prisons, lengthening prison sentences, making it easier
to convict the accused, and bringing greater certainty and swiftness to the
execution of death sentences. While not based solely in efforts to harm the
black community and its interests, or simply in the cynical pursuit of votes
by opportunistic politicians, the current political climate has a powerful
and undeniably racial subtext. The product of these trends is a potentially
widening gulf of perception, of understanding, of feelings, and of interests
across the color line.

Some, like Hacker and Bell, look at these complex problems, see no real
change, and see little hope for progress in the future, but that prognosis is
difficult to accept. Racial categories and identities are social constructs.
They are not given in nature, and they are subject to enormous variation
over historical time and space. To be sure, the black-white divide in the
United States is deeply entrenched structurally, culturally, and psychologi-
cally. But simply as a matter of logic and historical experience, the color
line is not unmodifiable.

If historical figures like Thurgood Marshall, Fannie Lou Hamer, Rosa Parks, and Martin Luther King Jr. had simply accepted Jim Crow racism rather than challenging it head on, we almost surely would not have had a *Brown* decision, the Civil Rights Act or the Voting Rights Act. We would not have witnessed the emergence of a black middle class that is at least modestly better residentially integrated and as large and accomplished as we have now. We would just as surely not have as many appointed and elected black public officials.

We stand at a moment of great ambiguity, uncertainty, and potentially momentous change in race relations. Lack of clarity about the future, however, does not warrant pessimistic certainty. The present is a time of deeply contradictory trends, not one of unequivocal backlash and polarization. Positive changes in racial attitudes and relations do not simply happen. They are made, in both intended and unintended ways. Laissez-faire racism, modern discrimination, and the current subtext of race in American politics are harder to confront directly than the obvious racism of the Jim Crow era. But the only path to transcending the color line is a continuous struggle to resolve the Myrdalian dilemma of race and to steadfastly pursue Dr. King's dream.

# PART TWO

# Affirmative Action

# CHAPTER THREE

# The Changing Meaning of Civil Rights, 1954–1994

## LAWRENCE H. FUCHS

The term "civil rights" has a long history in North America. Its essential meaning was laid out as early as 1641 in the Massachusetts Bay Colony with the promulgation of something called the "Body of Liberties," the main author of which probably was the Reverend Nathaniel Ward of Ipswich. The Puritans sought a code of law that would guarantee "such liberties, Immunities and priveledges as humanitie, Civilitie, and Christianitie call for as is due to every man . . . without impeachment and Infringement. . . ."[1] Various provisions prohibited authorities from depriving a citizen of life, liberty, or property without due process of law. Every adult male Puritan Christian adhering to the congregational form of worship was entitled to *habeas corpus* protection. They were not to be subject to inhumane and barbarous punishments. If accused of a crime, they were guaranteed counsel, and the testimony of more than one witness was necessary to convict them.

Heretics were not accorded civil rights, and laws were soon passed that excluded Anabaptists and Quakers from the colony. The Quaker, Mary Dyer, was hanged. But the idea that government could not take away certain rights from those designated as being under their protection would surface again in various colonial and state constitutions and come to full flower in the Virginia Declaration of Rights and in the Bill of Rights to the U.S. Constitution. The meaning of rights was clear to its authors, and so was the question of coverage and jurisdiction. When Madison wrote about civil rights in Federalist Paper No. 51, he had adult white males in mind. When he and other framers wrote the Bill of Rights, they had in mind prohibitions on the abuse of those rights by the new federal government. Later, the passage of the Thirteenth, Fourteenth, and Fifteenth Amendments purported to make clear that civil rights extended to African Americans as well.

Some opponents of the Fifteenth Amendment maintained that granting voting rights to African Americans would lead to a dismantling of the entire structure of caste. One opponent, Senator James Doolittle of Wisconsin, argued that if blacks could vote they could be voted for, and "if they can be voted for, they can be elected members of the legislature, . . . members of the Senate of the United States; generals in your army and . . . they might perhaps in the end elect some Negro as President of the United States." He went on:

If Negroes are to be elected Senators to this body, you cannot refuse to meet them at your reception, at your inauguration balls, at the President's table, and their wives with them, and their children also; and your children must meet them side by side, upon a footing of equality. Face the music, gentlemen; acknowledge the truth, that this is the necessary, direct tendency, and the inevitable result which must come if you force upon the states unrestricted and unqualified Negro suffrage.[2]

Doolittle had it exactly right. By the time of the civil rights revolution in the 1950s and 1960s, those of us who marched and demonstrated understood civil rights to mean precisely that: the tearing down of the boundaries of caste, and the full extension of constitutional rights to African Americans. The civil rights revolution began for me in 1954 with the *Brown v. Board of Education* decision and the Montgomery bus boycott led by Martin Luther King Jr. At that time, I had a regular radio news interview broadcast, and I had the privilege of interviewing Dr. King on one of his trips to Boston to raise money and gather support. Not long after, I became a member of the board of the Massachusetts chapter of the Congress of Racial Equality (CORE), whose strategy of direct nonviolent action appealed to me.

At Brandeis, I began to teach a course on the African American experience, and one question that interested me tremendously was the failure of Reconstruction. Although the U. S. Congress enacted five major civil rights and reconstruction acts between 1866 and 1875, these laws were so modified and so narrowly construed that their effectiveness was eroded. Then, in the *Slaughterhouse* cases in 1872 and in the civil rights cases of 1883, the U.S. Supreme Court destroyed those laws by asserting that the Fourteenth Amendment did not place under federal protection "the entire domain of civil rights heretofore belonging exclusively to the states" and that the Fourteenth and Fifteenth Amendments offered no federal protection against private action.

Although the federal courts gradually extended the protection of the Bill of Rights to individuals against acts by state governments before World War II, those extensions had no practical effect on the lives of most African Americans. John Harlan's famous assertion in *Plessy v. Ferguson* (1896) that "the law regards man as a man, and takes no account of his surroundings or his color when his civil rights as guaranteed by the supreme law of the land are involved," remained a dissent and nothing more until the Supreme Court began to chip away at some state segregation practices in the 1940s and 1950s, focusing particularly on the segregated practices of white primaries and of institutions of higher education. Then came the *Brown* decision and the Montgomery bus boycott.

Six years later, John F. Kennedy, seeking to shore up his support among liberals and African Americans, established the Civil Rights Advisory Committee for his presidential campaign, chaired by Hubert Humphrey. As a member of the committee, I recall our zealous pressure on the candidate to force a strong commitment to the issue of civil rights coverage for African Americans. Kennedy promised during the campaign to desegregate federally financed public housing with a stroke of the pen. Despite the almost daily urgings of Harris Wofford, then the President's Assistant for Civil Rights, in the weeks following Kennedy's inauguration, it took President Kennedy more than a year to fulfill that promise. In the meantime, I was in the Philippines as director of the Peace Corps, while demonstrations were taking place throughout the South demanding civil rights in every field from access to public accommodations to housing and employment. I returned home just in time for the massive interracial March on Washington on August 28, 1963, when Martin Luther King Jr. gave the civil rights movement its emblematic statement: "I have a dream that my four little children will one day live in a nation where they will not be judged by the color of their skin but by the content of their character."

The movement co-opted the Kennedy administration, which submitted comprehensive legislation on civil rights. Kennedy was assassinated, and the legislation was taken up by his successor, Lyndon Johnson. Congress passed the Civil Rights Act of 1964 with its comprehensive set of titles and strong enforcement mechanism to deny federal funds to programs that did not comply with its nondiscrimination requirements. Following the voting rights demonstrations in Selma, Alabama, and especially the march from Selma to Montgomery, in which I participated, Congress, aware of the ineffectuality of trying to enforce registration of blacks in the South under previous legislation, including the Civil Rights Act of 1964, passed a sweeping voting rights bill.[3] Now, the formal structure of caste in public education, public accommodations, employment, and politics had been toppled. Civil rights meant, for the first time, that the individual rights of African Americans would be protected by a proactive federal government. The meaning of civil rights had not changed, but there was no longer any question that civil rights were meant to cover all Americans in all government jurisdictions and that the federal government now had new powers to enforce them.

My own civil rights activity focused on education. Shortly after President Kennedy's death, I helped to persuade the secretary of education and the governor of Massachusetts to establish a racial imbalance commission, on which I served. The goal was to break down the de facto segregation in the schools of Boston and Springfield. The definition of racial imbalance was adopted by the state legislature in the Massachusetts racial imbalance law, and the remedies suggested—busing and magnet schools—also were adopted. Enormous turmoil and conflict ensued. I spoke and taught in freedom schools and even testified once in court on desegregation, but by the time of the assassination of Dr. King in April 1968, it was clear that our prescriptions for desegregation would be difficult to accomplish in the face of opposition in several ethnic communities in Boston, who believed that their neighborhood schools, which were often based on considerable ethnic solidarity, were being destroyed.

By this time, I had become involved as chairman of the executive committee of a major nonprofit educational research and development corporation called Education Development Center (EDC). Within twenty-four hours of Dr. King's assassination, we galvanized the staff to produce and publish a Martin Luther King curriculum consisting of four slender pamphlets, which we flew down to be taught in the schools of Washington, D.C., where the fury and despair of African American youngsters made normal teaching virtually impossible. I remember teaching for a few days myself in Abraham Lincoln High School, where I became aware of the value of such materials. After returning to Boston, one person on my staff made the suggestion that we produce a national curriculum around the issues of civil rights. With the help of the Ford Foundation, all three major television networks, public television, and *Newsweek* magazine, we were ready in six months with a television-based curriculum—*One Nation, Indivisible?*—that was seen by more than two million high school students over a period of five days. At the same time, I wrote a pamphlet addressed entirely to whites called "Where Is Racism?" and made it the centerpiece of a new organization started in my town: the Suburban Coalition Against Racism.

It was becoming apparent that the toppling of the legal caste system did not mean the end of searing, debilitating division between blacks and whites in the United States. The new civil rights legislation did not prevent the outbreak of 300 episodes of violence in 257 cities in the five years from 1964 through 1968. In 1965, not long after the ink was dry on the Voting Rights Act, African Americans were filmed throwing rocks and bottles at policemen in the Watts section of Los Angeles. In 1967, there were 164 disorders, with more than eighty people killed, nearly 90 percent of them black civilians and 10 percent policemen, firemen, and other public officials. Detroit and Newark had the worst violence. African American ghettos were growing, and the influx of drugs and violence into the ghettos was increasing too, along with anger and hatred toward whites. The struggle for civil rights had been supplanted by a struggle for identity and power. At the EDC, I raised money from the Danforth Foundation and other sources to begin a new four-volume curriculum called "Black in White America," published by Macmillan, that had its genesis in a curriculum I began in the early 1960s called "The Negro American." Also in 1968, I cashed in every chit I could at two successive Brandeis faculty meetings to help inaugurate a new Department of African and African American Studies.

As I look back, it is difficult to believe that we moved so swiftly from the era of civil rights to the era of "Black Power." How could it be that, only three years after passage of the Voting Rights Act, the Kerner Commission said that American society was becoming more divided by race, becoming two societies, one black and one white. How could such an assertion be made in the face of what was already an expansion of an African American middle class, the rise of African Americans to positions of leadership in major institutions, and what was beginning to be a trend, later accelerated, of increasing interracial marriage?

New black spokesmen who did not talk the language of civil rights had emerged. James Forman and Malcolm X began to talk about human rights. The Student Nonviolent Coordinating Committee (SNCC), Forman said, was a human rights organization working for the liberation of all oppressed persons everywhere in the world. Malcolm X spoke about pride and power, not about civil rights. Segregated, black-controlled institutions were the route to liberation for African Americans, not integration, the new spokesmen insisted, drawing on a deep, recurring theme in U.S. history of black nationalism. Group consciousness, apart from American identity, and group rights within the framework of a new kind of American racial pluralism, not individual rights regardless of color, would, Malcolm maintained, meet the needs of blacks.

These arguments were appealing because what progress there was did not meet the rising expectations and demands of many African Americans, who now openly expressed their hostility to those they saw as racist oppressors, or at least as the beneficiaries of racism. They saw little progress on the streets, where police often were still oppressive, or in the desegregation of housing, where the housing industry seemed able to thwart the antidiscrimination objectives of the law. And they saw whites and middle-class blacks and employers leaving the cities to which blacks had migrated from the South during and following World War II.

Where, therefore, was the progress that civil rights legislation had promised? The question became how to achieve faster progress toward economic and political parity with whites. It was a question addressed not only by angry separatist leaders but also by civil rights leaders, who worked hard to compete with the appeal of the separatists' rhetoric.

The civil rights leaders pressed litigation relentlessly to desegregate the schools and lobbied successfully to pass the Fair Housing Act of 1968, and they applied constant pressure to implement the Voting Rights Act. But for all their victories, and there were many, other blacks felt that the progress was too slow. Civil rights leaders needed more aggressive remedies than the usual antidiscrimination enforcement measures.

Of primary importance to civil rights leaders was the issue of equal employment opportunity. The opportunity to make a living was the most important civil right of all, and the caste system had depended on the segregation of blacks in jobs considered menial. How to break those enshrined patterns was the major task of civil rights enforcers. According to James Farmer, then head of the Congress of Racial Equality, the term "affirmative action" came from Lyndon Johnson himself. In a speech that Farmer made in 1978, he recalled a discussion with the then Vice-President Johnson in 1963. Farmer spoke to Johnson, who also was chairman of President Kennedy's Committee on Equal Employment Opportunity, about the need for what he called "compensatory preferential hiring." Johnson listened, then said: "Yes, it is a good idea, but don't call it compensatory. Call it 'affirmative action.' It's moving the nation forward! It is going out of our way to bring minorities in that have been excluded! That is positive affirmative action!"

Farmer and others had tried affirmative action through advertisement, recruitment, and training but were not getting results. When he went to a supervisor, a line manager, or a foreman, or whoever did the hiring, and asked: "You've been practicing affirmative action two years now. How many blacks do you have?" the employer would say: "I've tried hard, but I couldn't find any that were qualified." The problem, according to Farmer, became how to prove that he did try hard. "The only criteria we could come up with were numerical goals and timetables," said Farmer.[4]

The biggest boost to the results-oriented approach to affirmative action came during the administration of Richard Nixon. In 1969, the Nixon administration announced the Philadelphia Plan, which established the authority of the federal government to require companies doing business with the government to set up "goals and timetables" for the hiring and promotion of African Americans in craft union jobs. The goals and timetables remedy for achieving equal employment opportunity was incorporated in 1970 into regulations governing all federal procurement and contracting, thus affecting more than one-third of the nation's work force. Federal regulations, ready for implementation by 1971, urged "results-oriented procedures" and emphasized the concept of "under-utilization," which was defined as "having fewer minorities or women in a particular job classification than would reasonably be expected by their availability."

In addition to extending the meaning of civil rights beyond what either the authors of the Fourteenth Amendment or the Civil Rights Act of 1964 imagined, the Nixon regulations, as the language suggests, took another big step by defining four categories of minorities: Asians and Pacific Islanders; African Americans; Hispanics; and Native Americans and Alaskan natives. A new emphasis on designated minorities other than African Americans slipped into American law and policy at the very moment that the volume of immigration was going up swiftly and its composition was shifting away from immigrants of European origins as a result of passage of the Immigration Act of 1965.

Most liberals, including myself, tacitly or explicitly approved of this extension of affirmative action guidelines to Asian Americans and Latinos. The civil rights movement had inspired Mexican American leaders to develop new goals and strategies for advancing their claims, which they asserted as rights. After the Supreme Court ruled in 1974 that English-limited children who were being taught in English must be given special help to guarantee their equality under the law with students who spoke English as a first language, more than twenty states passed bilingual education acts, and the Office of Civil Rights of the Department of Health, Education, and Welfare was charged with implementing Title VI of the Civil Rights Act, which prohibited denial of access to education on the basis of a student's limited English proficiency. It directed that any school district in which children were effectively excluded from participation in the educational process because of English-language deficiency must take affirmative measures to rectify the deficiency. Mexican American leaders also lobbied hard in 1975 to require bilingual ballots if more than 5 percent of a district constituted a language minority and if the illiteracy rate of such persons was higher than the national rate. In this, they had the support of African American leaders, whose voting rights were protected in part by the requirement of the Voting Rights Act of 1965 that the English literacy requirement in state laws be banned by 1975, an objective that grew out of the long history of the discriminatory use of literacy tests. I believed in these remedies to effectuate voting rights and joined the board of directors of the Mexican American Legal and Education Defense Fund (MALDEF) in 1975, serving for four years.

The meaning of civil rights was intentionally being stretched in new directions both by me and by others who aimed to make the United States a more inclusive and just multiethnic society. At MALDEF we spoke of language rights, but not always with the greatest precision. The right to maintain one's ancestral language in essentially private associational activities, including the right to establish foreign-language schools, had been protected by Supreme Court decisions since the early 1920s. Now, the rights of English-limited children to equal educational opportunity, and of English-limited voters to equal access to the voting booth, were protected by law. Soon, one of the remedies used to provide English-limited children equal educational opportunity—bilingual education—was interpreted in practice by some bilingual educators to mean the maintenance of ancestral language and culture, and that sometimes was spoken of as a right too.

There were serious problems connected with counting by race to fulfill affirmative action goals for African Americans and members of other designated groups. How were the enforcers to test "good faith" conclusively unless employers (or admissions officers or contractors) made substantial progress toward meeting the numerical targets? How could employers avoid costly investigations and litigation unless they treated numerical goals as if they were quotas? How, if employers treated numerical goals as quotas, could they possibly avoid discriminating against those who were not members of the designated beneficiary groups under their affirmative action plans? How, if employers felt the pressure to hire and promote on the basis of ethnicity in order to meet targets they treated as hard and fast, could they avoid violating the Civil Rights Act of 1964, which barred preferential treatment and—in the case of state and local employers—the Fourteenth Amendment's insistence that no person be denied equal protection of the laws by the states?

The answer to this last question was provided by Supreme Court Justice Harry Blackmun in his assertion in *Regents of the University of California v. Bakke* case that "in order to get beyond racism, we must first take account of race. There is no other way. . . . In order to treat persons equally, we must treat them differently." The 1978 case involved an affirmative action plan by the University of California to set aside slots for admission to its medical school only for members of designated minorities. While the Court struck down the specific plan, Blackmun, speaking for a majority, made it clear that race and ethnicity could be taken into account in implementing results-oriented affirmative action programs and still pass constitutional muster. The Court decided in a series of cases that counting by race did not necessarily constitute illegitimate preferential treatment when undertaken on behalf of individuals who belonged to designated beneficiary groups, many of whose members had long suffered discrimination. Instead, they could be considered legitimate temporary remedies in order to effectuate the civil rights of individuals in those designated beneficiary groups, at least when they did not constitute blatant quotas that egregiously discriminated against others.

Because the effectiveness of remedies was to be measured by statistical results, it was not a long step for the leaders of African American and Mexican American groups to argue that the political access given to African Americans and to all Americans by the Voting Rights Act of 1965, as amended in 1975, did not translate into real power unless it could be shown that African Americans and Mexican Americans were being elected. The premise of that argument was (and is) that true or authentic representation depends on members of minority groups being able to elect persons of their own kind. The Leadership Conference on Civil Rights mobilized a strong lobbying effort in Congress in 1982 to pass additional amendments to the Voting Rights Act that made it possible for black or other minority plaintiffs to challenge any jurisdiction for engaging in electoral discrimination if election results showed that the number of blacks, Mexican Americans, or other designated minorities elected was not commensurate with the overall population proportions in a city, county, or other jurisdiction. It would no longer be necessary for plaintiffs to prove discriminatory intent on the part of those who had designed the electoral districts, as the U.S. Supreme Court had decided in a 1980 case; it would be enough to show that African Americans or Mexican Americans were not getting elected. Now, Justice Department attorneys routinely checked redistricting plans to make certain they were likely to result in the election of blacks and Hispanics wherever possible. Increasingly, many of those who vigorously advocated civil rights spoke of remedies to enforce them, such as ethnic gerrymandering, as if the remedies were the rights.

Members of the Supreme Court did not make that mistake. Those who were strongest in their advocacy of such remedies in the 1970s and 1980s—Justices Marshall, Brennan, and Blackmun—never wavered in maintaining that group-conscious measures based on race, ethnicity, or gender should be considered temporary remedies to protect the individual rights of individuals who were members of the designated beneficiary groups. In the *Bakke* case, which ruled against certain kinds of quotas, Justice Brennan wrote in his dissent that equality under the Constitution is linked "with the proposition that differences in color or creed, birth or status, are neither significant nor relevant to the way in which such persons are treated." Justice Marshall, in his dissent, echoed Martin Luther King Jr., saying that he wanted to live in a society "in which the color of a person's skin will not determine the opportunities available to him or her," and Justice Blackmun called for a society in which "persons will be regarded as persons," without regard to color or ethnicity. The protection of individual, not group, rights was the basis for their accepting group statistics as a rough but constitutionally permissible means to determine progress for African Americans and for members of other designated groups, as long as such programs were not seriously damaging to others. The criteria for judging such harm depended on whose programs were tested—federal, state, or private—and under what circumstances and in what historical context.

Because of its concern for individual rather than group rights, the Supreme Court did not rubber-stamp every results-based remedy defended in litigation before it. The ruling in *Bakke* was against a plan that denied a white male admission to medical school while setting aside sixteen places for minority students, against whom he was not allowed to compete. It was not against taking race into account in admissions policies. In 1984, in *Firefighters Local No. 1784 v. Stotts,* the Supreme Court ruled against another specific affirmative action plan without rejecting the concept of affirmative action. In that decision, the Court struck down a lower court order that had stopped the layoff of black firefighters who had been hired under an affirmative action plan. The city of Memphis, it said, could not fire white firefighters who had much more seniority than the recently hired blacks. The only circumstance in which Memphis could have done so, the Court said, would have been if the blacks had been actual victims of discrimination; but that was not the situation, and the Court decided that the harm to long-term white employees was too severe.

Two years later, in 1986, the Supreme Court again ruled against an affirmative action policy it believed went too far. The school board in the city of Jackson, Michigan, had a policy of laying off white teachers before minority group teachers who had less seniority. That too was unconstitutional under the Fourteenth Amendment. The Court was saying that it was one thing to give a qualified person a job or a promotion in order to advance the cause of equal opportunity, making someone else wait a little while longer on the assumption that there would be other jobs and opportunities for promotion, but that it was quite another thing to take a job away from someone who had seniority, and perhaps superior qualifications, in order to apply a broad social remedy.

In 1989 a majority of the Court again showed its concern with the principle of equal protection of the laws under the Fourteenth Amendment with regard to loosely drawn counting-by-race programs. In this case, the city of Richmond, Virginia, had passed an ordinance that required builders hired by the city to subcontract at least 30 percent of the dollar amount of each contract to one or more minority-owned and minority-controlled (51 percent) business enterprises. Richmond's ordinance violated the equal protection clause of the Fourteenth Amendment, said the Court, because it was drawn too loosely. Perhaps the Court was being sticky and even prickly in saying that the city of Richmond had to show a history of discrimination against black contractors. That would seem to be something that any of us could assume. But the Court had to draw a line somewhere on set-aside programs, and in this case insisted on strict scrutiny as a constitutional standard, perhaps because the Richmond city council and mayor were now black. Affirmative action had to be justified in such cases, it appeared to say, with considerable care. The fact that Richmond had included Aleuts among its beneficiary groups indicated a sloppiness in drafting the statute, which when tied to the lack of any attempt to establish a history of discrimination led five Supreme Court justices to say no to the Richmond ordinance.

The Court invoked the equal protection clause of the Fourteenth Amendment, stipulating that no state shall deny any person equal protection of the laws, because the Richmond ordinance involved state action. The test of strict scrutiny involving race-based remedies had not been applied under federal contracting programs until 1994, when the Court ruled that one such remedy went too far under a 1987 law that required the Department of Transportation to steer at least 10 percent of its funds to businesses owned by women or members of racial minorities. General contractors received a 1.5 percent federal bonus for hiring such firms as subcontractors. A white contractor in Colorado Springs, Colorado, challenged the program when, despite the lower bid submitted by his firm, the contract was awarded to a firm led by a Hispanic contractor. With the Richmond case, the Court agreed that the Fourteenth Amendment requires strict scrutiny of all race-based action by state and local governments. The new case, involving the Fifth Amendment's prohibition against depriving any American of due process of law, decided that such classifications must satisfy strict scrutiny too. Federal classifications are constitutionally permissible only to the extent that they serve important government objectives within the power of Congress and are substantially related to the achievement of those objectives.

Ethnic group leaders were not mollified by those who pointed out that a great many of the counting-by-ethnicity affirmative action remedies still could pass the constitutional test of strict scrutiny. Many of them had become so accustomed to speaking of civil rights as though they were rights only for members of designated beneficiary groups that they ceased to distinguish between remedies and rights altogether. To judge from a 1980 speech of Dr. Mary Frances Berry, then the vice-chair of the U.S. Commission on Civil Rights, almost any remedy aimed at helping members of designated victim-beneficiary groups could be advanced as a civil rights issue. She dismissed anyone who was concerned about the complexity of these issues as among those the people who "engage in oppressing other people [and] like to have them feel hopeless [and] like to characterize issues in terms that make them so complex that they cannot be dealt with."[5] She then proceeded to show just how loose the meaning of civil rights had become and how vastly different it was from its meaning at the time of the passage of the Civil Rights Act of 1964 and the Voting Rights Act of 1965.

In listing her civil rights agenda for the 1980s, Dr. Berry spoke of the admission of Cuban and Haitian boat people as a matter of civil rights. She spoke of limiting the recruitment by the Ku Klux Klan of students in junior and senior high schools as a question of civil rights. Civil rights were at stake, Berry said, when the federal government attempted to enforce mandates to pay a major portion of the cost of educating handicapped children by taking funds from other programs for nonhandicapped children. Another civil rights issue, she said, was the failure of federal and state governments to provide enough money for bilingual services in the schools. The unwillingness of institutions of higher education to spend more money to keep black and Hispanic students from dropping out also was a question of civil rights, she said. So was the failure to fund civil rights commissions adequately.

Some of the issues Dr. Berry listed were clearly matters of civil rights—that is, of constitutionally protected rights of all Americans: continuing discrimination in housing by realtors who steer minorities to minority neighborhoods; abuse by police of suspects because of their ethnicity or race; the defiance some institutions of higher education have shown regarding court decisions requiring them to integrate their student bodies. But much of Berry's agenda revealed how widely particular group claims were becoming confused with constitutionally protected civil rights.

By 1980, I was serving as executive director of the Select Commission on Immigration and Refugee Policy, having left the MALDEF board to avoid a conflict of interest. One issue of major importance was the proposal to penalize employers who knowingly and willingly hire illegal aliens, called "employer sanctions." That proposal had been made originally in the early 1950s by Senator Paul Douglas, a major leader in the fight for civil rights, who was joined by African American leaders, labor union leaders, and liberals generally. They saw employer sanctions as a remedy to protect the right of American citizens and resident aliens to work without being discriminated against by employers who could draw on an exploitable, cheap pool of illegal workers. But by 1980, as Carl Holman, the head of the Urban Coalition, explained to me, Mexican American leaders believed that employer sanctions endangered the civil rights of foreign-looking and foreign-sounding persons.

The main objection on the part of MALDEF and other Mexican American groups to employer sanctions was a fear that employers, anxious to protect themselves against the charge of hiring illegal aliens, would discriminate against those who looked and sounded foreign. It was a legitimate concern as long as the system for determining the culpability of employers was not linked to a secure, reliable, universal system of employee eligibility. Proposals for such a system also were opposed by what had come to be called the "civil rights community," whose black leaders generally rallied around the position of Mexican American leaders. Here was another case in which arguments on both sides of a proposed remedy to deal with a particular problem based their arguments on the cry of civil rights.

I became increasingly concerned about the growing tendency on the part of civil rights leaders to mix up remedies and interests with rights. It is one thing to advertise a selfish interest as being in the public interest, as when professors defend tenure or call for more federal research money to universities. But it is another thing to call such advocacy a matter of civil rights. I recall a recent conversation with a graduate student who was preparing to be a bilingual education supervisor. She told me she believed that Spanish-speaking children had a right to maintain their language and culture. I agreed that they did, and that they could do it if that was what they and their parents wanted to do. The Supreme Court had decided that back in the 1920s, I told her. But why, I asked, must the schools spend money to help these children maintain their ancestral language and culture? She replied: "Rich whites can send their children to private schools where they can learn second and third languages, but they don't want Latino children to retain the language of their parents." I replied: "Let us assume that your allegations are correct. What does that have to do with the rights, to say nothing about the educational needs of the children?"

The children do have a right under the law and the Constitution, as I discussed earlier, to get help from public tax dollars to learn English. But how the schools do that is a matter of educational policy. One can argue the desirability of a public school spending money on the maintenance of ancestral languages and cultures, but that is not a right, nor is a recent demand by "immigrant rights workers" (as the headline in *Asian Week*, an English-language weekly aimed primarily at Asian American readers, calls them) that health maintenance organizations and hospitals be credentialed for cultural and linguistic competency in the cultures and languages of the patients they serve.[6] If that policy is a matter of civil rights, every emergency room would have to give equal protection to Tamil, Urdu, and Tigrean speakers.

As executive director of the Select Commission on Immigration and Refugee Policy, I visited adult language classes in different parts of the United States and saw firsthand the proliferation of languages in the United States resulting from the post-1965 nondiscriminatory immigration policy, which had resulted in extensive immigration from Asian, West Indian, Latino, and African countries. The English-language classes did help newcomers participate in American society and did help speed their economic and civil assimilation. The message they received at such schools was not different from the message that had been given to immigrant generations in the past: acquire skills, and you can become an American in the marketplace and in political life, especially if you become a citizen. But when they had to fill out forms for employment or admission to college, they got a message that encouraged them to identify themselves as persons eligible for affirmative action because they were members of designated beneficiary victim groups. An increasing number of Americans and resident aliens were covered by affirmative action remedies each year, even though they arrived after the civil rights revolution had uprooted state-supported discrimination against Asians and Hispanics who either were born in the United States or came to the country before 1970.

It was predictable that the result would be increasing competition among leaders of different designated groups for whatever benefits affirmative action could bestow. Today we can see that results-oriented affirmative action plans, which measure success in terms of numbers, are having an increasingly divisive effect in multiethnic America. In 1993 the Republican governor of Ohio, George Voinovich, awarded nineteen contracts to companies owned by immigrants from India, provoking a strong protest from elected African American officials and a counterattack by one of the Indian businessmen, who said that the black-owned firms continue to get "all the work."

Another recent example came from the city of Oakland, where a new city council district was created in 1994 for the specific purpose of electing an Asian to the city council. African American leaders, claiming to represent the largest ethnic constituency in Oakland, became angry. The issue became contentious in the 1994 mayoralty campaign between the incumbent African American and a Chinese American challenger, even though neither candidate exploited it. In 1996 a Chinese American businessman in Arkansas challenged a consent decree, angry that the judges had imposed a district on him in order to elect an African American.

Given the exclusion of African Americans from the political process, and even from the jury box, through much of our history, a strong argument can be made for the ethnic gerrymandering that in 1994 helped to elect several of the thirty-nine members of the U.S. House of Representatives. The last African American to serve as a member of Congress from North Carolina after Reconstruction was George W. White, who was in the House from 1897 to 1901. When he left Congress, he told his fellow members: "This is perhaps the Negro's temporary farewell to the American Congress. But let me say: Phoenix-like, he will rise up someday and come again." White went on: "These parting words are on behalf of an outraged, heartbroken, bruised, and bleeding, but God-fearing people—faithful, industrious, loyal people, rising people, full of potential force."[7]

It is difficult to argue that the United States has not become a better and more unified nation with the election of thirty-nine members of the House and one Senator who are African American. But the remedy of creating districts that are earmarked for persons of a particular color or ethnic group can also become dangerously divisive. It tells newcomers to American politics that the American theory of political rights puts great emphasis on being represented by someone who looks and/or worships as you do, as opposed to someone who thinks the way you do.

As with other affirmative action remedies, the Supreme Court requires, under standards of strict scrutiny, a compelling reason to establish districts with tortured geographic lines just for the purpose of electing someone of a particular ethnic background. In *Shaw v. Reno*, decided on June 28, 1993, the Court decided by a 5 to 4 decision to uphold a lawsuit by white voters who claimed that creating a particular majority black district with an unusual geographic shape violated the Fourteenth Amendment's equal protection clause. The burden of proof, the Court held, is on the state to prove that such districts are "narrowly tailored to further a compelling government interest"—an extremely difficult burden of proof, but one that is appropriate for such extreme measures. The Court said that redistricting legislation that "rationally can be viewed only as an effort to segregate the races for purposes of voting" may be struck down. In this case, Justice Sandra Day O'Connor, speaking for the Court, said that the plan brought together faraway people who "may have little in common with one another but the color of their skin. . . ." Perhaps engaging in a bit of hyperbole, she said that the plan "bears an uncomfortable resemblance to political apartheid."

The Supreme Court revisited the issue again in 1996, when Justice O'Connor, speaking for a plurality of the Court, reiterated the view that any use of race in districting plans must come under strict scrutiny and serve a compelling public purpose. In no case, she argued in invalidating one congressional district in North Carolina and three in Texas, could race be the dominant factor.

Many African American, Asian American, or Latino American politicians and advocacy leaders denounced the decision as an assault on civil rights. They saw the Court as giving greater concern for regularly shaped districts than to principles of fair representation. Such critics apparently see no danger in promoting the notion that fair representation means there must be black districts, white districts, Asian districts, Hispanic districts, and perhaps subdivisions within those groups. Critics of *Shaw v. Reno* also point out that district lines are often jiggled to elect Republicans or Democrats, and they ask why these lines cannot be gerrymandered to elect members of designated minority groups. A. Leon Higginbotham Jr. and two associate authors argued that, by applying the equal protection clause in *Shaw v. Reno,* the Court *has* turned the meaning of the Fourteenth Amendment on its head. It is a mistake, they reasoned, to apply the equal protection clause "to preclude African-Americans from obtaining significant power."

> The decision, at least in part, is premised on the notion that irregularly shaped, minority-majority Congressional districts are somehow akin to apartheid and segregation. But apartheid and segregation are invidious policies intended, at bottom, to exclude citizens from civic life because of their race. Minority-majority districts, intended to include racial minorities into the politics from which they were so long locked out, are neither similar nor analogous to apartheid or segregation.[8]

But does that conclusion mean that every attempt at ethnic gerrymandering should be approved? Is there no gerrymander that would fail to pass constitutional muster?

Perhaps the fact-finding was wrong in the *Shaw* case, but the principle that there are limits to ethnic and racial gerrymandering must be upheld if one hopes to build, in John Higham's words, "a decent multiethnic society" in which Martin Luther King's goal for judging individuals on the basis of their character and not the color of their skin is nurtured. In recent years, black mayors in Los Angeles, Minneapolis, Seattle, and New York apparently were judged on the basis of their character and ability when they were elected with the votes of large numbers of whites, and an African American, Douglas Wilder, could not have been elected governor of Virginia without significant support from white voters. Other African Americans elected in overwhelmingly white districts in recent years include Carol Mosley Braun, the U.S. senator from Illinois, North Carolina's state auditor, the district attorney of Suffolk County (Boston, Massachusetts), and three members of the U.S. House of Representatives. That General Colin Powell should have been sought after by political power brokers from both parties to run for President of the United States is an indication that a black person could be elected president even though blacks constitute less than 10 percent of the voters in the largest district of all.

There are those who would question whether Colin Powell is capable of representing African Americans, as if there was not a vast diversity of interests expressed by African Americans. One of those critics might be Lani Guinier, who has been troubled by ethnic gerrymandering because conservative Republican whites in many state legislatures have seized the opportunity to create isolated black districts that ghettoize black voters and reduce their influence in formerly marginal districts that now go easily to conservative Republicans. In her article "The Triumph of Tokenism," Guinier distinguishes between blacks who are "authentic representatives" and blacks "who must appeal to white voters in order to get elected."[9] Such an elected politician may not be an authentic representative of blacks, according to Guinier, because the winner-take-all electoral system that generally prevails in the United States sends garbled messages, "producing winners while obscuring the reasons for their victories." She writes that "even where black support provides a critical margin, successful black candidates in majority white electorates do not necessarily feel obligated to black voters."

Such reasoning, as I have already indicated, can be extended to many groups on an ethnic basis—only Ibo politicians can represent Ibo speakers, only Gujarati politicians can represent the Gujarati, only Haitian politicians can represent Haitians, and so on. Systems of weighted representation or proportional representation may give a narrowly defined group the feeling that they have elected someone who is an authentic representative of that group, but they tend to make the task of governing in a democracy more difficult. One of Guinier's ideas for representative systems that would ensure the election of authentic blacks comes from John C. Calhoun, who put it forth as a theory of concurrent majorities, in which minority groups have a veto over certain propositions. What Calhoun wanted for the southern states, Guinier would like to see tried in different ways for African Americans and for other minorities. She calls for some system of weighted voting that could be justified as a way "to overcome the disproportionate power presently enjoyed by white voters in certain jurisdictions." Then, in a huge analytical jump, she writes that "the minority veto provides minorities with an equal opportunity to influence the political process and, consequently, comports with one person, one vote."

In the end, the position each of us takes on such proposals and on other aspects of affirmative action comes down to our vision for American society. Mine is for one in which the right to express group sensibilities, interests, and claims is protected and in which the individual's right to be protected against discrimination or coercion based on personal identity is also protected. The freedom to cross boundaries does not mean the end of diversity, but quite the opposite. It guarantees the freedom of individuals to form all kinds of groups to express themselves and to make claims on the polity on behalf of group interests. This kind of voluntary pluralism says to the children of interracial and interethnic marriages and to newcomer immigrants and the rest of us: You can be represented well in our system of geographic representation—based on one person, one vote—even by someone who does not resemble you physically or go to your mosque, synagogue, or temple or speak the language or follow the folkways of your ancestors. Your elected representative wants to hear your views and to satisfy your interests because he or she needs your vote as badly as the votes of others. Such a vision does not assume a monolithic black or white or any other so-called racial or ethnic voting interest. It accommodates the rising number of multiracial voters who are being born right now. It says to individuals, whether they are Jewish black male violinists or Buddhist Japanese American female carpenters, that their ideas and interests will be heard.

Nor does such a vision make every discussion about remedies to implement civil rights simple. Following *Brown v. Board of Education*, every African American child has a right to an education in an integrated school if it is at all possible. Many remedies have been tried to make it possible: extensive busing, magnet schools, and different standards for admission to schools that select students by competition. The remedies are not the right, but they are needed to fulfill the right. If the remedies trample on the rights of others, they create what Nathan Glazer called in 1982 "ethnic dilemmas."

An example of such a dilemma, and there are many, was presented in the Unified School District of San Francisco in 1995. Following a 1982 federal court consent decree that prevented any San Francisco public school from exceeding 40 to 45 percent of a single ethnic group, the Lowell High School required a competitive test for entrance, because it was supposed to be the most desirable high school in San Francisco. The remedy chosen by the school district to bring about integration at Lowell was to use different test scores to determine admission for members of separate ethnic groups. The school district required a score of 62 from Chinese American applicants, a score of 58 from other Asians and whites, and a score of 53 for African Americans and Latinos. Understandably, the parents and children with Polish, Ukrainian, or Chinese backgrounds were upset. Chinese American parents, anxious to get their children into this school, filed a class action suit against the California Board of Education and the San Francisco Unified School District. As a spokesperson for the Chinese American students said: "In our eyes, it's a very simple civil rights issue."[10]

Actually, it is a *complex* civil rights issue, but the Chinese American parents are closer to the 1954–64 meaning of civil rights than those who would jiggle the tests to produce an outcome based on ethnicity regardless of other factors. A policy that makes ethnicity such a critical factor in who is admitted to Lowell overlooked the possibility that some Vietnamese American or Polish American youngsters might come from broken homes, live in poverty, have speech impediments, or in some other way be disadvantaged as individuals. There is nothing more anguishing in our society than a dilemma caused by the claims of African American youngsters to have the state effect remedies that make integration real, as mandated by *Brown v. Board of Education* and subsequent court decisions, and the claims of Asian American and other students to be treated equally in competitive examinations. Even as we celebrate *Brown v. Board of Education* today, we have to face the reality of the fourth R: Resegregation. We have to think more creatively than ever about what we do to help educate all our youngsters, but especially those in the North's urban centers and suburbs and in the West, where black children find themselves increasingly in separate and unequal schools. We now face the irony that sees a black family moving to Georgia or Tennessee more likely to have their children grow up in integrated schools than if they remain in New York, Illinois, Texas, New Jersey, or California, which have the largest percentages of black students attending schools with 50 to 100 percent minority populations. But as we canvass the remedies today, they do not look nearly as simple as when I was a principal author of the Racial Imbalance Report as a member of the Massachusetts Racial Imbalance Commission in 1964.

Affirmative action remedies were intended to lead toward a more inclusive society. In many cases, they have been divisive, as the scramble of different groups to be counted as racial groups in the Census in order to qualify for affirmative action programs shows. Some Hispanic advocacy leaders, not content to have "Hispanic" listed as a separate, nonracial language minority category, have been arguing to be included as a fifth racial category in addition to "white," "black or African American," "Asian or Pacific Islander," and "American Indian and Alaskan native." The problem from their point of view is that most Hispanics call themselves white under the present listings, even if they check off "Hispanic" in the special nonracial category created for them. Leaders of Middle Eastern groups who do not want their groups limited to "black" or "white" want a separate category. Cape Verdean leaders who do not want to be forced to call themselves "black" or "white" have requested a separate category. Persons of mixed racial background do not want to be boxed in to the pentagon of categories that now exists and are clamoring for a multiracial category. One reason—but not the only one—that representatives of these groups want to be listed is to be able to make claims under the Voting Rights Act and under federal affirmative action plans in the areas of employment, housing, and education, and to obtain money under federal programs such as the Home Mortgage Disclosure Act and the Equal Credit Opportunity Act.

Believing as I do in an America that is as inclusive as possible for all who live legally in it and that has as its unifying principle that all women and men are created equal in dignity regardless of color, gender, religion, age, national ancestry, or sexual orientation, I want us to say to immigrants who come to the United States that we shall try our best as a society to protect them against any form of discrimination based on those benign qualities of their identity, but that no government will set aside contracts, jobs, or places at universities and colleges for them on the basis of those attributes. At the same time, we should be more vigorous than we have been in coordinating the activities of federal, state, and local agencies in preventing and punishing discrimination in education, employment, banking, and, that most difficult of all cases, housing. If we hold fast to the principle that the rights of all individuals should be protected regardless of ethnic background, we will see a way to phase out government-enforced affirmative action remedies that rely heavily on numbers as a measure of success in expanding opportunities for nonwhites. We can do that even as we retain and improve programs that emphasize recruitment and training to expand opportunities for all disadvantaged Americans, and as we refocus attention on the terrible problems of poverty that affect African Americans, Puerto Ricans, and Native Americans disproportionately, and that also affect a growing white underclass, Southeast Asian refugees—and others.

It is time for all of us who share a vision of a United States that is free from bigotry and discrimination to think and rethink about how we get from here to there. There is much to be done to overcome bigotry. Racism, expressed primarily in the treatment of blacks as inferior by whites and others, persists in the daily insults and indignities to which blacks are subjected. Affirmative action remedies are not the main cause of racial and ethnic tension in the United States. They are not the main cause of a racist backlash or of what appears to be the growing indifference of many Americans to the plight of those who suffer because of poverty and/or the color of their skin. But that does not mean that every affirmative action remedy will move us away from bigotry and discrimination and toward the humane multiethnic society we seek.

We all must answer a question: When is it desirable, as well as constitutionally permissible, for us to use ethnicity or so-called "race" as a basis for government policy to distribute benefits. For whom? For what purpose? In what way? By what rationale? For how long? Our answers to these questions depend on what we believe and what we are willing to do.

Our preoccupation with color and what is called "race" is negatively affecting our debate on many public policies, including crime, education, health, and welfare. The most important thing we can do to improve the life chances of African American youngsters in the United States is to make a commitment in those four areas on the order of the Manhattan Project or the Marshall Plan. This is not because I have so much confidence in the perfect wisdom of government or its ability to solve such complex problems, but because I believe we can do much better than we are now doing.

We should not cloud the debate by making these issues a matter of color or ethnicity. It is a question of building a more perfect union and establishing justice and providing for the common welfare to fulfill the promise of the preamble to the Constitution for the most vulnerable Americans, regardless of color or ancestry. I know that the budget deficit inhibits the ability of the nation to enhance basic human dignity and opportunity for those who live in poverty. In the face of that deficit, I also know that it is difficult to arrive at politically acceptable welfare, education, and health care reform measures. But one can accept the difficulty of dealing with these issues without giving up on the task of facing them in a humane way. I also believe that we are not doing enough to combat discrimination, particularly in the field of housing. The nation deserves a considerable amount of credit for its efforts against discrimination. We embarked on a civil rights compact and set up an extraordinary structure of civil rights enforcement. We read almost daily about settlements of job discrimination cases, the prosecution of civil rights discriminators, the allegations by the federal government of bias in this and that city in hiring police or firefighters, the exposure of the CIA and the FBI for not making greater efforts to hire minorities, and so on. But the most intractable, complex discrimination exists in the field of housing. Of course, if there were more and better jobs in inner cities, more police on the streets, more money for rehabilitation, and enterprise zones that generated business, those communities would be in better shape. But Douglas Massey's book with Nancy Denton, *American Apartheid*, shows that enforced segregation of African Americans is itself a major cause of the problems that cry out for remedy.

The unemployment rate for black youths between the ages of sixteen and nineteen is intolerable, and more can be done to reduce it. In some parts of the country in some sectors of the economy, illegal aliens are taking their place. But that is probably only a small part of the problem. White and other employers often have difficulty distinguishing between street kids, who they think will not stay on the job or will do it badly, and other youngsters who will make good employees. They do not want to hire young black males, particularly because they are afraid of them, as Elijah Anderson has said. We have got to do a better job of finding out why job-training programs are not more effective and the extent to which there is real discrimination in hiring and how to reduce it.

That many Americans share my beliefs regarding the urgency of another national effort to attack poverty is doubtful. But one consequence of the failure to do so will be the escalating anger of African Americans, even those in the middle class, as they watch what I believe they and I see as spreading indifference to the injuries of both race and poverty. As a result, we have seen increased support among African Americans for Afrocentric approaches to education and curriculum, rising anti-Semitism among black college students who cheer loudly for leaders of the Nation of Islam, and a growing acceptance among such black intellectuals as Derrick Bell of a theory of permanent racism to justify government policies that count by race. We also see growing support for segregation as a positive ideology and for reparations as a political agenda. I believe, as nearly everyone does, that the widespread use of drugs and the black-on-black violence in our cities promote indifference among whites and others while intensifying the pain and grievance most African Americans feel for the failure of the nation to make more progress toward a just society.

We need to face the fact that while the civil rights revolution was about extending the full protection of the U.S. Constitution to all Americans, it came about in the context of redressing the grievances of African Americans who, only becuase of their skin color, had been denied those rights. The decision of President Lyndon Johnson, and later that of President Richard Nixon, to go beyond antidiscrimination law—intended to cover everyone— to affirmative action was aimed specifically at redressing the grievances of African Americans. There never was a comparable historical justification for including others as designated beneficiary groups because of ethnicity. If possible, we should phase out proportionality-based affirmative action remedies for all groups except American-born African Americans by the year 2000. Most immigrants are now covered by numerical results-oriented affirmative action programs, something that was never contemplated when regulations were written in 1971 establishing categories of beneficiary groups to include Hispanic Americans and Asian Americans. Moreover, discrimination against Hispanic Americans and Asian Americans historically and to this date is much more like that suffered by many European immigrant groups and their children than it is like the history of slavery and caste suffered by the ancestors of African Americans. The lumping together of third- or fourth-generation Japanese Americans or Chinese Americans with recent H'mong and Mien refugees for purposes of affirmative action betrays some of the inherent weakness in the group-remedy approach to protecting individual rights. South Asian immigrants and African immigrants have high incomes in the aggregate. Japanese Americans in the aggregate have higher household incomes than any other ethnic group in California. But Southeast Asian immigrants have much lower household incomes, and refugees from Cambodia and Laos have high rates of welfare use.

Strong antidiscrimination enforcement should take place for Asian Americans, Latino Americans, and all Americans. Indeed, I believe in applying civil rights protections on the basis of sexual orientation. Although such constitutional protections already exist, they need to be explicit in legislation. But proportionality-based remedies should not be available to anyone but native-born African Americans.

The strict-scrutiny principle applied by the Supreme Court to race-based public policies is the correct one if we are to build a more perfect union with justice for all. Numerical-results remedies have been adopted in recognition of the difficulty of uprooting discriminatory practices, particularly against African Americans, through regular antidiscrimination methods of enforcement. Many of these numerical remedies have undoubtedly enhanced opportunities for African Americans, women, and others, but they should not be employed unless the program is narrowly tailored to implement a compelling public purpose. We must remember that membership in a racial or ethnic group is only a rough proxy for economic disadvantage and even for discrimination. Members of designated beneficiary groups may have grown up in loving, well-to-do families, and they may have had excellent, caring teachers. But because a white man from a severely disadvantaged background may be kept from a job or a promotion or admission to an educational institution solely because of skin color, the issue of equity—the equal protection question—cannot be ignored. When different competitive standards are used for members of different groups, even when uniform standards are clearly related to job performance (for example, a basic English competence test for entrance to teacher training schools in Texas or for the passage of a police sergeant's exam in New York), the equal protection clause should be considered under standards of strict scrutiny.

Not all objections to affirmative action remedies are driven by racist backlash or by an attempt to pretend that Americans are color-blind and that discrimination no longer exists. Another reason such remedies have been questioned by liberals with integrity and a powerful commitment to civil rights is that they may deprecate the achievements of members of designated groups. Still another is that set-aside programs are particularly vulnerable to fraud, as when women are used to front for men as owners or managers of companies seeking preferential treatment under Federal Communications Commission, Small Business Administration, or other government set-aside programs. They are also subject to abuse when Hispanic surnames are used inappropriately as a proxy for alleged discrimination and/or disadvantage. Despite these problems, however, numerical-results remedies can and should be applied under the Constitution for native-born African Americans when such remedies fulfill a compelling public purpose and are carefully tailored to do so. Desegregation plans fit into that category. A compelling public reason to count by race exists when there has been a pattern of discrimination in a particular sector of the economy or in a specific business. Such a purpose can exist when police departments, fire departments, and teaching staffs, needing to serve their populations better, count by race to achieve a greater presence of African Americans in their organizations. It also can exist at a university or college seeking diversity to enrich the education of all of its students. But goals should not be linked to fixed timetables. Race must never be the sole or dominant factor by which appointments, promotions, admissions, or contracts are approved. Fundamental standards and qualifications must not be compromised, even though some flexibility might meet the definition of a carefully tailored program in relation to the compelling public objective that is sought. The standard in the *Bakke* case is still a good one. Then, the Court ruled that it was permissible to take race into account in admissions as long as there are no quotas and race is not the sole or primary factor. The Court took a common-sense approach. Presumably, it would take the same kind of approach to the admissions program at the University of California at Berkeley, the most competitive of all of the universities in the California system, where in 1994 some 39 percent of the freshmen admitted were Asian, 32 percent were white, 14 percent were Hispanic, and 6 percent were black. Of these groups, Asians had the highest grade-point average from high school at 3.95; blacks had only 3.43. The young Asian student who was turned down with a 3.7 average would be justifiably angry. Yet the state clearly has an interest in encouraging the enrollment of African Americans at Berkeley.

Counting African Americans for the purpose of achieving an important public policy—diversity in college admissions, encouraging participation by blacks in politics, accelerating the number of role models in certain professions—should be permissible as a remedy to achieve those goals under conditions of strict scrutiny, which is to say that race should be one factor in the decision to allocate benefits and that numerical targets should never be quotas. Counting-by-race remedies can still be considered good medicine aimed at making Americans a more perfect union, but we must all recognize that medicine taken for too long or in concentrations that are too high is frequently poisonous. Counting-by-race remedies are dangerous, and wise public policy would aim at eliminating them altogether and concentrating on color-blind and ethnic-blind policies to broaden opportunities for the disadvantaged. That is not because Americans are or should be color-blind, any more than they should be ethnic-blind. We all can be enriched by an appreciation of the traditions, values, and sensibilities of others. A genuinely multiethnic society is not one that has many ethnocentrisms but one in which the boundaries are so fluid that those traditions and values can be freely shared. But in the end the Constitution must be color-blind. Remedies, even counting-by-race remedies just for native-born African Americans, must be temporary when they are based on counting by race or ethnicity if we are to build a humane multiethnic society based on individual rights.

It would be wise to set a date by which to eliminate all counting-by-race remedies, perhaps by the year 2010. Most Americans want to be assured that the idea of group rights based on color or ethnicity has not become entrenched in the American political and legal system. They want to know that numerical-results affirmative action remedies, as opposed to other measures taken in a proactive way to promote equal opportunity, will not last forever. By setting a date certain to end counting-by-race remedies, we will give agencies in the government strong impetus to shift their energies to programs of outreach and training and to vigorous antidiscrimination action. We would focus again on the nonracially class-based policies to solve problems that are disproportionately hurtful to African Americans. We would make clear our commitment to civil rights protections around a unifying definition of civil rights that is not ambiguous or easily subject to abuse. We would trim the incentives that intensify ethnic grievance and conflict. Without neglecting or ducking for a moment the terrible scars of race that are so deeply etched in American history, we must pay at least as much attention to the requirements of the *unum* as we do to the demands of the *pluribus*. That is the way to help both democracy and diversity flourish. It is the way to nourish our dream of equal opportunity for all, regardless of race, ethnicity, or gender.

## CHAPTER FOUR

# Making Sense of the Affirmative Action Debate

## ERWIN CHEMERINSKY

No issue is currently more controversial or more divisive than affirmative action. Those who support affirmative action argue that it is an essential technique to remedy the long legacy of racism in American society. Opponents of affirmative action contend that it is reverse discrimination and that it is simply wrong for the government ever to use race in conferring benefits such as government contracts, jobs, or admissions to schools.

Both advocates and foes of affirmative action cloak their positions in noble rhetoric. Supporters of affirmative action describe a history of subjugation of African Americans that includes the horrors of slavery, the government-mandated segregation of the Jim Crow laws, and racial discrimination in every facet of society. Opponents, in contrast, believe that it is imperative to have a color-blind society where every person is treated as an individual and evaluated on his or her own merits.

The author wishes to thank Melanie Petross for her excellent research assistance. He is also grateful to Catherine Fisk for all that he has learned in many conversations with her about this topic.

An enormous amount is at stake in this debate. Jobs, admission to colleges and universities, government licenses and contracts, and elected political office are the tangible benefits at issue. More generally, the debate is about how American society should think about and deal with race. Enormous disparities between whites and blacks remain in every measure of educational and economic achievement. Must this be tolerated, or can the government use affirmative action as a step toward greater equality?

The major problem with the debate over affirmative action is that it treats affirmative action as if it were one type of government action for a single purpose. Both defenders and attackers of affirmative action frequently fail to recognize that affirmative action can take many forms to achieve many different goals. Far too often, debates about affirmative action involve opponents attacking the most extreme forms of affirmative action, such as rigid quotas adopted based on a general desire to help minorities, while supporters defend using race to help proven victims of past discrimination. A meaningful discussion of affirmative action cannot focus on affirmative action as if it is a monolithic concept, but rather must focus on what types of race-based actions are permissible under what circumstances.

The first section of this chapter, "The Goals of Affirmative Action," considers the different purposes that affirmative action might serve: remedying past discrimination; enhancing diversity; increasing the political power of minority groups; providing role models; enhancing the wealth and services provided to minority communities. The initial focus of the affirmative action debate should be on which, if any, of these goals are a permissible basis for using race in decision-making.

The second section, "The Techniques of Affirmative Action," considers some of the forms that affirmative action can take. Techniques of affirmative action in hiring or admissions, for example, can range from efforts to encourage minorities to apply for positions, to goals and timetables, to rigid quotas.

The third section, "The Need for Affirmative Action," concludes by arguing that some types of affirmative action are desirable and indeed essential under some circumstances. It also responds to some of the major objections to all affirmative action efforts.

The central thesis of this chapter is that the debate over affirmative action will be inherently misguided so long as it treats affirmative action as if it were a unitary concept. A meaningful discussion of affirmative action must be particularized, focusing on the specific types of actions that are permissible under certain circumstances. For the sake of clarity and simplicity, "affirmative action," as used throughout this chapter, simply refers to the government's use of race in decision-making to benefit racial minorities. Gender-based affirmative action is also an important and related topic, but not the focus here.

In addition, this chapter focuses primarily on government affirmative action efforts, although the same analysis often applies when affirmative action is undertaken by the private sector. The primary difference is that government actions are limited by the Constitution, whereas the Constitution does not apply to private conduct. Because this chapter is concerned with whether and when affirmative action efforts are and should be constitutional, the focus is on government efforts.

# The Goals of Affirmative Action

Affirmative action is used to achieve many different objectives. An essential starting point in the debate over affirmative action must be to identify which goals are permissible, or even compelling, and which are unacceptable.

## Remedying Past Discrimination

The most frequently identified objective for affirmative action is to remedy past discrimination. No one can deny the legacy of racism that has plagued American society. Those who advocate affirmative action say that it is not enough to stop current discrimination, that efforts must be made to erase the effects of past discrimination—and this necessarily involves affirmative action. Those who oppose affirmative action say that it is sufficient to prohibit race discrimination and to allow all American citizens to be considered based on their merits.

The problem is that remedying past discrimination can mean many different things and cannot be treated as a single concept. For example, in its most limited sense, remedying past discrimination can mean providing a benefit to an individual who personally suffered discrimination in the past. If a person can prove that he or she was denied a job on account of race, a court order to hire that person is a form of affirmative action; the person is now being hired to remedy past discrimination. Even the most conservative members of the U.S. Supreme Court who vociferously oppose affirmative action are willing to accept it under these circumstances.[1] Remedying past discrimination in this limited sense means using race to help a person who is a proven victim of race discrimination.

Remedying past discrimination can also have a broader meaning: it can be used to remedy a class of persons who were the subject of discrimination, even though the benefits are not limited to the individuals that were the proven victims of the discrimination. The Supreme Court's decision in *Paradise v. United States* is illustrative.[2] A federal district court had found that the Alabama Department of Public Safety had engaged in intentional racial discrimination in hiring and promotions. As a remedy, the court ordered that every time a white was hired or promoted a qualified black had to be hired or promoted, until the effects of the past discrimination were eradicated.

The beneficiaries of this order were not limited only to individuals who could prove that they were denied jobs or promotions. The reality is that many blacks never applied because they knew about the discrimination, and therefore it would be far too limited to restrict the remedy to those who could prove that they personally had suffered. The Supreme Court upheld the federal court's order as an appropriate remedy for past discrimination.

Similarly, in *Fullilove v. Klutznick*, the Supreme Court upheld a federal law that set aside public works monies for minority businesses, because it concluded that Congress had found a long history of discrimination in the construction industry.[3] Again, affirmative action was used to help a group that had suffered past discrimination, although the remedy was not limited to those who could prove that they specifically had suffered discrimination.

When affirmative action is employed in this fashion to remedy past discrimination, the issue inevitably becomes what type of proof of prior discrimination is needed—how specific must it be? Must it be proof of discrimination by a single department or agency, as in *Paradise*, or may it be proof of discrimination in a more general sector of society, as in *Fullilove?*

Even more broadly, affirmative action might be used to remedy general social discrimination. In other words, these efforts are based on the legacy of racism and discrimination that pervaded all aspects of American society. For example, preferential treatment for minorities in hiring or admissions to schools can be justified in light of the history of discriminatory treatment. In one sense, this approach to affirmative action is about trying to place minorities where they would be if the centuries of discrimination had not occurred. In another sense, this type of affirmative action is sometimes described as reparations—giving a form of compensation to the class of persons who have suffered.

One problem with the affirmative action debate is that supporters and foes of affirmative action often mean different things when they discuss affirmative action to remedy past discrimination. Frequently, opponents of affirmative action argue that reparations are not appropriate, and point to other groups that also have suffered a long history of discrimination but do not benefit from affirmative action. In contrast, supporters of affirmative action often speak of remedying past discrimination in a more limited sense of helping the victims, individually or as a class, that have suffered discrimination. The key point is that it is not enough to speak of whether affirmative action is justified to remedy past discrimination. There must be a much more particularized definition of what that means.

Within that discussion there then needs to be consideration of what it means to be a victim of past discrimination. What counts as past discrimination, and how particular must the proof be and how narrowly tailored must the remedy be?

## Enhancing Diversity

Another important objective of affirmative action is enhancing diversity. Entirely apart from remedying past discrimination, race might be used to provide more diversity than would exist through a completely color-blind system.

This justification for affirmative action is most frequently invoked with regard to decisions by colleges and universities, both in admitting students and in hiring faculty members. The argument is that race is a powerful factor influencing a person's experiences and perceptions. Therefore, education is enhanced when there is a diverse student body and faculty.

For example, in fifteen years of teaching constitutional law, I have had classes that were almost all white and classes where there were a substantial number of minority students. The discussions about race and affirmative action were vastly different, depending on whether there were a significant number of minority students.

I have no doubt that my students learned more and benefited more from the discussion when minority students were present.

In *Regents of the University of California v. Bakke,* Justice Lewis Powell argued that colleges and universities have a compelling interest in having a diverse student body.[4] Ideally, such diversity would exist through color-blind admissions and hiring policies, but where diversity will not result from color-blind admissions, and because of the legacy of discrimination still often it won't happen, then affirmative action is used to enhance diversity.

Although increasing diversity is most frequently used to justify affirmative action in the educational context, there are other situations where this goal is invoked. For example, in *Metro Broadcasting v. FCC*, the Supreme Court upheld a federal system to give preference to minority businesses in licensing of broadcast stations.[5] Justice Brennan, writing for the Court, emphasized the value of diversity of views and programming over the broadcast media and accepted the government's argument that racial diversity in licensing will enhance this goal.[6]

Discussing affirmative action to enhance diversity requires consideration of the circumstances in which diversity is valuable, the extent of diversity without affirmative action, and the degree of diversity that should be sought through affirmative action. Rarely, though, do discussions about affirmative action become that specific.

## Increasing the Political Power of Minorities

The reality is that African Americans, Latinos, and Asians are underrepresented in elected office relative to their proportion of the population. Through much of American history, the franchise was denied to minority voters. Although the Fifteenth Amendment declares that the right to vote shall not be denied on account of race, it was met "by a near century of unremitting and ingenious defiance."[7] The 1965 Voting Rights Act and its amendments in 1982 were crucial to ensuring the enfranchisement of minorities and ending techniques designed to dilute their political power. Even after the law ordered that minorities be allowed to vote, and even after discriminatory techniques such as literacy tests were abolished, there remained ways in which minority political strength was diluted—such as with at-large elections and by dividing the minority population into different districts.

One possible goal of affirmative action is to enhance minority political power, such as by drawing election districts to increase the number of minority representatives likely to be elected. Again, though, this argument can take many different forms, and care must be taken to identify precisely why such an effort is made.

One possibility is simply using race to group voters because of the likely common interests that track racial lines. As Justice Ruth Bader Ginsburg recently observed, "To accommodate the reality of ethnic bonds, legislatures have long drawn voting districts along ethnic lines. Our Nation's cities are full of districts identified by their ethnic character—Chinese, Irish, Italian, Jewish, Polish, Russian, for example."[8]

Race also might be used in drawing political districts to achieve rough proportionality in representation. If a state is 25 percent African American, election districts might be drawn so that 25 percent of them are majority black, in order to create the possibility that the representation will parallel the demographics of the population.

Most generally, it might be argued that the only way to remedy the legacy of discrimination is to provide racial minorities political power. This requires drawing election districts in a manner that is likely to increase the number of minority voters.

Recent Supreme Court decisions have been hostile to using race to increase minority political representation. In *Shaw v. Reno* (1993)[9] and in *Miller v. Johnson* (1995),[10] the Court strongly disapproved using race in drawing election district lines and said that this would be tolerated only if strict scrutiny is met.

## Providing Role Models

Affirmative action can also be justified as a way to provide role models in society. For example, affirmative action in hiring faculty members can be justified as a means to providing positive role models for minority students. At the same time, white students undoubtedly benefit from seeing minorities in positions of authority and by having these positive role models. More generally, affirmative action in college and university admissions might be justified because it is likely to provide good role models in the long term. For instance, increasing the number of black doctors and black lawyers will provide desirable role models in the future.

However, the U.S. Supreme Court has rejected the role-model argument as a justification for affirmative action. In *Wygant v. Jackson Board of Education*,[11] the Court declared unconstitutional a school system's plan to lay off white teachers who had more seniority than minority teachers. Writing for the Court, Justice Lewis Powell explained that providing role models for black students was not a sufficiently compelling objective to support affirmative action:

> The role model theory allows the Board to engage in discriminatory hiring and layoff practices long past the point required by legitimate remedial purpose. . . . Moreover, because the role model theory does not necessarily bear a relationship to the harm caused by past discriminatory hiring practices, it actually could be used to escape the obligation to remedy such practices by justifying the small percentage of black teachers by reference to the small percentage of black students.

Evaluating the Court's position requires careful analysis of the importance of role models in society. How important is it to provide such role models, and what degree of affirmative action is necessary to supply the appropriate number of role models? Again, unfortunately, discussion of affirmative action rarely gets this specific.

## Enhancing the Wealth and Services Provided to the Minority Community

The legacy of discrimination is that minority communities have less access to professional services and, more generally, are more economically disadvantaged than white communities. Affirmative action can be justified as a way to deal with these problems. For example, affirmative action in medical school admissions might be explained as a way to improve the delivery of health care services to communities currently underserved.[12] The hope is that training more African American doctors will increase the number of doctors who want to practice in the African American community. Affirmative action in awarding government contracts can also be justified as a way of benefiting economically disadvantaged areas. Preferences for minority businesses and set-asides will ideally help to cure the enormous disparities in wealth and poverty between whites and minorities.

But the Supreme Court has been hostile to this rationale for affirmative action. In *Bakke,* Justice Powell explained that training more black doctors would not necessarily mean that there would be more doctors actually practicing in black communities,[13] and that this goal might be achieved more directly, such as by providing incentives for doctors to work in areas that are underserved. The Court never has accepted affirmative action as a legitimate form of wealth transfer.

The basic question is whether it is permissible to use affirmative action to increase the wealth and services provided to minority communities. Often this argument is not considered separately, either because it is politically unpalatable or because it is subsumed in arguments about the need for affirmative action to remedy past discrimination.

## Conclusion

These five justifications for affirmative action are not exhaustive of all the possible goals that might be advanced, nor are they mutually exclusive. Particular affirmative action plans obviously might be justified on more than one of these grounds, but not all these rationales might be applicable in all circumstances. For example, the desire for diversity might be seen as a powerful reason for affirmative action in college admissions, but it is less likely to be used to justify set-asides in awarding government contracts.

The central point is that care needs to be taken in identifying the particular reason for affirmative action in specific circumstances. Affirmative action can be undertaken for many different reasons, and meaningful discussion requires attention to the justification in each context.

# The Techniques of Affirmative Action

Although the goals for affirmative action are varied, the means of affirmative action are even more numerous. There is a vast array of techniques for affirmative action depending on whether it is affirmative action in employment, in education, in contracting or licensing, or in political representation.

For example, just in the context of employment there are many different forms that affirmative action can take. Affirmative action can be voluntarily undertaken by a government employer or it can be involuntarily imposed by a court. Affirmative action might be limited to encouraging minorities to apply. Even if the ultimate hiring process is color-blind, it is still affirmative action to the extent that more is done to encourage minorities to apply than is done for whites.

Affirmative action might take the form of aggressive recruitment of minorities for particular positions. Again, even if the decision-making will be race neutral, affirmative action can be taken in active steps to find qualified minorities and encourage them to apply for particular positions.

Alternatively, affirmative action can be taken through goals and time-tables. An employer can declare that its objective is to have a certain percentage of minorities in specific positions by a designated point in time. Goals and timetables have been a key aspect of affirmative action efforts used by the federal Equal Employment Opportunity Commission.[14]

Employers also can engage in affirmative action by using race as one factor among many in hiring decisions. For example, as a law school faculty member, I have seen our appointments committee pursue many objectives simultaneously: faculty to teach particular subjects, individuals with prestigious academic credentials, and racial diversity. There are many factors being considered and race is one of them.

Another form of affirmative action is race-norming. For example, an employer that uses tests in hiring might choose to hire the top-performing white, the top-performing black, the top-performing Hispanic, and the top-performing Asian. Likewise, even without the use of a test, an employer could rank applicants by race and choose the top from each racial list.

Affirmative action could take the form of set-asides if there are qualified applicants. An employer could say that a certain percentage of slots is held for qualified minorities. If there are less than that number of qualified minority applicants, then the slots will go to whites. If there are more than that number of qualified minority applicants, then more minorities would be hired than the percentage specified in the set-aside.

At its most extreme, affirmative action can take the form of rigid quotas, where a certain percentage of slots are designated exclusively for minorities. To understand the obvious, such quotas are the most controversial form of affirmative action and the example that critics most frequently focus on when attacking affirmative action.

This list of affirmative action techniques in employment is not exhaustive even in that context. Nor are the techniques mutually exclusive; an employer can use many of these simultaneously. Also, the line between many of these techniques often is blurred. Conceptually, there is a difference between goals and timetables as opposed to quotas, but in practice the distinction is often difficult to draw.

Likewise, in admissions to colleges and universities there are a great many forms that affirmative action can take. As with employment, it can include everything from encouraging minorities to apply, to aggressive recruitment, to using race as one factor in admissions decisions, to goals and timetables, to race-norming, to set-asides, to quotas. And this list is by no means comprehensive. For example, as a way of increasing minority enrollment, colleges and universities might use scholarships targeted for minority students[15] or special programs designed for minorities.

All too often the debate about affirmative action proceeds as if affirmative action were a single type of government action that always takes the same form. This is incorrect and inevitably produces an unproductive dialogue. Opponents of affirmative action direct their criticism at the most extreme techniques, such as rigid quotas, while supporters focus on much more modest efforts.

## The Need for Affirmative Action

It should be clear by now that affirmative action must be contextualized. Debate about whether affirmative action is good or bad is inherently misleading because affirmative action can take so many different forms to achieve so many different goals. To be productive and enlightening, the debate must be about what types of affirmative action are appropriate to achieve which objectives.

For example, I strongly believe that it is essential that there be diversity in the classroom. Education is enhanced immeasurably when students are exposed to others who are different from themselves in background, class, and race. Ideally, the admissions process would produce a diverse student body without any attention to race but unfortunately that is not the reality of American society. The legacy of past discrimination, and the continuing enormous disparities in educational expenditures for black and white children, means that completely race-blind admissions often result in an entering class with little diversity. Therefore, as the Supreme Court approved in *Bakke*, it is desirable for colleges and universities to use race as one factor in admissions decisions in order to increase the diversity of their student bodies.

There are circumstances in which more aggressive affirmative action efforts are required. For example, as mentioned earlier, in *Paradise v. United States*, a federal district court found that the Alabama Department of Public Safety had systematically excluded blacks from employment and, if hired, had discriminated against them in promotions.[16] The court ordered that, for a period of time, 50 percent of the hires and 50 percent of the promotions had to go to African Americans. The Supreme Court upheld this as a constitutional remedy for proven past discrimination.

On the other hand, there are certainly instances when particular types of affirmative action are inappropriate. Few would defend a quota, such as the one used in *Paradise*, in the absence of past discrimination or other compelling circumstances.

Those who oppose all affirmative action have a heavy burden to meet: they must show that all affirmative action efforts under all circumstances are inappropriate. I believe this burden cannot be met, but by treating affirmative action as if it were a unitary concept, opponents can avoid the burden by simply arguing against the worst forms of affirmative action under the most extreme circumstances.

Consider the arguments that are typically advanced against affirmative action and why they fail. One frequent argument against affirmative action is that the Constitution commands that the government be color-blind. This argument takes its inspiration from the powerful words of Justice John Harlan, dissenting in *Plessy v. Ferguson:* "Our Constitution is color-blind, and neither knows nor tolerates classes among citizens. In respect of civil rights, all citizens are equal before the law."[17] Few would deny that ideally government would be color-blind in all of its decision-making.

Yet color blindness is a means to the end of equality and not synonymous with equality. There are times when government must be color-conscious in order to achieve equality. For example, if it is proven that the government engaged in intentional race discrimination in hiring and promotions, then a remedy must be crafted in terms of race. Those who have been treated wrongly by an employer are entitled to a remedy that would place them where they would have been without the discrimination. Commanding color blindness is not a sufficient remedy for these victims of proven discrimination.

Nor is color blindness appropriate in circumstances where color might make a difference. For example, in a racially tense city it might be very desirable to ensure that a significant number of African American police officers are assigned to a predominantly African American community. Likewise, for the reasons discussed above, racial diversity is often extremely important in colleges and universities. If color blindness fails to produce diversity, then there are times when color-consciousness is necessary.

The simple reality is that our race matters in our background, our heritage, the way we are treated, and the way we perceive the world. There are times when it does not make sense to pretend that this is not so or to insist that color blindness be followed even where color matters greatly.

A second argument that is often made against affirmative action is that it wrongly interferes with decision-making based on merit. This argument rests on many assumptions. For example, there is the assumption that decisions would truly rest on merit absent affirmative action efforts. Consider admissions to colleges and universities, for example. The selection process has long favored applicants whose parents or relatives have attended the institution; many colleges admit athletes who do not meet the usual definition of merit; and sometimes universities give preference to applicants from diverse geographic areas.

In the employment context as well, it would be a mistake to assume that all hiring is merit-based except for affirmative action hiring. The reality is that nepotism and favoritism for friends and family always has existed.

Moreover, the argument based on merit assumes that the traditional measures of merit are accurate and are exhaustive of the definition of merit. For instance, in law school admissions the assumption is that grades and LSAT scores accurately measure who is most deserving of admission *and* that these are exhaustive of how merit should be evaluated. Yet, both parts of this assumption seem highly problematic. Undergraduate grades and LSAT scores often fail to predict many of the skills needed to succeed in law school and especially to excel as an attorney. More important, "merit" must include all that makes a person deserving of entrance. Because of the importance of diversity, merit should often include what a person will add to the education of other students.

This is perhaps even clearer in the context of faculty hiring. Faculty members are hired, in part, because of what they can teach students. In choosing a new faculty member, a school often will consider what the teacher can add to the education of students beyond what is already present on the faculty. For example, if a law school does not have a corporations teacher, it likely will make hiring one a priority because it believes that adding a corporations teacher will do the most to add to its students' education. By the same notion, if a school has no black faculty members, it can believe that adding black faculty—and the experiences and perspectives they bring to the school—can do a great deal to enhance the education of its students.

A third argument frequently made against affirmative action is that affirmative action is inherently undesirable because it inevitably harms innocent people. But affirmative action does not in all circumstances injure others. For example, if affirmative action takes the form of aggressive advertisement of positions in minority communities and active recruitment of minority applicants, it is difficult to see how anyone can claim an injury deserving of consideration.

Another illustration where affirmative action occurs without real injury is when race is used in drawing election districts to increase the number of minority representatives. All people are equally represented: one person, one vote is maintained; no one's political strength is diluted. Creating an additional majority black district seems to harm no one, except perhaps for a white candidate who has less chance of being elected.[18]

Moreover, in matters such as employment, education, or government contracting, benefiting minorities inevitably means taking away something from whites. To describe the injury of whites as an argument against affirmative action is to assume that whites are presumptively entitled to what they have and that their loss is a harm to be avoided. That entitlement, however, must be established in each context and cannot be assumed. For example, if an employer engages in overt discrimination and fails to hire a black person solely because of race, the remedy might be that the particular victim must be hired. Virtually no one questions the propriety of this remedy, even though its effect is to deny the position to a white person who is personally innocent of wrongdoing.[19]

In other words, the question is whether affirmative action is justified in favoring some over others based on race. If the answer supports affirmative action, some might be hurt by that, but affirmative action still is justified in order to achieve the desired advantages.

This is not to say that affirmative action is always justified or to ignore the harms to those who lose as a result of affirmative action. The point is that there must be careful consideration of whether affirmative action is justified in particular circumstances, and this analysis must consider who will be hurt by the affirmative action effort. Once it is decided that affirmative action is nonetheless justified, it is not sufficient to attack it just by pointing to its victims. There needs to be a much more detailed discussion about whether the harms are justified by the need for affirmative action under the circumstances.

A fourth argument against affirmative action, one that is increasingly common, is that it should be based on social class and not on race. The contention is that affirmative action exists to help those who have been disadvantaged and that therefore social class, and especially income, are better targets for such efforts.

Under some circumstances, this argument makes sense, but in other instances substituting social class for race is not sufficient. For example, if affirmative action is used to remedy proven discrimination against a racial minority, it is not an adequate remedy to help those with less income. The remedy must be targeted to the victims of the prior discrimination.

Also, if the goal of affirmative action is to increase the diversity in the classroom, social class should not be substituted for race. Ideally, diversity will mean differences among the students both as to race and to income. Social class should be added to the criteria used in admissions, but it should not replace race because it does not replace the need for minority students regardless of their income.

Many contend that what is really wrong with affirmative action is that it does not treat people as individuals, but instead looks at people as members of minority groups. The flaw in this argument is that people are both individuals and members of racial groups. Often it is essential to recognize their race in order to treat them appropriately and properly. If an employer or an educational institution has engaged in race discrimination, the remedy is necessarily directed to members of that racial group. Where race is relevant, it makes no sense to ignore that characteristic and focus on all of the other and less relevant characteristics.

For example, Justice Kennedy recently objected to affirmative action in drawing election district lines on the ground that it wrongly stereotyped blacks and treated them as members of a group and not as individuals.[20] But any black person is both an individual and a member of a racial group. Sometimes color is relevant, and in those instances appraising the person requires considering his or her race. Election district lines have long been drawn to keep ethnic communities together. This is based on the recognition that groups often share common interests and goals. Likewise, drawing election lines to create majority African American or Latino districts recognizes that such individuals are both individuals and members of a group and that group identity can matter.

Finally, opponents of affirmative action sometimes argue against it based on the reactions of the larger white society. The argument is that affirmative action exacerbates racial tensions and that affirmative action stigmatizes minorities because others then assume that any minority who is hired or admitted is there because of affirmative action.

That the reactions of the white majority should doom affirmative action is questionable.[21] Desegregation and the end of Jim Crow caused enormous tensions, yet few deny that the changes were necessary regardless of the tensions engendered. Similarly, the focus of affirmative action has to be its necessity in particular circumstances and not on whether white people like it.

At the same time, the question of stigma is a complicated one. Are blacks, as a group, better off having more spaces in colleges and universities with the danger of stigma, or would they be better off with few slots but less stigma? Affirmative action does create stigma. Yet, at least under some circumstances, minorities are probably much better off with more jobs or positions in schools, even at the cost of such stigma.

None of this is to say that the arguments against affirmative action are always wrong under all circumstances. There are instances where affirmative action is undesirable and where these harms will be manifest. Some affirmative action efforts undoubtedly have been misguided. The point is that there are many situations where these harms do not result from affirmative action and that it is wrong to assume that the harms are an inherent and inevitable part of all affirmative action efforts.

This chapter is a plea for a change in the way that affirmative action is discussed. Countless times, I have been invited to participate in debates about whether affirmative action is good or bad. A practice that is as varied as affirmative action cannot be deemed either good or bad. It all depends on the goals sought and the means chosen. Therefore, discussions about affirmative action should not be at the general level concerning its overall desirability, but rather about specific practices under particular circumstances.

There are instances where affirmative action is essential and times when it is unnecessary. There are techniques of affirmative action that are highly questionable and means that are easily defended. A meaningful discussion of affirmative action must therefore focus on context. Unfortunately, that is what has been all too often lacking in debates about affirmative action.

CHAPTER FIVE

# Residential Segregation and Persistent Urban Poverty

## DOUGLAS S. MASSEY

Although the Kerner Commission of 1968 singled out the ghetto as a fundamental structural factor promoting black poverty in the United States, residential segregation has been overlooked in recent academic debates and
policy discussions on the urban underclass. Even though a large share of
African Americans continue to be segregated involuntarily on the basis of
race, thinking within the policy establishment has drifted toward the view
that race is declining in significance and that black poverty is largely a class-
based phenomenon.

Given this emphasis, research into the causes of urban black poverty has
focused largely on race-neutral factors such as economic restructuring, family dissolution, education, culture, and welfare. Although researchers often
use the terms "ghetto," "ghetto poor," and "ghetto poverty," few see the
ghetto itself as something problematic and few have called for dismantling

This chapter by Douglas S. Massey originally appeared in *Social Service Review*
68 (1994): 471–87, and is reprinted here by permission. Copyright © 1994 by the
University of Chicago.

it as part of a broader attack on urban poverty. Despite its absence from policy discussions, however, residential segregation is not a thing of the past or some neutral fact that can be safely ignored. A large share of black America remains involuntarily segregated, and because life chances are so decisively influenced by where one lives, segregation is deeply implicated in the perpetuation of black poverty.

As a result of their residential segregation, African Americans endure a harsh and extremely disadvantaged environment where poverty, crime, single parenthood, welfare dependency, and educational failure are not only common but also all too frequently the norm. Because of the persistence of white prejudice against black neighbors and the continuation of pervasive discrimination in the real-estate and banking industries, a series of barriers exist in the path of black social and geographic mobility. The federal government has not only tolerated this state of affairs but, at key junctures over the past several decades, has intervened actively to sustain it. Residential segregation by race is an imbedded feature of life in the United States that is deeply institutionalized at all levels of American society, and as long as high levels of racial segregation persist, black poverty will be endemic and racial divisions will grow.

## Trends in Black-White Segregation

In the years following the civil rights movement of the 1960s, urban blacks came to experience one of two basic conditions. Those in metropolitan areas with large black populations experienced extremely high levels of segregation that showed little tendency to decline over time.[1] Suburbanization of blacks lagged well behind the levels of other groups, and the African Americans who did manage to achieve suburban residence remained racially isolated. In sixteen metropolitan areas, blacks were so highly segregated across so many dimensions simultaneously that Nancy Denton and I coined the term "hypersegregation" to describe their situation. Together these metropolitan areas—which include Baltimore, Chicago, Cleveland, Detroit, Los Angeles, Newark, Philadelphia, St. Louis, and Washington, D.C.—contained more than one-third of all African Americans in the United States.[2]

In urban areas where blacks constituted a relatively small share of the population, however, such as Tucson, Phoenix, and Seattle, levels of black-white segregation *declined* after 1970, at times quite rapidly.[3] In these urban areas, African Americans were dispersed widely throughout the metropolitan environment, and in contrast to the situation of large urban black communities, suburbanization brought significant integration and interracial contact. Unfortunately, relatively few African Americans experienced these benign conditions.

The dividing line between these contrasting trends is a metropolitan black fraction of 5 percent. Below this level, desegregation occurred; above it there was little change. Andrew Gross and I developed an index of the degree of segregation required to keep the probability of white-black contact at 5 percent or less.[4] The difference between this index and the level of segregation actually observed in 1970 closely predicted the decline over the ensuing decade. During the 1970s, in other words, urban areas in the United States were moving toward precisely the level of segregation needed to keep the likelihood of white-black contact at 5 percent or less. In areas with small black populations, this pattern implied rapid desegregation; in areas with large black communities, it meant continued segregation and racial isolation.

Preliminary work on the 1990 Census suggests that this split in the urban black experience has continued.[5] Urban areas with large black populations remain highly segregated and have shown little tendency to decline; areas with small black populations continue their move toward integration. Declines were especially rapid in urban areas of the South and West that contained sizeable Hispanic populations and large military bases, in addition to small black populations. Although black access to suburbs increased, in areas with large African American populations settlement was restricted to a small number of suburban communities whose racial segregation was increasing; the small number of blacks entering suburbs was not sufficient to affect the overall pattern of high racial segregation within the urban area as a whole. As a result, metropolitan areas that were hypersegregated in 1980 generally remained so in 1990, and some new areas were added to the list.[6]

The high degree of black residential segregation is unprecedented and unique. No other group in the history of the United States has ever experienced such high levels of segregation sustained over such a long period of time. Despite recent declines, the average level of black segregation is still 50 percent greater than that observed among Asians or Hispanics, and the lowest levels of black segregation generally correspond to the highest levels observed for Hispanics and Asians.

# The Causes of Racial Residential Segregation

This distinctive pattern of high black segregation cannot be attributed to socioeconomic factors—at least as of 1980, when the last study was carried out.[7] As of that year, black families earning more than $50,000 were just as segregated as those earning under $2,500; and in metropolitan areas with large Hispanic as well as black populations, the poorest Hispanic families were *less* segregated than the most affluent blacks. Similar patterns are observed when data are broken down by education and occupation. Controlling for social class makes little difference in considering the level of black segregation: blacks in large cities are segregated no matter how much they earn, learn, or achieve.

High levels of black segregation are attributable not to a lack of income but to three other factors: prejudice, discrimination, and public policy. White racial prejudice yields a weak demand for housing in integrated neighborhoods and fuels a process of neighborhood racial transition. Pervasive discrimination in the real-estate and banking industries keeps blacks out of most neighborhoods, providing prejudiced whites with an avenue of escape when faced with the prospect of black settlement in their neighborhoods. Finally, the federal government itself institutionalized the practice of mortgage red-lining and supported state and local governments in their use of urban renewal and public housing programs as part of a deliberate attempt to segregate urban blacks.

Although whites now accept open housing in principle, survey data show that they are reluctant to accept it in practice. Whereas almost 90 percent of white respondents to national surveys agree that "black people have a right to live wherever they can afford to," only 40 percent would be willing to vote for a law stating that a homeowner cannot refuse to sell to someone because of their race or skin color.[8]

Moreover, when questions are posed about specific neighborhood compositions, it becomes clear that white tolerance for racial mixing is quite limited. One-third of whites responding to a 1992 Detroit survey said they would feel uncomfortable in a neighborhood where 20 percent of the residents were black, and about the same percentage would be unwilling to enter such an area.[9] When the black share rises to one third, 59 percent of all whites said they would be unwilling to enter, 44 percent would feel uncomfortable, and 29 percent would seek to leave. At a 50–50 racial mixture, neighborhoods become unacceptable to all but a small minority of whites: 73 percent said they would not want to enter, 53 percent would try to leave, and 65 percent would feel uncomfortable.

In contrast, in both principle and practice African Americans express strong support for integration. Blacks are unanimous in agreeing that "black people have a right to live wherever they can afford to," and 71 percent would vote for a community-wide law to enforce that right.[10] When asked about specific neighborhood racial compositions, they consistently select racially mixed areas as most desirable. Although the most popular choice is a neighborhood that is half-black and half-white, 87 percent of African Americans would be willing to live in a neighborhood that is only 20 percent black.[11]

Although black respondents do express a reluctance to enter all-white neighborhoods, this apprehension does not indicate a rejection of integration per se, but stems from a well-founded fear of hostility and violence. Among black respondents to a 1976 Detroit survey who said they would be reluctant to move into an all-white area, 34 percent believed that white neighbors would be unfriendly and make them feel unwelcome, 37 percent believed they would be made to feel uncomfortable, and 17 percent expressed a fear of violence; four-fifths rejected the view that moving into a white neighborhood would be deserting the black community.[12]

If it were up to them, then, blacks would live in racially mixed neighborhoods. But it is not solely up to them, because their preferences interact with the preferences of whites to produce the neighborhoods we actually observe. Whereas most blacks pick a 50–50 racial mixture as most desirable, the vast majority of whites are unwilling to enter such a neighborhood, and most would try to leave. This fundamental disparity has been confirmed by surveys conducted in Milwaukee, Omaha, Cincinnati, Kansas City, and Los Angeles, all of which show that blacks strongly prefer a 50–50 mixture and that whites have little tolerance for racial mixtures beyond 20 percent black.[13]

These contrasting attitudes imply a disparity in the demand for housing in integrated neighborhoods. Given the violence, intimidation, and harassment that historically have followed their entry into white areas, blacks are reluctant to be first across the color line. After one or two black families have entered a neighborhood, however, black demand grows rapidly, given the high value placed on integrated housing. This demand escalates as the percentage of blacks rises toward 50 percent, the most preferred neighborhood configuration; beyond this point, it stabilizes and falls off as the black percentage rises toward 100 percent.

The pattern of white demand for housing in racially mixed areas follows precisely the opposite trajectory. Demand is strong for homes in all-white areas, but once one or two black families have entered, white demand begins to falter as some white families leave and others refuse to move in. The acceleration in residential turnover coincides with the expansion of black demand, making it likely that outgoing white households are replaced by black families. As the percentage of blacks rises, white demand drops more steeply and black demand rises at an increasing rate. By the time black demand peaks at the 50 percent mark, almost no whites are willing to enter and the large majority are trying to leave. Thus, racial segregation is fomented by a process of racial turnover fueled by antiblack prejudice on the part of whites.

Although prejudice is a necessary condition for segregation of blacks, however, it alone is not sufficient to maintain the residential color line. Active discrimination against black home-seekers must also occur: some neighborhoods must be kept nonblack if whites are to have an avenue of retreat following black entry elsewhere. Racial discrimination was institutionalized in the real-estate industry during the 1920s and well established in private practice by the 1940s.[14] Discriminatory behavior was open and widespread among realtors at least until 1968, when the Fair Housing Act was passed. After that year, outright refusals to rent or sell to blacks became rare, given that overt discrimination could lead to prosecution under the law.

Black home-seekers now face a more subtle process of exclusion. Rather than encountering "white only" signs, they encounter a series of covert barriers surreptitiously placed in their way. Although each individual act of discrimination may be small and subtle, together they have a powerful and cumulative effect in lowering the probability of blacks entering white neighborhoods. Moreover, because the discrimination is latent it is not noticeable, and the only way to confirm whether or not discrimination has occurred is to compare the treatment of black clients and white clients with similar social and economic characteristics.

Differences in the treatment of white and black home-seekers are measured by means of a housing audit.[15] Teams of white and black auditors are paired and sent to randomly selected realtors to pose as clients seeking a home or apartment. The auditors are trained to present comparable housing needs and family characteristics, and to express similar tastes; they are assigned equivalent social and economic traits by the investigator. After each encounter, the auditors fill out a report of their experiences and the results are tabulated and compared to determine the nature and level of discrimination.

In 1987, George Galster wrote to more than 200 local fair housing organizations and obtained written reports of 71 different audit studies carried out during the 1980s: 21 in the home sales market and 50 in the rental market.[16] Despite differences in measures and methods, he concluded that "racial discrimination continues to be a dominant feature of metropolitan housing markets in the 1980s." Using a conservative measure of racial bias, Galster found that blacks averaged a 20 percent chance of experiencing discrimination in the sales market and a 50 percent chance in the rental market.

He also studied six real-estate firms located in Cincinnati and Memphis and found that racial steering occurred in roughly 50 percent of the transactions sampled during the mid-1980s.[17] Racial steering occurs when white and black clients are guided to neighborhoods that differ systematically with respect to social and economic characteristics, especially racial composition. Homes shown to blacks tended to be in racially mixed areas and were more likely to be adjacent to neighborhoods with a high percentage of black residents. Whites were rarely shown homes in integrated neighborhoods unless they specifically requested them, and even then they were guided primarily to homes in white areas. Sales agents made numerous positive comments about white neighborhoods to white clients but said little to black home-buyers. In a review of thirty-six different audit studies, Galster discovered that selective comments by agents is probably more common than overt steering.[18]

In 1988 the U.S. Department of Housing and Urban Development (HUD) carried out a nationwide audit survey.[19] Twenty audit sites were randomly selected from among metropolitan areas having a central city population exceeding 100,000 and a black percentage of more than 12 percent. Real-estate ads in major metropolitan newspapers were randomly sampled and realtors were approached by auditors who inquired about the availability of the advertised unit; they also asked about other units that might be on the market. The Housing Discrimination Study (HDS) covered both the rental and sales markets, and the auditors were given incomes and family characteristics appropriate to the housing unit advertised.

The HDS provides little evidence that discrimination against blacks has declined. Indeed, previous studies appear to have understated both the incidence and the severity of housing discrimination in American cities. According to HDS data, housing was made systematically more available to whites in 45 percent of the transactions in the rental market and in 34 percent of those in the sales market. Whites received more favorable credit assistance in 46 percent of sales encounters and were offered more favorable terms in 17 percent of rental transactions. When housing availability and financial assistance were considered together, the likelihood of experiencing racial discrimination was 53 percent in both the rental and the sales markets.

In addition to measuring the incidence of discrimination (that is, the percentage of encounters where discrimination occurs), the HDS study also measured its severity (the number of units made available to whites but not blacks). In stark terms, the severity of housing discrimination is such that blacks are systematically shown, recommended, and invited to inspect far fewer homes than comparably qualified whites. As a result, their access to urban housing is substantially reduced.

Among advertised rental units, the likelihood that an additional unit was shown to whites but not to blacks was 65 percent, and the probability that an additional unit was recommended to whites but not to blacks was 91 percent.[20] The HDS auditors encountered equally severe bias in the marketing of unadvertised units: the likelihood that an additional unit was inspected by blacks was only 62 percent, whereas the probability that whites alone were invited to see another unit was 90 percent.[21] Comparable results were found in urban sales markets, where the severity of discrimination varied from 66 percent to 89 percent. Thus, no matter what index one considers, most of the housing units made available to whites were not brought to the attention of blacks.[22]

Although these audit results are compelling, they do not directly link discrimination with segregation. Using data from an earlier HUD audit study, however, George Galster related cross-metropolitan variation in housing discrimination to the degree of racial segregation in different urban areas.[23] He not only confirmed an empirical link between discrimination and segregation, but also discovered that segregation had important feedback effects on socioeconomic status. Discrimination not only leads to segregation, but segregation, by restricting economic opportunities for blacks, produces interracial economic disparities that incite further discrimination and more segregation.

Galster has also shown that white prejudice and discrimination are connected to patterns of racial change within neighborhoods.[24] In a detailed study of census tracts in the Cleveland area, he found that neighborhoods that were all-white or racially changing evinced much higher rates of discrimination than areas that were stably integrated or predominantly black.

Moreover, the pace of racial change was strongly predicted by the percent-age of whites who agreed that white people have a right to keep blacks out of their neighborhoods.

The final factor responsible for black residential segregation is govern-ment policy. During the 1940s and 1950s the Federal Housing Administra-tion (FHA) invented the practice of red-lining and effectively established it as standard practice within the banking industry.[25] As a condition for underwriting a mortgage, the FHA required a neighborhood assessment; neighborhoods that contained black residents, were adjacent to black areas, or were thought to be at risk of attracting blacks at some point in the future were colored red on the agency's Residential Security Maps and systematically denied access to FHA-backed loans. Private lenders originat-ing non-FHA loans took their cue from the government, and the practice of red-lining became institutionalized throughout the lending industry.

Black and mixed-race areas were thus denied access to capital, guarantee-ing that housing prices would stagnate, dwellings would steadily deterio-rate, and whites would be unable to purchase homes in integrated areas. As a result of federal policy, therefore, racial turnover and physical deterio-ration became inevitable following black entry into a neighborhood. During the early 1970s, lawsuits and pressure from the civil rights community fi-nally forced the FHA to open up its lending program to black participation. Since then, however, whites have deserted the FHA lending program in favor of conventional loans.

Studies show that blacks are still rejected for conventional loans at rates far higher than whites of comparable economic background.[26] Moreover, because of red-lining, black and racially mixed areas do not receive the amount of mortgage capital that they would otherwise qualify for on eco-nomic criteria alone.[27] Paradoxically, the recent opening up of FHA lending to blacks has only fueled neighborhood racial transition, with FHA loans being used by blacks to buy homes in racially mixed areas from whites, who then flee to all-white neighborhoods using conventional loans that are denied to blacks.

During the period 1950–70 the federal government also promoted segre-gation through urban renewal and public housing programs administered by HUD. As black in-migration and white suburbanization brought rapid racial turnover to U.S. cities, local elites became alarmed by the threat that expanding ghettos posed to white institutions and business districts. With federal support, they used renewal programs to clear black neighborhoods that were encroaching on white districts, and employed public housing as a means of containing the families displaced by "renewal." White city councils blocked the construction of minority housing projects outside the ghetto, however, so most were built on cleared land in black areas, thereby driving up the degree of racial and class isolation.[28]

## Racial Segregation and Socioeconomic Mobility

If segregation is imposed on African Americans involuntarily through an interlocking set of individual actions, institutional practices, and government actions that are prejudicial in their intent and discriminatory in their effect, then significant barriers are placed in the path of black social mobility. Because where one lives is such an important determinant of one's life chances, barriers to residential mobility inevitably end up being barriers to social mobility. If one group of people is denied full access to urban housing markets because of skin color, then that group is systematically denied access to the full range of benefits in urban society.

Housing markets are especially important because they distribute much more than a place to live; they also distribute any good or resource that is *correlated* with where one lives. Housing markets do not just distribute houses. They also distribute education, employment, safety, insurance rates, services, and wealth in the form of home equity, and they also determine the level of exposure to crime and drugs and the peer groups that children experience. Research consistently shows that, dollar for dollar of income, year for year of schooling, and unit for unit of occupational status, blacks achieve much less in the way of residential benefits than other racial and ethnic groups.[29]

Because of persistent segregation, blacks are far more likely than whites with the same income to experience inferior schools, isolation from jobs, crime and violence, excessive insurance rates, sagging home values, and peer environments where expectations run to gang membership and teenage pregnancy rather than college attendance. As a result, black families who have improved their lot are much less able than the upwardly mobile of other groups to consolidate their gains, move ahead further, and pass their achievements on to their children.

## Segregation and the Concentration of Poverty

Segregation not only harms the interests of individual people and families who experience barriers to residential mobility; it also undermines the community as a whole by concentrating poverty at extraordinary levels. Concentrated poverty occurs because segregation confines any general increase in black poverty to a small number of spatially distinct neighborhoods. Rather than being spread uniformly throughout a metropolitan environment, poor families created by an economic downturn are restricted to a small number of densely settled, tightly packed, and geographically isolated areas. Given a high level of residential segregation, any increase in the poverty rate *must* produce a spatial concentration of poverty; no other result is possible.[30]

Because rates of poverty and levels of segregation differ so much between whites, blacks, and Hispanics, individual members of these groups are structurally constrained to experience markedly different levels of neighborhood poverty. The geographic concentration of poverty is built into the experience of blacks but is alien to the experience of whites, even if the whites themselves are quite poor. Moreover, the basic effect of segregation in concentrating poverty is significantly exacerbated by public housing, which was used during the period 1950–70 in a racially discriminatory manner to confine and isolate urban blacks. Neighborhoods that contain public housing projects have concentrations of poverty that are at least double what they would otherwise be.[31]

In concentrating poverty, segregation acts simultaneously to concentrate anything that is correlated with poverty: crime, drug abuse, welfare dependency, single parenthood, and educational difficulties. To the extent that individual socioeconomic failings follow from prolonged exposure to concentrated poverty and its correlates, therefore, these disadvantages are ultimately produced by the structural organization of metropolitan areas in the United States. The mere fact that blacks are both highly segregated and poor means that individual African Americans are more likely to suffer joblessness and to experience single parenthood than either Hispanics or whites, quite apart from any disadvantages they may suffer with respect to personal or family characteristics.

A growing body of research has linked individual socioeconomic difficulties to the geographic concentration of socioeconomic disadvantage that people experience in their neighborhoods.[32] One study directly linked the socioeconomic disadvantages suffered by individual minority members to the degree of segregation their group experiences in urban society. Using individual, community, and metropolitan data from the fifty largest U.S. metropolitan areas in 1980, myself, Andrew Gross, and Mitchell Eggers show that segregation and poverty interact to concentrate poverty geographically within neighborhoods and that exposure to neighborhood poverty subsequently increases the probability of male joblessness and single motherhood among individuals.[33] In this fashion, the structural condition of segregation is linked to individual behaviors that are widely associated with the underclass through the intervening factor of neighborhood poverty.

According to their estimates, increasing the black poverty rate from 10 percent to 40 percent under conditions of no segregation has a relatively modest effect on the neighborhood environment that blacks experience, raising it modestly from about 8 percent to 17 percent. Although the probabilities of male joblessness and single motherhood are sensitive to the rate of poverty that people experience in their neighborhood, this modest change in neighborhood poverty is not enough to affect individual outcomes much. The probability of male joblessness rises only from 36 percent to 40 percent as a result of increased poverty concentration, and the likelihood of single motherhood increases from 23 percent to 28 percent.

In a highly segregated urban area, by contrast, increasing the overall rate of black poverty causes a marked increase in the concentration of poverty with black neighborhoods. As the overall rate of poverty increases from 10 percent to 40 percent, the neighborhood poverty rate likewise goes from 10 percent to 41 percent. This sharp increase in neighborhood poverty has a profound effect on the well-being of individual blacks, even those who have not been pushed into poverty themselves, because segregation forces them to live in neighborhoods with many families who are poor. As a result of the increase in neighborhood poverty to which they are exposed, the probability of joblessness among young black males rises from 40 percent to 53 percent and the likelihood of single motherhood increases from 28 percent to 41 percent.

Thus, increasing the rate of poverty of a segregated group causes its neighborhood environment to deteriorate, which in turn causes individual probabilities of socioeconomic failure to rise. The same rise in poverty without segregation would hardly affect group members at all because it would have marginal effects on the neighborhoods in which they live. In other words, segregation is directly responsible for the creation of a uniquely harsh and disadvantaged black residential environment, making it likely that individual blacks themselves will fail no matter what their socioeconomic characteristics or family background. Racial segregation is the institutional nexus that enables the transmission of poverty from person to person and generation to generation, and it is therefore a primary structural factor behind the perpetuation of the urban underclass.

# Public-Policy Needs

In the United States today, public-policy discussions regarding the urban underclass frequently devolve into debates on the importance of race versus class. By presenting the case for segregation's role as a central cause of urban poverty, I seek to end this specious opposition. The issue is not whether race *or* class perpetuates the urban underclass, but how race *and* class *interact* to undermine the social and economic well-being of black Americans. I argue that race operates powerfully through urban housing markets and that racial segregation interacts with black class structure to produce a uniquely disadvantaged neighborhood environment for many African Americans, an environment that builds a variety of self-perpetuating processes of deprivation into black lives.

Public policies must therefore address both race and class issues if they are to be successful. Race-conscious steps need to be taken to dismantle the institutional apparatus of segregation, and class-specific policies must be implemented to improve the socioeconomic status of African Americans. By themselves, programs targeted to low-income blacks will fail because they will be swamped by powerful environmental influences arising from the disastrous neighborhood conditions that blacks experience because of segregation. Likewise, efforts to reduce segregation will falter unless African Americans acquire the socioeconomic resources that enable them to take full advantage of urban housing markets and the benefits they distribute.

The elimination of residential segregation will require the direct involvement of the federal government to an unprecedented degree, and two departments—Housing and Urban Development and Justice—must throw their institutional weight behind fair-housing enforcement if residential desegregation is to occur. If the ghetto is to be dismantled, HUD in particular must intervene forcefully in eight ways.

First, HUD must increase its financial assistance to local fair-housing organizations in order to enhance their ability to investigate and prosecute individual complaints of housing discrimination. Grants made to local agencies dedicated to fair-housing enforcement will enable them to expand their efforts by hiring more legal staff, implementing more extensive testing programs, and making their services more widely available.

Second, HUD should establish a permanent testing program that is capable of identifying realtors who engage in a pattern and practice of discrimination. A special unit dedicated to the regular administration of housing audits should be created in HUD under the assistant secretary for fair housing and equal opportunity. Audits of randomly selected realtors should be conducted annually within metropolitan areas that have large black communities, and when evidence of systematic discrimination is uncovered, the department should compile additional evidence and turn it over to the attorney general for vigorous prosecution. Initially these audits should be targeted to hypersegregated cities.

Third, a staff should be created at HUD under the assistant secretary for fair housing and equal opportunity to scrutinize lending data for unusually high rates of rejection among minority applicants and black neighborhoods. When the rejection rates cannot be explained statistically by social, demographic, economic, credit histories, or other background factors, a systematic case study of the bank's lending practices should be initiated. If clear evidence of discrimination is uncovered, the case should be referred to the attorney general for prosecution; if no discrimination, an equal opportunity lending plan should be negotiated, implemented, and monitored.

Fourth, funding for housing certificate programs authorized under Section 8 of the 1974 Housing and Community Development Act should be expanded, and programs modeled on the Gautreaux Demonstration Project should be more widely implemented. Black public housing residents in Chicago who moved into integrated suburban settings through this demonstration project have been shown to experience greater success in education and employment than a comparable group who remained behind in the ghetto.[34]

Fifth, given the overriding importance of residential mobility to individual well-being, hate crimes directed against blacks moving into white neighborhoods must be considered more severe than ordinary acts of vandalism or assault. Rather than being left only to local authorities, they should be prosecuted at the federal level as violations of the victims' civil rights. Stiff financial penalties and jail terms should be imposed, not in recognition of the severity of the vandalism or violence itself but in acknowledgment of the serious damage that segregation does to the well-being of the nation.

Sixth, HUD should work to strengthen the Voluntary Affirmative Marketing Agreement, a pact reached between HUD and the National Association of Realtors during the Ford administration. The agreement originally established a network of housing resource boards to enforce the Fair Housing Act with support from HUD, but during the Reagan administration, funds were cut and the agreement was modified to relieve realtors of responsibility for fair-housing enforcement; new regulations also prohibited the use of testers by local resource boards and made secret the list of real-estate boards that had signed the agreement. In strengthening this agreement, this list should once again be made public, the use of testers should be encouraged, and the responsibilities of realtors to enforce the Fair Housing Act should be spelled out explicitly.

Seventh, HUD should establish new programs and expand existing programs to train realtors in fair-housing marketing procedures, especially those serving black neighborhoods. Agents catering primarily to white clients should be instructed about advertising and marketing methods to ensure that blacks in segregated communities gain access to information about housing opportunities outside the ghetto, whereas those serving the black share of the market should be trained to market homes throughout the metropolitan area and be instructed especially in how to use the multiple-listing service (MLS). HUD officials and local fair-housing groups should carefully monitor whether realtors serving blacks are given access to the MLS.

Eighth and finally, the assistant secretary for fair housing and equal opportunity at HUD must take a more active role in overseeing real-estate advertising and marketing practices, two areas that have received insufficient federal attention in the past. Realtors in selected metropolitan areas should be sampled and their advertising and marketing practices regularly examined for conformity with federal fair-housing regulations. HUD should play a larger role in ensuring that black home-seekers are not being systematically and deliberately overlooked by prevailing marketing practices.

For the most part, these policies do not require major changes in legislation. What they require is political will. When there is the will to end segregation, the necessary funds and legislative measures will follow. For America, the failure to end segregation will perpetuate a bitter dilemma that has long divided the nation. If segregation is permitted to continue, poverty inevitably will deepen and become more persistent within a large share of the black community, crime and drugs will become more firmly rooted, and social institutions will fragment further under the weight of deteriorating conditions. As racial inequality sharpens, the fears of whites will grow, racial prejudices will be reinforced, and hostility toward blacks will increase, making the problems of racial justice and equal opportunity even more insoluble. Until we decide to end the long reign of American apartheid, we cannot hope to move forward as a people and a nation.

PART THREE

# Multiculturalism
# Reassessed

# CHAPTER SIX

# Multiculturalism and a New America

## NATHAN GLAZER

To refer to a "new America," one that multiculturalism is expressing, or helping to bring about, is likely to lead to a number of very different reactions. One reaction might be alarm and regret—what was wrong with the old America? some might ask. It absorbed tens of millions of immigrants, it made them part of one nation speaking a single language, loyal to its principles, living in a common culture. Why do we need a new America at all?

Then there is the contrasting and opposite reaction, which looks back in anger at the old America and its various failings—with regard to blacks, preeminently, but also to Native Americans (American Indians, as some of us might know them), Hispanics, Asians, women—and the list can be extended. Those with such a reaction might look forward to a new and different America, with hope or enthusiasm or simply the firm determination that it will be built regardless of opposition.

My own stance is neither one nor the other. In my view, the defects of the old America have been progressively repaired over the past fifty years. I myself doubt that much more, if anything, is needed at the level of law or constitutional interpretation to make this a free and democratic nation, and one in which equality is a prevailing principle. We have serious social problems, and they center most significantly on the gaps between blacks or African Americans and other Americans, but they direct us to consider how our social policies can be more effective, rather than to any major legislative initiative or new constitutional interpretation, which was our objective in the 1950s and 1960s. We have become a much more equal country from the point of view of rights or law; public or government discrimination in various spheres against women and nonwhite groups has disappeared and been replaced by substantial preferences. Public opinion has changed, to become more welcoming of ethnic groups, racial groups, groups that were once considered deviant, all now considered equal parts of the common American society. The system worked, and it is still working, to fully incorporate all elements into our society and polity. That is my view, and so I have to join those who feel regret to some degree if the old America is passing.

How public opinion polls would divide us on the old America and the new I do not know. Congressmen and legislators seem to prefer the old America, and because they reflect public opinion one would think the crusaders for a new America must be in a minority. But the matter is not so simple. In 1944, a school board in Florida demanded that pupils be taught that America is the best society. This would not have been a matter of much dispute forty years ago, in the days of the old America, and those who would have been doubtful then might well have stayed silent. Indeed, there would have been no necessity for such an action then: that is the way I and others were taught as a matter of course. In the Florida case, the action of the board was roundly ridiculed in the national mass media, and, surprisingly, in the next election the board was replaced. Did those who voted against the board think ours *was not* the best society? Or did they think it was not good manners to insist on it publicly and teach it to our children? Or were they embarrassed that the community was being ridiculed for this insistence and therefore believed it would be better to keep their opinion that America was the best society to themselves?[1]

"Multiculturalism," a word that is not even in the spellcheck dictionary of my word-processing program, is the term that sums up the conflicts and the confusions around this issue of the defects of the old America and the need to recast our practices, particularly in the field of education, to build a new and better America. But what does it mean, what does it refer to? We do not determine the meaning of a word by fiat or by resorting to dictionaries, and certainly not in the case of a word like "multiculturalism," which is both new and endlessly changing in its implications. We learn what a word means by its usage.

Richard Bernstein, in his interesting and important book *The Dictator-ship of Virtue*, uses as his subtitle "Multiculturalism and the Battle for America's Future." It seems that the word "multiculturalism" evokes apocalyptic images. Having searched the term in NEXIS, an electronic databank with the complete texts of most major American newspapers, Bernstein tell us that the words "multicultural" and "multiculturalism" appeared in 40 articles in 1981 and 2,000 in 1992.[2] It can scarcely have meant the same thing in those two different years. Struggling with the various meanings of the term, I have explored what Bernstein and others today have in mind when they use the term "multiculturalism." Bernstein deals with a diverse set of issues. He begins his book with the story of how "sensitivity training" was introduced for the staff of a major newspaper as a result of an editorial that angered the newspaper's black staff members. Sensitivity training is found not only in newspapers. A great deal of sensitivity training, considered necessary to prepare people for an increasingly diverse work force, goes on in American corporations, government offices, and schools. Thus, one expression of "multiculturalism," both in Bernstein's account and in general use, is this awareness that the language we use, the points of view we hold, may hurt and outrage others.

Consider as a classroom example of the need for sensitivity an account from a program in Boston schools designed to expose students to multicultural issues. A student teacher says to his class that any student who flunks the test will be "shot." An experienced mentor takes the student teacher aside to explain that this kind of language is inappropriate with inner-city students, who are too often exposed to shooting and guns and violence. One assumes that the student teacher was joking, but he learned that this kind of exaggeration was multiculturally insensitive—that being shot was something his pupils had to consider seriously as a real possibility every day of their lives. Were those guiding him in becoming multiculturally more sensitive themselves being oversensitive? Is it possible that the pupils would have seen this as allowable hyperbole? These are the kinds of issues multi-culturalism raises.[3]

Multiculturalism raises issues of how we conceive, celebrate, or decry key moments in our national history. Bernstein discusses, for example, the conflicts over how or whether to celebrate the 500th anniversary of Columbus's voyage. Here was an exemplary case of how multicultural sensitivities are changing the old America. For the 400th anniversary of his voyage, the greatest world's fair in American history was launched in Chicago, commemorative stamps were issued, and there was a huge national party to celebrate what was then called his discovery. The 500th anniversary in 1992 took place in a very different America. This was no longer an event to be celebrated, and no longer to be described as a discovery. Many raged against this downplaying of Columbus's voyage, but the expected national party was not held. Our memorials, monuments, rememberings, are deeply affected by the new multiculturalism. And thus we are led to consider what we have lost, what we have gained, when we contrast the celebrations of 1892 with the conflicts of 1992.

But the key area we have in mind when we use the term "multiculturalism" today is education, at the college level and at the elementary and high school level. Bernstein reviews programs in universities and colleges for incoming freshmen on diversity—training courses for dorm residents on how to respond to a diverse student body, which seem to focus, in his account, on gay and lesbian students. I assume this is not true of all such training programs. Bernstein deals with a number of cases in which universities have come down with a heavy hand on faculty in response to charges of insensitivity, racism, or sexual harassment. He deals most extensively with battles over curriculum at the University of Texas and the Brookline High School. Issues in higher education dominate his account.

In general, multiculturalism on the campus has received more attention in the press and in book-length treatments than multiculturalism in public schools—elementary and secondary. One can understand this, because our colleges tend to be much more diverse ethnically and racially and in the open expression of homosexuality than our high schools or elementary schools, many of which serve relatively homogeneous student bodies. Because so many of our elementary schools and high schools can be dominantly of one minority group, we have in many of them a type of multiculturalism that we might call monoculturalism—concentration on one group, its history and travails and achievements. Such programs have been among the most controversial in the gamut of issues we consider under the rubric of multiculturalism. They raise the specter of separatism in a nation that is formally dedicated to making one people out of many.

Multiculturalism thus raises a host of diverse issues in response to a variety of changing circumstances: the increasing diversity, in race and ethnic background, of work forces; the greater assertiveness of minority groups or their leaders in demanding that the common culture take account of minorities; the increased number of students, faculty, and staff from ethnic and racial minorities in higher education; their increasing number and influence in such major institutions as newspapers and television stations; the almost simultaneous rise of a powerful women's movement, changing the consciousness of many women to the point where the once unobjectionable practices of an old America are seen as offensive and discriminatory; the encouragement this process gives to gays and lesbians to claim public recognition and respect; the growing political weight of such groups; the growing responsiveness of political figures, the media, and educational institutions to the points of view of such groups.

Conflicts over curriculum—whether at Stanford, Berkeley, or Texas, or in Brookline or New York City—are central issues in multiculturalism. Issues of sensitivity loom almost as large. The two are of course connected. Those arguing for more multicultural curriculums believe that will make people more sensitive to the problems of minorities and women and sexual lifestyle groups that now cluster under the banner of multiculturalism.

Affirmative action often comes up in discussions of multiculturalism, and undoubtedly it has contributed to the diversity of work forces and student bodies, but that is not at the heart of the issue of multiculturalism. Affirmative action operates under its own legal requirements, with heavy involvement of the courts. Multiculturalism is something that is truly happening in the culture, primarily in schools and colleges, with much less involvement of law and courts and lawyers—not that they are absent. But what has happened in the field of affirmative action may tell us much about what may happen to multiculturalism and will alert us to the forces involved and the kind of power they may be able to deploy.

Affirmative action reminds us that it is possible for a point of view and a policy that do not receive majority approval to become dominant and established. Consider again the case of the Florida school board, which may well have expressed majority sentiment when it acted but which found that its action was considered retrograde, insensitive. In the case of multicultural education, as in that of affirmative action, I want to consider the possibility that what I take to be majority opinion is cowed by a distinctive array of forces. The majority of the American people do not like affirmative action. (How much they don't like it depends on what kind of question you ask them and on how important it is to them in comparison with other issues.) Two U.S. Presidents in the 1980s had conducted campaigns in which they indicated their disapproval of affirmative action, and both, despite twelve years in office, were able to do nothing to reduce the legal basis for affirmative action, which rests primarily on an executive order by the president. Legally, a stroke of the pen could have eliminated the requirements for most affirmative action programs. The pen might have been lifted but never came down.

Why, one may ask, does affirmative action remain as a significant determinant of employment decisions in many government offices and services and among many major private employers? Affirmative action has become a norm. We may not like it, but that is the way to behave. When in the Reagan administration it was proposed to modify affirmative action programs, there was a storm of protest. The protest from civil rights organizations was expected, but the more effective protest came from many cities that were operating under consent decrees requiring a pattern of hiring by race and sex, and from many corporations that had affirmative action programs in place. It would upset the apple cart to change things now, they said. Thus, the regulations, despite the technical simplicity of changing them, were not changed.

I see much in this story that resembles what is happening in multicultural education. Multiculturalism asks us to consider how something becomes institutionalized, becomes a norm, in the face of a widespread and perhaps majority skepticism and disagreement. Most national media treatments of multiculturalism, insofar as they have taken a stand, have been critical.[4] In covering the parts of school curriculums that multiculturalism most affects—social studies, history, literature—the media usually see nothing much wrong with the old America. Those who were educated under the old regime seem to be nostalgic about the education they received and believe that the education their children are getting today is inferior to it.

So, one of the mysteries of multiculturalism is why it is so strong in the schools, in the colleges, despite ridicule from much of the media and much of the American elite. The case of affirmative action, despite the large differences from multiculturalism, is instructive. Very different social groups were responsible for the success of affirmative action and for the spread of multiculturalism. In the story of affirmative action, one can point to the power of civil rights groups spearheaded by committed constitutional lawyers who acted with the conviction that their cause possessed a higher morality. This was, of course, hardly sufficient. Affirmative action also needed the intervention of presidents (Kennedy, Johnson), the acquiescence of other presidents in having it continue (Nixon, Ford, Carter), and the reluctance of yet other presidents ostensibly opposed (Reagan, Bush) to intervene. It needed victory in many court battles, and it needed the acquiescence (scarcely the approval—that would have been hard to get) of Congress.

In this complex of elements, however, I would emphasize the role of the conviction of its chief proponents that they were acting out of a higher morality—for what was right and against those who uphold a decayed formalism or who simply express retrograde values. We see the same thing again and again in battles over multiculturalism. The institutors and defenders of affirmative action always felt they held the high ground of morality against their opponents. They saw themselves as simply pressing the idea of equality somewhat further, fighting for yet another notch upward in the interpretation of the meaning of equality and the interpretation of the Fourteenth Amendment. They presented themselves as—and indeed were—the continuators of the civil rights revolution, the most important movement for the common good in twentieth-century American history. Their opponents also claimed they were acting for a higher morality, even though they were attacked for defending selfish interests. They saw themselves as defending the Constitution too, and in particular its emphasis on liberal individualism.[5] But this did not have much potency against the mantle of the civil rights revolution.

Of course, in time this moral advantage of the proponents of affirmative action was reduced. From a crusade, affirmative action became an interest, supported by interest groups, and its claim to the higher moral ground no longer was so convincing. The issue had become who gets the job. But by then affirmative action had become a norm, institutionalized. The moral advantage helped institutionalize affirmative action. Then a combination of legal precedents, interests, expectations, maintained it, though we still see struggles over the details.

Those who have brought multiculturalism to American colleges and public schools represent a very different constellation of forces. Lawyers are involved very little, courts play almost no role, presidents are not involved. Yet one element is the same. The proponents have the same sense of representing the future and of fighting against the past. And in the case of multicultural education, as in the case of affirmative action, the resisters, despite the powerful arguments they can bring, despite their conviction that they act out of no racist or sexist sentiments, sense that the multiculturalists hold the moral advantage. When multiculturalists tell their opponents that they represent the past, that is undoubtedly true. When they say their opponents represent elitist values, that too is true, and the answer—but we want everybody to be part of the elite—rings hollow.

Multiculturalism has the disadvantage of being tarred with the nonsense of Afrocentrism (which is part of, and encouraged by, multiculturalism) and the silliness of "politically correct" speech, and it has the burden of defending the rights of groups that have been and still are by many considered morally "deviant," gays and lesbians. One would think these disadvantages would make multicultural education futile, yet it flourishes and expands, as we can see from the recent National Standards for United States History, which is supported by the National Education Association, the National Council for the Social Studies, and the American Federation of Teachers and was funded by the National Endowment for the Humanities and the U.S. Department of Education.[6] What gives it this strength is the advantage of taking up, in the wake of the civil rights revolution, the same cause: the interests of blacks. Affirmative action is undoubtedly more closely connected with the civil rights movement than is multicultural education; it is a direct outgrowth of the legal battles of the civil rights revolution. Yet I believe a key basis for the strength of the multicultural movement in education, despite its various sillinesses, is that, certainly more than its opponents, it represents still the civil rights cause.

One of Richard Bernstein's longest accounts tells of a battle at the University of Texas concerning a proposed required composition course that was to be based on Supreme Court civil rights cases and that presented only one point of view on them—the chief opponent of the course found it necessary to defend himself by pointing to his own civil rights credentials. And Bernstein, trying to account for the intensity of conviction of the multiculturalists in this conflict, writes: "There is little doubt, in my mind, that much of the moral fervor with which the campaign [for the new course] was waged stemmed from the belief that changing the curriculum . . . would advance the battle against racism and for inclusion."[7]

Despite the confusing spread of multiculturalism beyond what we might think of as distinctive ethnic cultures to encompass women, gays, lesbians, and other groups, I believe both the origins and the strength of the tremors that are shaking American education make sense only in the light of the black experience. Multiculturalism is not, for example, a case of the revival of ethnicity owing to a large new immigration. The immigrants do not press for bilingual education or multicultural education. If most school programs for immigrants consisted of immersion in English-language classes and the teaching of American history and general studies in their form of twenty or even forty years ago, I do not think we would hear much complaint from immigrants. Immigrants today, as was the case with immigrants of the past, come to become Americans. They are willingly assimilated in many key respects. They want to learn English and become American citizens much the way the earlier immigrants did, with some variation from group to group. Spanish-speaking groups, it is true, are interested in seeing the language survive among their children, but no more than earlier immigrant groups were. Were it not for mandates for bilingualism at the state and national level, adopted in the wake of the civil rights movement, I believe most of the parents in these groups would have accepted the pattern of imposition of English that was typical for earlier immigrant waves. Multiculturalism as an educational movement coincides with the period of growing immigration since the late 1960s, but that is more a coincidence than a cause.

The most persuasive explanation of the power of multiculturalism lies in the disappointments of the period after the great legal victories of the civil rights movement—from the mid-1970s on. The key development of that period was that the expected rise of the black population to near-parity with whites did not materialize. The progress of the black population, which was considerable in the 1960s, was checked in the mid-1970s. A chief example of that check was that blacks were not able to take advantage of the new educational opportunities open to them. Blacks' scores on tests showed little improvement, and of course education is the key to economic and professional advancement. It is no accident that one key area in which blacks responded to disappointment and frustration at their slow advance was in education. And here they bore on their banner the heady claim that they were only completing what the civil rights revolution failed to do.

The civil rights revolution expected that improved education for blacks would come through integration of the schools, but for the most part that was not to be. As in so many cases in race relations, what happened was given a radically different interpretation, by blacks and by whites. Blacks believed that, despite the apparent enlistment of the Supreme Court and despite national civil rights legislation, the integration of schools was subverted because of the enormous power whites still held. Whites believed that the rapid increase in the black population in northern cities, and their concentration in black areas in the 1960s, 1970s, and 1980s, made integration in many cases impossible. Even where integration took place there were problems: slurs and more than slurs from students and teachers and administrators; conflicts between white students and black students, some indeed based on what we might call cultural differences; resegregation of blacks in "special education" classes; the high proportion of black boys who were disciplined; and a host of other second- and third-generation problems. Integration was downgraded on the agenda of black leadership.

Blacks have lost interest, and whites are quite content to accept the demographic realities that ensure that many all-black schools will remain all black, and that substantial parts of the black school population will be educated in them. But if not integration, what can we count on to raise the level of education of black children in all-black schools?

There are very different answers current to this question. Some black educators see no reason to change the overall pattern of the American school curriculum—just do it better, they say, and with more money. Indeed, one leading and successful black educator believes that black students should learn Shakespeare, and from quite a young age. But many black educators see older curriculums as defective because black students do not see themselves in the books or in the teachers. Affirmative action will provide the teachers and the administrators; multiculturalism must provide the new curriculums. You and I might protest that that is not the answer, that good teaching, better texts, a restructured organization of schools, national norms, and state requirements are what is needed. But in our typical big-city school systems, which often have a majority of black students because large sections of the city are entirely black, and in which it becomes the norm to have a black school superintendent and in which blacks are prominent on boards of education (as of course they will be in black majority cities, with black mayors), there is a powerful opening for the answer of multiculturalism. But in this case (as in so many) "multiculturalism" might be considered a misnomer, because it is actually one culture that is being emphasized. We could argue over whether the culture of black America fully qualifies as a distinct culture, separate from the culture of the nation in which it is embodied, but that does not affect what is happening on the ground, where curriculums are being changed, in many all-black schools and in many other schools too.

The building blocks for such a change are available: eminent black writers, a key role for blacks in American history, and black leaders. And so Martin Luther King replaces George Washington on the school walls (who would be so crass as to put up portraits of Washington and Jefferson with their funny haircuts on the school wall today?), textbooks begin to include more pictures of blacks, and the story of American history is recast more sharply as the story of slavery, the battle over slavery, Reconstruction, Jim Crow, and civil rights. And why not, for that is a very important part of the story. Much of this change has already taken place, as we can see by studying recent textbooks.[8]

To my mind, it is the disappointment in the wake of the political successes of the civil rights movement that explains the power of multiculturalism. The civil rights movement succeeded in getting passed key laws that brought a much greater number of blacks into politics, that increased the number of blacks in colleges and major public and private institutions, and that eliminated all forms of public discrimination, but it did not change the circumstances of large numbers of blacks in the central cities. Perhaps most important, it did not change the fact of a predominant residential segregation that marked blacks off from all other ethnic and racial groups, and it did not change the fact that blacks did not participate in assimilation to a common society the way all other ethnic and racial groups had. Continued residential and educational segregation was one evidence of this difference. A distinctively low rate of intermarriage with whites was further evidence.[9]

It would seem inevitable that this distinctive placement of American blacks in the spectrum of ethnic and racial groups in American life would lead to some distinctive response in the sphere of education. This response could be seen all through the 1970s and 1980s, steadily gaining power. By the end of the 1980s, the multicultural revolution in curriculums had already scored major victories, even without the publicity that has accompanied battles over multiculturalism in recent years. Textbooks had changed to give large and sympathetic treatments, more than in the past, to the story of Native Americans and blacks. Examinations had changed, as in the case of the SAT, to give a large place to black history, black leaders, and famous blacks in various areas. Did the exams change in response to the textbooks, or did the textbooks change in response to the change in examinations? No matter, they changed together on a national scale.

Other factors too explain the strength of multiculturalism, even if one ascribes the major influence, as I do, to the unsatisfactory position of blacks. The change could not have occurred without major ideological changes in American society at large, particularly affecting educated Americans—not necessarily the elite, but the educated of all types who write the textbooks and make up the examinations. The textbook writers and presumably the examination makers were responding to pressures, but they could have resisted them. The pressures for multiculturalism were not overwhelming, and textbook publishers do resist some pressures. After all, how many respond to the pressures of Christian fundamentalists? But the textbook writers and publishers, the test-makers and educational leaders, for the most part accepted the demands of the critics of the old America. The nature of this change in the ideological atmosphere has been much discussed, and I have no special insight on why it occurred—it could have been the Vietnam War, weariness over the extended cold war, revelations as to how the government was conducting it, the assassinations of national leaders, and the relative decline of American economic power.

I shall discuss two anomalies in this development. In the late 1960s and early 1970s, in response to the rise of black self-assertion, there was a correlative if smaller surge of interest in older ethnicities: the immigrants of the last great wave. These groups are the special interest of the Balch Institute. If there was to be multiculturalism, why not courses on Irish, Italians, Jews, Poles, and other groups? Why should not their story be incorporated into the textbooks and the exams? They were not, as Reed Ueda and I discovered when we reviewed major texts in American history ten years ago. They might be mentioned in passing in discussions of industrialization, the rise of the city, or mass immigration, but there was no attention to them as distinctive groups.[10] As the multicultural surge has extended, one might have expected more reference to these groups in textbooks and curriculums, but that has not happened, and it won't. These groups have not become part of the "multicultural" story because its driving force comes from the black situation.

Multiculturalism has been called "oppression studies" by some of its critics, but older oppression, and oppression in foreign countries, will not do. One form of oppression dominates the making of multiculturalism: the oppression of blacks, and by extension oppression on the basis of race. Asians will be welcomed but probably won't be interested. Hispanic Americans are welcomed into the category of those who can legitimately lay claim to multiculturalism, but they are not as committed to it as blacks, and commitment varies from group to group. The most committed are perhaps the Puerto Ricans; the least committed are the immigrants from Central and Latin America; and Mexican Americans are, as Peter Skerry has dubbed them, the "ambivalent minority,"[11] torn between the ethnic path of assimilation and the distinctive path of minority politics as developed by black Americans. Latinos play a major role among ethnic and racial groups in multiculturalism, but it pales next to the role blacks play. For Latinos the immigrant path of assimilation is available, and in any case their place in American history and literature is much more modest.

If the black condition is the major explanation of the rise and force of multiculturalism, why do women and women's interests play such a large role in multiculturalism? Women's studies have been more successful in the colleges than black studies, and women have seized a place in the textbooks and the examinations for social studies and literature as large as that of blacks. Their oppression, if we consider that term suitable for cultural patterns that had prevailed for millenniums and were found in almost all societies, was of a completely different order from that of blacks. This is an aspect of multiculturalism that I observe in wonder rather than have any explanation for. One can make a case that blacks, and other groups separated from the larger society in greater or lesser degree, preserved or created subcultures and that recognition of that subculture is properly part of a "multicultural" education. The case is harder to make when it comes to women, who live in the same culture as the men they marry or raise as children. Whatever its unsuitability, the term "multiculturalism" has been stretched to cover women's issues, and material on women has established as secure a role in multicultural curricula as material on American blacks.

One could ask the same question about the recent prominence of gays and lesbians and their demands, extensively recognized in higher education and beginning to be recognized in public secondary education. There have even been proposals that elementary school students should be sensitized to the presence and distinctive family patterns created by gays and lesbians.[12] Despite the controversies about bringing such issues into the public schools, one suspects that in time they will be accepted. No conflict in this area ends with the demands of a group that claims oppression being swept under the rug. It seems that the "wave of the future" favors the ever-expanding extension of the concept of equality. It is this overarching historical umbrella that gives a moral self-confidence to those who demand multicultural education, whether blacks or gay and lesbian advocates.

I have been impressed recently by the term "identity politics," which I think is quite new but which one begins to see everywhere, in academic conferences, of course, in academic literature, but even now in newspapers. It is an odd term, because it recognizes the importance of some identities and does not seem to cover some others. For example, it does not cover the identity "working class" or "American." "Identity politics" refers only to groups that lay claim to oppression by dominant social forces—state, businesses, employers, schools, parents—on the basis of race or ethnicity, sex, sexual lifestyle, or some distinctive disadvantage (physical disability for example). The term "working class" perhaps reminds the disaffected of the organized labor movement and its history, at least in large parts of it, of hostility to blacks and indifference to the claims of women. To place an emphasis on the working class would seem to have the effect of depreciating the claims of blacks and women. If one were to argue for the significance of the "American" identity—and all Americans gain some advantage from the identity—it would be considered gross or crass, nationalistic certainly, chauvinistic possibly. Consider the case of the Florida school board.

The battles over multiculturalism during the last few years have been fought in the media and in books, and on occasion in curriculum committees. Except for a few well-known and well-publicized cases, they have not been fought in the schools and in schools of education, because there some degree of multiculturalism is simply accepted as a matter of course in curriculums in social studies and literature. Of course, in many schools multiculturalism has little impact. Teachers are still on the whole conservative. But I have been impressed by the acquiescence of teachers and administrators and writers in educational journals and professors in schools of education to the ever increasing attention to issues affecting blacks and women in curriculum, to the ever greater emphasis on the ethnic and racial backgrounds and sex of students, to the ever wider and more open and severe criticism of the America of the past.[13] All this takes place even in schools and school systems that have few minorities. Never has an educational trend come so far with so few advocates of real intellectual distinction—all of those seem to be on the other side. But while they argue for retaining the virtues of an older America and older styles of education, the kind that ignored ethnic and racial differences and taught everyone that Washington and Jefferson were our founding fathers, the crescive process that has already established a substantial measure of multiculturalism in the schools continues. It was already well established more than ten years ago.

Phrases like "the wave of the future," whatever their attractiveness, explain nothing. Real people have to do things to change history. Everyone now accepts that some degree of multiculturalism is inevitable in American education. There are those who use the term as an epithet. But one will not commonly find them in real schools, in real school debates.

Multiculturalism of some sort is now taken as a given. Whatever the causes that make it so prominent an aspect of education today—the failure of the civil rights revolution and its achievements to raise the condition of many blacks, as I believe; and the resultant frustration, or the new resurgence of immigration, which some credit, or the decline in American self-confidence—something has happened. It leads to steadily more critical reconsideration of the curriculums that once seemed to serve us in good stead, educating Americans, assimilating immigrants, preserving connection with the past.

The wave of change has left behind the old immigrant groups, which after relatively modest changes that barely recognize their presence and role in American history have made their peace with the curriculums of the public schools. These curriculums never paid much attention to the old immigrant groups, and now these groups do not care whether the school does or does not recognize them. But blacks have not yet made their peace, I am not sure that women are ready to make their peace, and gays and lesbians are now beginning to make their demands.

"Multiculturalism" is a term that many of us who have studied immigration and ethnic diversity might have found perfectly satisfactory to cover our sense some decades ago that American history and social studies needed to incorporate a larger recognition of American diversity. But terms can take on a life of their own, totally unexpected by their original users. It has become a contested term, to use contemporary jargon—an epithet to some, a banner to others. The fight now is not over multiculturalism, pro or con, unless one accepts the interpretation of the term given to it by polemicists. It is how much, what kind, for whom, at what ages, under what standards. This is work that will have to be done in national and state commissions, in state agencies, in local school boards, in schools, with textbook publishers, with test-makers. Having some modest experience with a state commission on social studies curriculum, I have discovered how hard such work is, how various are our conceptions of America, how surprisingly we can disagree on what seem to me to be obvious truths.[14] Short of the extremes, there remains a good deal of commonalty. The new America will not, like the old, take it for granted that this is the best of countries as well as the strongest. It will become more self-conscious about making any claim to a distinctive goodness and superiority, and that is all for the best. There is much in the education of the old America that would grate on us today, but there is also much that gives us some basis for pride, and I hope that can be retained in the teaching of and for a new America.

CHAPTER SEVEN

# Our Pluralistic Common Culture

## DIANE RAVITCH

The United States is a nation, not a confederation of independent states nor a collection of disparate nationality groups. It has a common civic culture that can be briefly summarized in a single sentence: "We the people of the United States, in Order to form a more perfect Union, establish Justice, insure domestic Tranquility, provide for the common defence, promote the general Welfare, and secure the Blessings of Liberty to ourselves and our Posterity, do ordain and establish this Constitution for the United States of America." This sentence, surely the most important sentence in American history, implicitly poses a question: Who are "We the people of the United States"? At the time the sentence was written, only a part of the population—white males—enjoyed the full rights of citizenship. And yet there was that sentence. It said "We the people," not "We the white male citizens." Much blood has been spilled over the years to expand the definition of "We the people" to include all Americans.

Today, the principle is well established that anyone born in the United States or naturalized as a citizen is an American. Citizenship is not conditioned by race, religion, ethnicity, language, or gender. Yet the very broad heterogeneity of our nation raises questions as to whether there are any ties that bind us together as a nation and a people. Do we as citizens have anything in common? Does it matter whether we have anything in common? Is there such a thing as American nationality and American identity? How should our understanding of nationality and identity affect public policy in general, and educational policy in particular?

Others have ably surveyed the history of the idea of American nationalism and American identity, and I will not recapitulate a story that has been well told by, among others, Philip Gleason,[1] John Higham,[2] Arthur Mann,[3] Milton M. Gordon,[4] and Lawrence H. Fuchs.[5] The very nature of American nationhood—its fluidity and openness—guarantees that we, and our posterity, will be addressing these questions again and again, shaping answers as best we can in light of our generation's experience. It is in this spirit that I intend to revisit some of the ideological dilemmas of American national identity and consider how these affect the way that we govern ourselves and educate the rising generation.

Harold Isaacs asked in 1975: "How can we live with our differences without, as always heretofore, being driven by them to tear each other limb from limb?"[6] Isaacs described the continuing fragmentation of human society as "an ironic, painful, and dangerous paradox: the more global our science and technology, the more tribal our politics; the more universal our system of communications, the less we know what to communicate; the closer we get to other planets, the less able we become to lead a tolerable existence on our own; the more it becomes apparent that human beings cannot decently survive with their separatenesses, the more separate they become."[7] Isaacs listed thirty-four bloody intergroup conflicts between 1945 and 1974 that had taken more than 10 million lives. The list included 2 million people killed in clashes between Hindus and Muslims during the partition of India and the creation of Pakistan; 2 million killed in civil war in Biafra; 500,000 Sudanese blacks killed by Sudanese Arabs; more than 500,000 Pakistanis killed by other Pakistanis; 200,000 Watusi and Bahutu slaughtered during the separation of Burundi and Rwanda; and 150,000 Kurds killed by the Iraqis. An updated list would surely include many millions more slaughtered in racial, ethnic, and religious conflicts around the world. These are not, unfortunately, remote or unknown events; not long ago, the world watched in mute and passive horror as hundreds of thousands of people were brutally massacred in Rwanda.

Racial, ethnic, and religious tensions have caused nations to disintegrate. Ethnic conflicts have caused murders and massacres in many nations, including Ireland, Bosnia, Hungary, Romania, India, Somalia, Lebanon, Israel, Syria, Egypt, Liberia, Sri Lanka, Cambodia, Burma, and Indonesia. Let us not forget: It is hard, very hard, for people to live in peace alongside others who are different from themselves. Sometimes conflict erupts because of large racial, religious, or linguistic differences. Sometimes it explodes between peoples who are more alike than different, as in Bosnia or Northern Ireland. A recent article about the psychological roots of ethnic violence noted that when differences between neighboring groups are small, minor distinguishing features assume great importance. The article cited Cyprus, a hotbed of ethnic conflict, where both Greek and Turkish men wear identical black baggy pants and shirts; the Turks, however, always wear red sashes and smoke cigarettes from a red pack, while the Greeks wear blue sashes and smoke cigarettes from a blue pack.[8]

In 1990 I encountered what Freud called "the narcissism of small differences" in a visit to Prague. There I met a politically active doctor who tried to explain to me why Czechs and Slovaks could not possibly coexist within the same state. "I don't understand," I said. "You are the same race, the same religion, and you speak a similar language. What is the problem?" She answered, "We are very different peoples; they are an eastern people, we are a western people. We have little in common." So now this country of 16 million people has become two nations.

The roll call of death, genocide, hatred, and massacres stemming from ethnic conflict should convince us of one thing: A successful multiethnic society is a rare and wondrous achievement in the world. Scholars, policymakers, educators, parents, and other citizens must ask, "What should we do to encourage a spirit of mutual respect and tolerance among people who may differ in many ways?" and "How can public policy nurture comity among the nation's citizens?"

As Emerson, Melville, and Whitman long ago prophesied, America has become the world's first universal nation. We count as citizens people from all the world's regions, races, religions, languages, and cultures. This remarkable demographic diversity may be a source of enormous vitality, as many hope, or it may be a source of perpetual tension and conflict, as many fear. Which is it to be? The answer is not obvious, nor is it foreordained. It will be determined by our own institutions, policies, and values. Diversity does not necessarily promise either harmony or conflict, although experience here and abroad suggests that it is more likely to be associated with conflict than with harmony.

How do we build a sense of the common good in an ethnically diverse society? It is not likely that we will be able to forge a sense of the common good unless we identify and build a common civic culture that overrides all of our particularities. Absent a common civic culture, the people who live within our borders would be neither a people nor a nation. The population would be a random collection of unrelated groups and individuals, sharing nothing but geographical space in the middle of North America. Were this the case, there would be no reason for anyone to pay taxes to help anyone outside his own group; there would be no patriotic spirit on which to draw for the common defense or the general welfare; there would be no grounds on which to appeal to vindicate anyone's rights. Each group would be left to fend for itself, unable to call upon the pocketbook or conscience or fellow feeling of anyone outside the group. In the absence of a common civic culture, a shared sense of national identity, Americans would relate to each other with as much concern and interest as they do to people in faraway lands.

Fortunately, the United States does have a common civic culture, which provides the foundation for American national identity. It is vital and real, and it holds the allegiance of the American people. This civic culture is the sum of the institutions, values, and ideals that Americans share. Our recognition of our frequent failure to live up to our ideals serves to remind us that we accept the reality of common ideals. Even the most severe critics of this nation ultimately invoke the nation's ideals as a benchmark for their critique.

The institutions, values, and ideals that constitute the American civic culture can be succinctly described, because they are familiar to us all; their sources are to be found in the Declaration of Independence, the U.S. Constitution, and the Bill of Rights. These documents contain three fundamental ideas—liberty, equality, and government based on the consent of the governed—and have provided the ideological seeds for countless reform movements seeking justice and equal treatment for everyone who has been excluded from the full protection of the laws. From these documents have emerged a democratic civic culture that is based on majority rule, the rule of law, equal rights for every citizen, freedom of expression, and protection of the rights of minorities. These documents establish legal, democratic political processes for resolving disputes at the ballot box and in courts of law. The institutions and political processes of this society promote certain values: tolerance, equality, freedom, fairness, individualism, optimism, civic participation, and self-reliance.

Because Americans treasure their own rights and freedoms, they tend to give a wide berth to people with whom they disagree, saying, "It's a free country" or "Live and let live." Most Americans are undisturbed by people who do or say what they please, so long as they don't trample on anyone else's basic rights. The extent to which Americans volunteer to help out in their communities and through their associations has always amazed foreigners; volunteer activities in churches, synagogues, schools, the workplace, and the neighborhood continue to be a staple of American civic culture. Of course, some Americans do not share in these consensual values; some people are bad citizens—they are unfair, intolerant, and unwilling to do their share. But they are not typical.

The civic culture is the heart of the American common culture. It is not grounded in race, ethnicity, gender, or anything else peculiar to a group or individual. It belongs to all Americans. It is widely shared among native-born citizens, naturalized citizens, and newcomers. It promises freedom, opportunity, equality, and the right to be a self-governing member of a self-governing polity. Any person or group with a legitimate grievance relies on the existence of the civic culture to validate his or her claims for justice. Most Americans willingly perform their civic responsibilities and voluntarily pay their taxes, because they are glad to be Americans.

Real as it is, the civic culture is not the totality of American culture. People are defined in many ways, only some of which are included in the civic culture. The civic culture ensures that no one can be excluded from participation in civic duties because of his or her race, religion, ethnicity, or gender, but it does not make those characteristics unimportant in people's lives. Indeed, those characteristics are frequently the basis on which people organize to participate in public life as well as in private life. Thus, a paradox: How should the civic culture relate to group life when part of the purpose of civic culture is to treat each individual without regard to group identification?

The extensive literature that has addressed these issues recognizes that American nationality includes tendencies toward both assimilation and differentiation. Some advocates embrace only one definition of American identity, but experience demonstrates that Americans can assimilate and be different from one another at the same time. Typically, the definitions of American identity range across the following spectrum.

First, *assimilation*. The chief argument for assimilation is that the United States will be a stronger, more unified society if differences among its citizens are minimized. When immigration reached a peak in the early years of the twentieth century, public policy and private actions promoted the rapid assimilation of all citizens. Historically, there have been at least two varieties of assimilation. One was an idealistic appeal to Americans to merge and become a new race and a new nation, different from any other in the world. The presumption was that everyone—whatever their race, religion, or culture—had something of value to contribute to the emerging new America. The metaphor for this kind of assimilation has been the melting pot, which suggested the melting and blending of disparate cultures into a new whole. The other version of assimilation, familiar to many today from their experience in public schools of the first half of the century, was Anglo-assimilation. This approach pressed newcomers to embrace the culture, history, and literature of the Anglo-American founders of the nation. This was a fairly mild sort of assimilation, since non-Anglo immigrants were free to speak their native language outside of public school, to worship as they chose, and otherwise to live in accordance with their own choices.

Second, *cultural pluralism*. Reacting against assimilationism in 1915, Horace Kallen called for a movement toward greater differentiation, for "a democracy of nationalities."[9] His view, which he later called cultural pluralism, was posited on the belief that cultural groups were distinct, that individuals achieved their greatest sense of freedom and satisfaction to the extent that they were members of a cultural group, and that public policy should encourage national groups to flourish. In essence, the United States would be a better nation if it became a nation of nations. Kallen's ideas were embraced by those who sought an alternative to coercive assimilation, but they have been criticized for "racial romanticism" by implying that every nationality has its own peculiar cultural and biological inheritance.[10] The metaphor for cultural pluralism, as Kallen envisioned it, was an orchestration of many different groups, each playing its own instrument in a grand national harmony. In our own time, the early Kallen concept of cultural pluralism is represented by the metaphor of a mosaic, a collection of separate stones linked together in a common project; the stones, however, are each distinct and relatively unchanging.

Third, *dynamic pluralism*. Over the decades, the concept of cultural pluralism has evolved into a tendency toward assimilation, not differentiation. Today it refers to the ways that groups interact and influence each other. Lawrence H. Fuchs uses the metaphor of the kaleidoscope to describe a situation in which cultural groups intersect, interconnect, and interact; in contrast to a melting pot, it might be called a stir-fry or a lightly cooked stew, each ingredient seeping into the other while retaining its own flavor. Dynamic pluralism describes the ways that cultures blend and change each other; I think, for example, of a restaurant in Central Texas that serves both bratwurst and tacos, or a Puerto Rican bagel factory in Manhattan, or the popularity among all kinds of audiences, without regard to ethnicity, of jazz, ragtime, salsa, reggae, the blues, and the polka, all of which began as ethnic musical expressions, but have become universal.

Fourth, *separatism*. The ultimate version of differentiation is separatism. A small minority of Americans, animated mostly by religious beliefs, choose to avoid intermingling with other groups. They include the Amish, Hutterites, certain Orthodox Jewish sects, and certain Muslim groups. These groups maintain their own schools to avoid the assimilating qualities of American public schools. They do not want to be melted or otherwise assimilated, and they choose to limit their interactions with other ethnic and religious groups.

Which of these ways of life best describes the national identity? Are we to be a melting pot, an orchestra, a salad bowl, a mosaic, or something else? Whatever the metaphor, the fact is that all these ways of life coexist and all are viable in modern American society. All these paths intersect with the civic culture, which nurtures and protects them. Even those who choose to live in separate groups are not entirely separate; they too make use of public roads, the common currency, the judicial system, and the other protections supplied by the state, such as fire, police, and military defense. One person may live simultaneously in several of these ways of life. An American citizen today can at one and the same time be assimilated in some facets of his or her life (for example, at work or at college); can be a member of a vigorous ethnic culture; and can be a participant in dynamic pluralism who happily enjoys the products of other cultural groups. Americans do not choose among these ways of living; most move easily from one mode to another or live simultaneously in several. As American citizens, we are free to make our choices, unconstrained by government, so long as we do not break the law or injure others.

For all practical purposes, assimilation (voluntary and unconscious) goes forward every day in the United States. As people in other nations frequently remark, American popular culture is a powerfully assimilative instrument; the movies and television disseminate common ideas about dress, behavior, language, music, clothing, and values. Most people, regardless of their racial, religious, or ethnic origins, work in settings that have no racial, religious, or ethnic dimension; as workplaces become more diverse, workers adapt to each other, and assimilation continues apace. Without legislation or regulation, English is the language of the public sphere. The melting pot keeps on melting.

Among new immigrants, assimilation moves ahead, slowly but surely. Even what seem to be intensely ethnic communities to the outsider are almost always multicultural. Asians live side by side with other Asians from very different cultures, because the word "Asian" encompasses diverse cultures; so do Hispanics. Similarly, urban black communities contain people who trace their origins to many different cultures in the Caribbean, Latin America, Africa, and the United States. It is only public policy that sees a single culture, defined by race or language, when in fact most of these ethnic communities contain many cultural groups living side by side. For newcomers, exposure to American schools, workplaces, television, and politics also has an assimilative effect. Within a generation or two, newcomers are very different from those they left behind in their native land, even though they are still bearers of the ethnic culture.

There is another sense in which it must be said that the melting pot did work. Many Americans are products of mixed marriages that long ago crossed racial and/or ethnic lines; some do not even know their ethnic origins. Can it be that we celebrate ethnicity because we fear that it is slipping away? Can it be that the homogenizing effects of American culture cause many Americans to magnify or re-create ethnic attachments that make their lives more interesting? When almost everyone wears green on St. Patrick's Day, when almost everyone eats pasta, and when almost everyone sings music of African American origin (for example, jazz, the blues, spirituals), then we must acknowledge that ethnic experiences have been transformed and made available to nongroup members. The melting pot keeps bubbling.

At the same time, cultural pluralism also persists. There are many ethnic groups that have chosen to retain their group identity. It may not be the same as in its country of origin, but it is still quite different from the assimilated lives of most urbanites and suburbanites. There are many Americans who, for reasons of their own, choose to live in close proximity to people of the same group. Those Americans who prefer to live with easy accessibility to ethnic foods, ethnic churches, ethnic schools, and ethnic companionship maintain their culture on their terms, without in any sense diminishing their sense of identity as American citizens.

It is also true that dynamic pluralism has become a common experience in modern America, especially for people who live in metropolitan areas. They may be Protestant, Catholic, Jewish, Muslim, or Hindu, but their religious affiliation does not define their circle of friends or their place of residence. They may be of German, Irish, Korean, Italian, African, Polish, Lebanese, or Cuban descent, but they regularly interact with people who are not, whether at work, in school or college, or in their social life. Their interaction with other cultures is not simply accidental. They like to eat foods that are not unique to their heritage; to go to movies, exhibits, or plays about people different from themselves; to live in a neighborhood where ethnic diversity is the rule. They enjoy their own ethnic origins, but they also enjoy experiencing those of others.

In the midst of all this vigorous and unselfconscious pluralism, separation survives too. Most Americans respect the rights of those who choose to live apart. Live and let live. No matter how peculiar they may seem to others, those who separate are still Americans. In most instances, their ancestors came here to find freedom, and there is a general presumption that they should have it.

The civic culture is not threatened by the coexistence of these different ways of life. On the contrary, these different ways of life rely on the civic culture to provide the mechanism to resolve disputes as well as the consensus that allows individuals to shift easily from a cosmopolitan world to an ethnic world and back again, without undue psychic stress.

Yet it should be noted that the civic culture is not an impregnable fortress, impervious to assault, needing no defenders. It has been jeopardized in the past and will surely be jeopardized in the future by demagogues who seek to set group against group; who seek out, exploit, and fan the grievances that can easily be found in a pluralistic society. Every generation has known its nativists, Ku Kluxers, anti-Catholics, anti-Semites, racists, and ethnocentrists. They define themselves by whom they are against. They reject the values of the common civic culture: tolerance, fairness, equality, respect for those who are different. Instead, they preach hatred and conspiracy.

Fortunately, ethnocentrists and tribalists usually have limited staying power. Most Americans do not like to be told that they must think and act on the basis of their blood. Most prefer the freedom that the civic culture provides. The alternatives are not broadly appealing.

The all-encompassing civic culture is the best guarantee of our individual liberties; few are willing to exchange them for an ethnic cocoon. The civic culture assures us that our ethnic worlds are not ghettos or shtetls; the elders cannot force us to stay against our will. We are free to leave our ethnic enclaves, bound by nothing more than our internal sense of commitment to family and heritage. In recent years, the civic culture has also reassured us that it is praiseworthy to enjoy our ethnic diversity. We do not have to straighten our hair, change our names, shorten our noses, or discard our distinctive garb. Indeed, given the voracious appetite of the American consumer culture for variety, we may expect to see the ethnic garb that was cast away by our grandparents featured in national advertising as the latest fashion.

What I am proposing as public policy and educational policy has two components: First, teach the civic culture that belongs to all of us and that protects our basic rights. Second, adopt a stance of toleration regarding the nature of American identity, acknowledging that the civic culture does not dictate only one way to be an American. Recognize that American citizens make different choices, which is their right. Accept that Americans are free to assimilate or to diffentiate themselves, or to do both on different days of the week, and that these choices are protected by our common civic culture. Understand that it is not the role of the government to impose assimilation or differentiation on its citizens against their will. Essential to their freedom as Americans is their freedom to define their way of life for themselves.

My proposal may be summarized as *e pluribus unum*, with equal weight given to *pluribus* and *unum*. It draws upon the civic culture for the values of tolerance and liberty. It is at bottom a *pluralistic* theory, for it accepts that there is no single pattern of group life that is right for everyone. Every citizen is entitled to the same rights and liberties, and every citizen is entitled to make his or her own choices about how or whether to participate in group life.

Is it paradoxical that I say, on the one hand, "Do not impose pluralism," but that, on the other hand, I advocate a pluralistic theory of group life? Yes and no. Public policy should not force pluralism on those who prefer to live separately. But separatist communities depend on appeals to pluralism ("live and let live") for their survival. Thus the best protection for real diversity—in which different cultures persist—is pluralism. Modern American life is so relentlessly assimilative, and so aggressive in promoting cultural blending, that separatist communities should be left alone so long as they respect the law.

John Higham has written that "an adequate theory of American culture will have to address the reality of assimilation as well as the persistence of differences."[11] Higham further argued that a constructive educational policy must confront these three dilemmas:

First, arousal or restraint? "Should scholarship and teaching arouse or subdue ethnicity as a social force? . . . The problem is that ethnic mobilization rapidly spreads to other groups, creating situations full of danger for all of them."[12]

Second, convergence or divergence? Do we want a future of greater or reduced separateness and autonomy between ethnic groups? "On the surface, one would think that the goal of equality would not be well served by highlighting or increasing differences among people."[13]

Third, preserving or creating? Higham perceives a conflict between those who hark back to a glorious past and those who want to create something new.

"All three of these unexamined dilemmas have a common source. Multiculturalism is silent on problems of arousal, divergence, and direction because . . . it lacks a vision of what it wants the country to become. For young people in search of some common purpose beyond the confines of their own endowment, multiculturalism offers no nourishing center or beckoning horizon."[14]

## Arousal vs. Restraint

Educational policy should teach students about ethnic diversity but avoid arousing ethnic pride or ethnic antagonisms. Ethnic diversity is a reality in the world and in the nation, and students need to learn about the history and traditions of the many groups in this nation, as well as the major world civilizations. It has become commonplace in American schools to teach racial pride and ethnic pride, but this is a dangerous practice. As Higham points out, that is a two-edged sword that can be wielded to stir ethnic hatreds. Frederick Douglass argued in 1884 that appeals to race pride were "a positive evil." He asked, "What is the thing we are fighting against, and what are we fighting for in this country? What is the mountain devil, the lion in the way of our progress? What is it, but American race pride; an assumption of superiority upon the ground of race and color? Do we not know that every argument we make, and every pretension we set up in favor of race pride, is giving the enemy a stick to break our own heads?"[15] Karl Popper warned more than fifty years ago that the idea "we think with our blood" or "our national heritage" or "our race" divides the world into friends and foes and makes political egalitarianism "practically impossible."[16] For this reason, any educational policy that embraces racial or ethnic arousal is not only at odds with the civic culture but directly undermines the egalitarian demands of minorities.

A public opinion poll released in the fall of 1994 showed that most Americans believe in the importance of reinforcing the common civic culture and avoiding ethnic arousal. This study by Public Agenda (whose president is Daniel Yankelovich) found that the public wants the schools to teach those values "that allow a diverse society to live together peacefully." By overwhelming majorities, Americans want the schools to stress tolerance and equality (95 percent say that schools should teach "respect for others regardless of their racial or ethnic background"). Large majorities oppose lessons that are seen as socially divisive, such as bringing in "a guest speaker who advocates black separatism" (a proposition opposed by equal numbers of white and black parents).[17]

## Convergence vs. Divergence

Pluralism demands neither convergence nor divergence, but a balance between *pluribus* and *unum*. In recent years, however, schools and universities have tended to replace pluralism with uniculturalism. Under the guise of multiculturalism, some educational institutions have introduced separatist courses, separatist curriculums, and separatist programs. Although such actions are often described as promoting multiculturalism, they obviously promote the opposite of multiculturalism. Critics have commented unfavorably on the separatist interpretation of contemporary multiculturalism. Richard Rorty of the University of Virginia complained that the new multiculturalism repudiates the idea of national identity and seeks to keep the nation's many communities "at odds with one another."[18] Robert Brustein of Yale University chastised multiculturalists who embrace tribalism and ethnocentrism. "Total absorption in a separate culture," he wrote, "like the adoption of separate tables, separate houses, separate clubs, separate studies, and separate schools, represents not multiculturalism, but the return of segregation in voluntary form, the abandonment of hope for a national identity, the death of pluralism, the rejection of the great ideal of integration."[19] Separatist communities must be free to pursue their agendas and support their schools, but it would be socially destructive to endorse separatism in public policy.

## Looking Back or Looking Forward

An educational policy that balances *pluribus* and *unum* would teach the history of our civic culture and of the American people, warts and all. The history and literature that we teach must encompass the richness and diversity of our people. But at the same time it must be a forward-looking story, a story of a nation that is becoming, a people in the process of becoming a people, a polity ever striving to fulfill the common purposes described in the first sentence of the American Constitution.

There are paradoxes aplenty in the emerging American identity. As I have written elsewhere, the American common culture is multicultural. Even academic celebrations of ethnocentricity seem slated to feed the thirst of the common culture for new heroes, new models of American accomplishment. The cultural mainstream is a broad stream indeed, which encompasses people of every race, religion, and ethnic group. The American of our generation who does not know the poetry of Langston Hughes, the fiction of Alice Walker, the music of Scott Joplin, the architecture of I. M. Pei, the films of Spike Lee, or the soaring rhetoric of Martin Luther King Jr. is out of touch with the common culture. We can be sure that the next generation of Americans will add to and subtract from the common culture that we know. The great instrumentalities for shaping the common culture—films and television—celebrate diversity, individuality, and talent. The remarkable success of American movies in a world market testifies to the fact that they were produced for an audience that finds universality in particularity.

Years from now, when future historians review this period in American life, they are likely to be struck by the blending and borrowings among the nation's cultures, by the way that Americans of different cultural origins exchanged art, literature, humor, music, cuisine, dress, technology, and ideas. Living in the present, we worry about the eruption of tribalism and ethnocentrism and about the danger that they pose to genuine pluralism, as well as to the possibility of building political coalitions for social progress. But future historians are likely to see instead the absorption, domestication, and commodification of these movements. They will become, I suspect, an identifiable feature of the American common culture, providing fodder for books, films, T-shirts, and academic conferences.

I do not suggest that fundamentalism is to be taken lightly—much of the ethnic slaughter earlier described was the result of rampant fundamentalism. The American civic culture is not comfortable with extremism. The U.S.

Constitution is a testament to the virtues of checks and balances; the national motto, *e pluribus unum*, requires a balancing of opposites; the American people are themselves a demographic refutation of the principle of racial, ethnic, or religious purity. I recall Nathan Glazer, some twenty years ago, warning about the danger of absolutizing anything. The most prominent victim of fundamentalism in our own time is author Salmon Rushdie. In hiding after receiving a death sentence because of his novel *The Satanic Verses*, he wrote that the novel

> celebrates hybridity, impurity, intermingling, the transformation that comes of new and unexpected combinations of human beings, cultures, ideas, politics, movies, songs. It rejoices in mongrelization and fears the absolutism of the Pure. Melange, hotch-potch, a bit of this and a bit of that is *how newness enters the world.* . . . Throughout human history, the apostles of purity, those who have claimed to possess a total explanation, have wrought havoc among mere mixed-up human beings. Like many millions of people, I am a bastard child of history. Perhaps we all are, black and brown and white, leaking into one another, as a character of mine once said, *like flavours when you cook.*[20]

"Like flavours when you cook." Rushdie was saying essentially what John Higham argues about the universalist vision, "that we are all multicultural and increasingly transnational—that minority and majority cultures alike are becoming more and more interconnected, interpenetrative, and even indistinguishable."[21]

At the conclusion of the world war in 1918, John Dewey spoke about the ideas that Americans might contribute to help in the reconstruction ahead. First, he recommended to the devastated nations the principle of *e pluribus unum*, "where the unity does not destroy the many, but maintains each constituent factor in full vigor." Then, he offered this idea:

> One of the greatest problems which is troubling the Old World is that of the rights of nationalities which are included within larger political units—the Poles, the Irish, the Bohemians, the Jugo-Slavs, the Jews. Here, too, the American contribution is radical. We have solved the problem by a complete separation of nationality from citizenship. Not only have we separated language, cultural traditions, all that is called race, from the state—that is, from problems of political organization and power. To us, language, literature, creed, group ways, national

culture, are social rather than political, human rather than national, interests. Let this idea fly abroad; it bears healing in its wings.[22]

Dewey's analysis was wrong in that the United States had not done what he said; at that very time, it did restrict the rights of black Americans on the basis of their race, it assertively classified people by race, and it actively imposed assimilation on its immigrant population. But his statement should be read as a description of the American ideal, the American Creed that Myrdal later wrote about. The choice to assimilate or not must remain with the individual, not the state; the choice to preserve cultural traditions belongs to individuals and groups, not to the state.

The state must teach the civic culture on which all of us rely. Through its schools and institutions of higher education, it must provide equal opportunity for individuals to improve themselves, regardless of where they live or who their parents were. It owes to every American an education that enables them to take part, either individually or in concert with others, in establishing justice, ensuring domestic tranquility, providing for the common defense, promoting the general welfare, and securing the blessings of liberty for themselves and their children.

PART FOUR

Toward the Future

# CHAPTER EIGHT

# Race and Civil Society

## A Democratic Conversation

## JEAN BETHKE ELSHTAIN and CHRISTOPHER BEEM

We've all seen them—the World War II films in which the airplane crew or the platoon has a group of guys—all GIs and proud of it—with names like LaRosa, O'Brien, Goldberg, Chavez, Olafsen, Mickweicz. They're Americans to the man, and they are making a point—we're different from the people we are fighting.[1] America is open to all comers. You don't have to be of a particular race, or adhere to a given religion, or bear an identifiable ethnic name from one of a handful of accepted groups to be one of us. But the picture is by no means perfect. You don't see an African American or a Japanese American in the group.[2] The Armed Services were segregated until after World War II, and Japanese Americans fought in a separate Nisei regiment. But the point could be taken nonetheless: America was different because it enabled people who were "different" to nevertheless hold something in common: their identity as citizens, their aspirations as free men and women, their determination to make life better for their children. That seems rather a long time ago—a frozen tableau from another time and place; a time when we were innocent, perhaps, or naive, or just "didn't get it."

A "reading" of the "text" of a World War II war film, in today's jargon, would probably go something like this: Men from various ethnic groups were unwittingly co-opted to conform to the model of the hegemonic, phallogocentric, dominant Anglo-Saxon Protestant male, save for those the society implacably refused to normalize—namely, blacks and, in this era, Japanese Americans. Having encoded this dominance more generally, such men, already oppressors in their own households by virtue of their superior standing in patriarchal society, became even more eager embodiments of the normative standards of a racist, sexist, imperialist society. End of story.

We exaggerate a bit—for comedic effect or shock value, depending on how familiar the reader is with the coinage of the academic marketplace—but not by much, for we are all now enjoined to see the past in harsh and dismissive terms: Christianity is nothing but the violent re-encoding in new guise of the violent Jewish God; the U.S. Constitution is nothing but the writing into law of the privileges of a dominant, male class; Abraham Lincoln, as one mightily exercised soul shouted after a lecture Elshtain had delivered, should never be quoted because he was nothing but a racist. The relentless drumbeat goes on. Harsh criticism—trashing, as it is called in the vernacular—has become an end in itself. But we worry about this willful contempt for the past, a contempt that stokes arrogance and fuels the flames of historicist prejudice. In short, we do not believe that the way we have "wised up" is so much a victory for wisdom as for cynicism. And that isn't so smart. A free society cannot long survive widespread cynicism among its citizens. Cynicism, the assumption that one's words and deeds always mask an ulterior and crassly self-interested motivation, breeds a politics of resentment. And resentment, finally, drains our normative institutions, including education and politics and even the family, of their ethical legitimacy and deters them from doing the tasks they are there to do.

The sad thing is that much of what we here decry is undertaken in the name of putting some things right, of correcting some wrongs, of celebrating what is called "multiculturalism." But in this area as in so many others, things are not necessarily what they claim to be. We propose that we take a closer look at this new multiculturalism. What do its proponents assume? What do they claim? What do they aim for? What are the effects of these aims and claims on relations between the races? What are their effects on citizenship and responsibility in a free society?

We want to begin to answer these and other questions by reminding us all, once again, of what is at stake. There are two false and dangerous stories about ethnic and racial diversity and American identity. The first is drawn from a historical era, now past; the second, from the present moment. We shall rehearse these two tales that pose or posed particular threats to the generous dream of a democracy as the way free citizens come to know a good in common that they cannot know alone.

Our first cautionary tale is the story of a quest for unity and homogeneity that assaulted diversity in the process: a too strong and too overreaching homogeneous identity was deemed necessary as a prerequisite for citizenship and responsibility. We want to take the reader back to the World War I era, when the allure of an overarching, collective civic purpose took a statist turn that seemed to be a cure for what ailed the republic, at least in the view of those who lamented an excessive diversity. Nationalizing progressives were disheartened at the cultural impact of both the rampant, unbridled industrialism of the Gilded Age and the messy, cacophonous sprawl brought on by wave after wave of immigrants. Desirous of finding some way to forge a unified national will and civic philosophy, these progressives saw the coming of World War I as a way to attain at long last a homogeneous, ordered, and rational society.[3]

Evincing the spirit of the times, John R. Commons, a progressive labor economist, maintained that national greatness required a new singularity of purpose and identity—one nation, one mind. Walter Lippmann likewise assailed the evils of localism and fretted that American diversity was too great and had become a block in the way of order, purpose, and discipline. Progressives like these saw World War I as the great engine of social progress. Conscription would serve, in historian David Kennedy's words, as an "effective homogenizing agent in what many regarded as a dangerously diverse society. Shared military service, one advocate colorfully argued, was the only way to 'yank the hyphen' out of Italian-Americans or Polish-Americans or other such imperfectly assimilated immigrants."[4]

President Woodrow Wilson, who had already proclaimed that "any man who carries a hyphen about him carries a dagger that he is ready to plunge into the vitals of the Republic,"[5] thundered, in words of unifying excess:

> There are citizens of the United States, I blush to admit, under our generous naturalization laws born under other flags but welcomed to the full freedom and opportunity of America, who have poured the poison of disloyalty into the very arteries of our national life. . . . Such creatures of passion, disloyalty, and anarchy must be crushed out. . . . The hand of our power should close over them at once.[6]

"Americanization" became the goal, the watchword—for some, the threat: one nation indivisible.

To be sure, genuine regard for the welfare of immigrant groups lay at the base of much progressive sentiment, the fear that separatism and heterogeneity were synonymous with inequality and marginality. One must also acknowledge that this drive for national unity was in large measure born of pressing political demands. There was, after all, a war going on. For all this, progressive and liberal opinion proved particularly susceptible to the cry for unity because of its emphasis on the notion that the voice of America must speak as one. The temptation to forge a unity that is indistinguishable from stifling conformity is great; it invited figures from Woodrow Wilson down to trim the sails of free speech on the grounds that the war against dissent was a war against civic dismemberment, a war for great national aspirations, and an opportunity to forge a community that might encompass the entire continent. The coming of the first world war offered this particular progressive mind-set an optimistic set of "social possibilities."

Perhaps, then, the current practitioners of the "hermeneutics of suspicion" are right. Perhaps the entire thrust of American history has been to destroy our particular identities, even our dignity, in order to create some common identity, some homogenized product. There is a kernel of truth to such claims, but it is not the truth unadorned, for even in the midst of the rush to yank out the hyphens there were dissenting voices. One was that of Randolph Bourne, himself a member of the progressive crowd and a regular correspondent for *The New Republic* until he fell out with the publishers over their newfound war fervor. Bourne wrote a wonderful piece at the height of war suspicion and fanaticism and attacks on aliens and immigrants. Against the effort to cement a homogenized and decidedly Waspish American identity, he yearned for a politics of commonalties that cherished the bracing tonic of perspicuous contrasts. Bourne celebrated a cosmopolitan enterprise, a social world within which many voices were heard:

America is coming to be, not a nationality but a trans-nationality, a weaving back and forth, with other lands, of many threads of all sizes and colors. Any movement which attempts to thwart this weaving or to dye the fabric any one color, or disentangle the threads of the strands, is false to this cosmopolitan vision.[7]

No "tight and jealous" nationalism for Bourne, he called for an experimental ideal in which each of us is left free to fashion our own ways of living.

Yet Bourne also believed in the possibility of politics. To be sure, politics requires a common set of terms, but Bourne believed those terms could not be wholly imposed from above. They must rather emerge organically through the vibrant interplay of cultures and individuals.

This Bournian ideal (or, perhaps, Bournian mean) is necessarily hostile to any overly robust proclamation of the American identity that demands a single, overarching collective unity, under the aegis of the state, to attain or to sustain its purposes. But his ideal also alerts us to a second false and dangerous story: the harsh particularism, now under way in American civic and scholarly life, in which we reduce ourselves to ethnic, racial, or gender categories, cynically dismissive of the possibility for reaching outside one's own group. In the name of diversity and multiculturalism, this rigidifying of difference types people by racial, ethnic, gender, or sexual orientation categories and says in effect, that *these* are the differences that matter—not the quality of a person's intellect, the depth of a person's commitment to community, the scope of a person's understanding of the human condition, the dignity of a person's life, or the ill-dignity heaped on a person by an unjust social circumstance. Bourne's rich tapestry contrasts mightily with the multiculturalist's quilt, a collection of solid patches representing this color, this gender, and this or that identity, all kept separate and each threatening at any moment to detach itself. This second story is also a perversion of the dream of democracy and the civic life constitutive of it.

Rather than negotiating the complexity of public and private identities and embracing the notion of the "citizen" as the way we have to sustain a public identity not reducible to the terms of our private selves, more and more we are told that we must gain recognition exclusively along race, gender, or sexual preference lines. The public world becomes a world of many "I's" who form a "we" only with others like themselves in these prefixed categories. Of course, Democrats recognize in the demand for recognition a powerful concern. Some forms of equal recognition are surely not only possible in a democracy but form its very lifeblood. The question is: What sort of recognition? Recognition of what? For what? To claim "I am different. You must recognize me and honor my difference" tells us nothing that is interesting. Should you or I honor someone, recognize her, simply because she is female or proclaims a particular version of her sexual identity? This makes little sense. We may disagree with her about every current political issue we find important—from what American post–cold war foreign policy ought to be, to what needs to be done to stem the tide of deterioration and despair in America's inner cities, to whether violence on television is a serious concern or just an easy target for riled and worried parents and educators.

Indeed, one could even insist that it is incorporation within a single civic body that makes meaningful diversity possible. Our differences must be recognized if they are to exist substantively at all. As political philosopher Charles Taylor writes, "My discovering my own identity doesn't mean that I work it out in isolation, but that I negotiate it through dialogue, partly overt, partly internal, with others. . . . My own identity crucially depends on my dialogical relations with others."[8] What this means is that we cannot be different all by ourselves. A political body that brings people together, creating a "we," but that enables these same persons to separate themselves and to recognize one another in and through their differences as well as in what they share in common—that was the great challenge. Bourne's call for transnationality was thus a call for balance, a balance that is at the core of democratic life. The worst excesses of the multicultural movement are just as destructive to this balance as the progressive's unbridled call for unity. Thus, in our time and our society, the great challenge remains.

A survey of the landscape of fin de siècle America makes it apparent that the drive for identity politics is merely one manifestation of our contemporary troubles. Although a dwindling band of pundits and apologists insist that Americans are suffering the pangs of dislocation en route to salutary change, even progress, such reassurances ring increasingly hollow. Experts and ordinary citizens lament the growth of a culture of mistrust, cynicism, and scandal. Our suspicion is that this broader cultural crisis is also properly characterized as a problem of imbalance. If this is so, then exploring this crisis affords us an opportunity to reconnect our discussion about race with these basic questions about American politics, society, and culture. We therefore want to focus for a moment on another source for, and manifestation of, this cultural pathology—namely, the overall weakening of that world known as democratic civil society.

By any standard of objective evidence, our society has experienced serious growth of corrosive forms of isolation, boredom, and despair, and declining levels of involvement in politics and community life—from simple acts like voting and exchanging pleasantries with a neighbor, to more demanding participation in political parties and in local and other civic associations. Collectively, these myriad opportunities for social interaction and civic engagement constitute democratic civil society, for that is where Americans forge the bonds of social and political trust and competence. Yet in our contemporary social world, these opportunities are increasingly passed over, and American society manifests the unhappy results. Social scientists who have researched the matter argue for a causal relationship: This sharp decline in participation has led to a notable decline in social trust. Ultimately, the evaporation of American civil society points to nothing less than a crisis in "social capital formation." Just like identity politics, the decline of civil society at once manifests and reinforces the increasing inability of American society to pursue a good that is common.

Historically, democratic theorists have either taken for granted the web of mediating institutions, vibrant informal and formal civic associations, or they have pointed specifically to those institutions as the means by which a society maintains the relationship between democracy and the everyday actions and spirit of a people. In the latter group, the most famous thinker is Alexis de Tocqueville. Democracy requires laws, constitutions, and authoritative institutions, but Tocqueville also insisted that it depends on democratic dispositions. These include a preparedness to work with others for shared ends; a combination of often strong convictions coupled with a readiness to compromise in the recognition that one cannot always get everything one wants; a sense of individuality, and a commitment to civic goods that are not the possession of one person or of one small group alone. The world that nourished and sustained such democratic dispositions was a thickly interwoven social fabric, the web of mediating institutions already noted.[9] The tale here gestured toward is a story of the unraveling of the institutions of civil society, and hence the dramatic upsurge in all forms of social mistrust and generalized fearfulness and cynicism.

The pernicious effects of the resultant mistrust, privatization, and anomie are many. For example, there is empirical support for the popularly held view that where neighborhoods are intact—that is, where there is a strong sense of common interest and a fairly strong moral consensus—drug, alcohol abuse, crime, and truancy among the young diminish. Because neighborhoods are less and less likely to be intact, all forms of socially destructive behavior are on the rise. Children, in particular, have borne the brunt of negative social trends. All one has to do is look at any American newspaper any day of the week to learn about the devastating effects on the young. The stories paint a picture of a continual downward spiral—what Elshtain has called a spiral of delegitimation. The decline in neighborhoods leads to further strain on families and child-rearing. Family breakdown generates unparented children who attend schools that increasingly resemble detention homes rather than centers of enduring training and discipline, and declining levels of education and training further contribute to out-of-wedlock births and violence at unprecedented levels.

This cultural crisis and its various causes—the fact that we are hunkered down into bristling "identity groups," isolated and fearful, expecting the worst from each other—to explain the quaint, faraway feeling that is likely to be evoked by the platoon full of GIs. But perhaps there is still something to be learned from them. Consider the social world that those GIs are supposed to symbolize. If those men are indeed representative, then it is clear that the earlier efforts of Wilson, Croly, Lippmann, and others to yank out the hyphens were at best only partially successful. Twenty years or so after strict immigration quotas were imposed, the men portrayed in these movies likely lived in neighborhoods and towns where theirs was the dominant ethnic group. Strong lines of demarcation separated these neighborhoods, and they were often crossed only with impunity. They likely went to church, and that church probably would have reflected a strong ethnic and cultural heritage. They were not members of the Lutheran church, they went to the Norwegian Lutheran Church; they didn't belong to a Catholic parish, they belonged to Santa Lucia's or Saint Patrick's. Some of these men came to know members of other ethnic groups through the public school, or later, through the workplace; for many World War II veterans their cultural experience was a singularly hyphenated one, and their first and most significant exposure to the other cultures, other ideas about what it means to be an American, took place during the war itself. In other words, those war movies celebrated a shared sense of identity and community for which the war itself was largely responsible.

Yet this does not mean that their message was pure propaganda. Indeed, social scientists concerned about civil society argue that these experiences within a very cohesive neighborhood enabled that commonalty to happen. The mediating institutions of civil society—like family, neighborhood, and church—bridge the gap between the individual group and the nation. At their best, they inculcate a shared sense of national identity and solidarity even as they express and reinforce a specific and unique ethnic identity. If this is true, then it is precisely their strong and unique identities, and ultimately their strong ethnic neighborhoods, that enabled or at least facilitated their coming together. It also means that, willy-nilly, something like Bourne's vision triumphed in World War II America. Americans maintained their separate identities even as they were able to come together in pursuit of a common cause.

But again, the movie scene is notable for what is left out—most relevant here, African Americans. Lest we forget, the war had a remarkable impact in this respect, as well. The shameful reality of segregation, in light of the notable heroism and sacrifice of Negro units, helped accelerate the black migration to the North, as well as Truman's first fitful steps toward civil rights. Yet the exclusion of African Americans in the movie is representative only of society at large. All the ethnic enclaves of the 1940s were notable in their ability to inculcate a strong sense of ethnic identity and civic virtue; thereafter, they also became notably united in their desire to keep blacks out.

As the civil rights movement came alive, the idea of segregation—whether manifested at drinking fountains, in movie houses, or in neighborhoods— was rejected as an inherently illegitimate structural impediment to full citizenship and full humanity. A new ideal of a color-blind society was put forward, and desegregation was championed as the indispensable means for achieving this end. In his famous speech at Howard University in 1965, President Lyndon Johnson noted that the "deep, corrosive, obstinate differences" between "Negro poverty" and "white poverty" were "simply and solely the consequence of ancient brutality, past injustice, and present prejudice." He therefore "dedicated the expanding efforts of the Johnson administration" to addressing these differences, so that the nation might someday "reach the time when the only difference between Negroes and whites is the color of their skin."[10]

Surveying the sorry state of race relations and civil society at the end of the century, we can see that Johnson's hopeful exhortations seem like a long time ago too. To be sure, it is easy to forget or belittle the remarkable achievements of this era, but it is nevertheless the case that thirty years after these words were spoken, fifty years after World War II, most interaction between whites and blacks takes place where it always has: in the schools, in the workplace, and in the military. Integrated neighborhoods are more common, but they remain a rare commodity, and even when they exist in fact, it is even more unlikely that they manifest the kind of ethical cohesion that characterized neighborhoods past. As for the idea that our commonality might someday be limited only by our pigmentation, even the goal seems a far-off memory.

Historical hindsight allows us to suspect that, in this case, our faraway feeling is born of the fact that while President Johnson's intentions might have been wholly benign, his goals were not. In the end, the goal of desegregation as Johnson outlines it bears a striking similarity to the Progressive's idea of national community. Johnson too sought to yank the hyphen out of the American experience, and he wanted to use the power of the national government to further that end. To be sure, both movements were hopeful and even noble ideals, born of the best intentions, seeking to address serious problems. Wilson and Johnson might have put forward a different understanding of the evils of localism, but both described it as evil. And at least in the later case, one must be clear about the successes. The civil rights movement brought down the social ethos of Jim Crow. Indeed, in some large measure it achieved the goals outlined by Croly and Lippmann. Scenes of firehoses, attack dogs, and blown-up churches instigated a national mandate, a national moral consensus, that ultimately crushed the localism of the old South. But just like the Progressive movement, desegregation sought community at an unsustainable level—the nation—even as it compromised the viability of community-sustaining institutions at the local level. It also sought to redress the wrongs of prejudice by slowly extinguishing ethnic identity and cultural difference. From a contemporary perspective, it appears that for all their noble intentions, both movements failed in their ultimate objectives because both goals were misguided from the start.

There is a similar connection on the reverse side as well. Notice that a kind of ethnic isolation attaches both to identity politics and to the neighborhoods of World War II America. Whatever goods this isolation might achieve within their own community—a point that is surely debatable— there is clearly an intolerant and isolated quality to both which undermines a commitment to the common, transethnic group good. There are clear differences between the two. The America of the 1940s was for the most part able to achieve a common good, but it was a racially constricted conception. The identity politics associated with contemporary America seeks to identify and reject that conception, but in doing so it makes the search for a common good not more possible but more distant, and tends, disastrously, to see "culture" as an outgrowth of "race." In both cases, commitment to the group undermines and invalidates the search for a common good that is truly common.

This long and unhappy jaunt through twentieth-century American history reveals that there is, finally, a shared dimension to the problem of race and the problem of civil society. Living in the aftermath of Wilson and Johnson has shown us that real, sustainable community is local and that a national community is at best a temporary reality. Desegregation can address serious historical injustices, and a strong national government may be able to ameliorate the inequities of unbridled capitalism, but neither can create community and neither can legitimately or profitably seek to homogenize the American experience.

Nevertheless, in both instances, a serious problem remains. On the one hand, we want to reinvigorate the institutions of civic culture, the virtue-building neighborhoods of two generations ago, and we guardedly question whether such kinds of neighborhoods do not depend on or at least thrive on a kind of ethnic identity that sustains long-standing prejudices. On the other hand, we want to ameliorate, and finally eliminate, the remaining vestiges of a racist culture, and that requires a commitment to a specific conception of fairness and justice that is almost universal and that surely transcends the insulary ethos of an ethnic community. In a culture brimming with cynicism and despair, it no doubt sounds as if we want to have our cake and eat it too, but what we want is a Bournian ideal for race relations. Fortunately, that ideal has already found an able advocate, and we therefore close by turning to the words of Martin Luther King Jr.

King championed much of Johnson's program—indeed, he repeatedly noted that desegregation, and the dismantling of Jim Crow laws, was a good in and of itself. King acknowledged that while these changes "may not change the heart" they could "restrain the heartless."[11] Nevertheless, King was equally adamant that desegregation was not enough. "Our ultimate goal," King said, "is integration." King argued that desegregation was merely a physical description and "only a first step on the road to a good society."[12] True integration was a spiritual reality. It reflected the belief in the sacredness of all persons and required nothing less than a change of heart.

It is true that King's rhetoric often reflected the tone of the time. His writings sometimes echo Johnson's strategy of bringing all races together by eliminating cultural differences. King also used terms that are reminiscent of the Progressives, even talking about "a national community." But these words are not the whole story. Because true integration is a spiritual goal, and because it respected the status of all persons, King would not allow that race or ethnicity could or should be yanked out of a person's identity. In short, true integration did not constitute homogenization. His words are worth quoting at length:

> The Negro is the child of two cultures—Africa and America. The problem is that in the search for wholeness all too many Negroes seek to embrace only one side of their natures. Some, seeking to reject their heritage, are ashamed of their color, ashamed of black art and music,

and determine what is beautiful and good by the standards of white society. They end up frustrated and without cultural roots. Others seek to reject everything American and to identify totally with Africa, even to the point of wearing African clothes. But this approach also leads to frustration because the American Negro is not an African. . . . The American Negro is neither totally African nor totally Western. He is Afro-American, a true hybrid, a combination of two cultures.[13]

In short, Martin Luther King Jr. believed that the spiritual ideal of integration requires that equality and commonality coexist with racial and ethnic pride, cultural diversity, and spirited, challenging exchange. So understood, King's objectives for race relations echo Bourne's objectives for American culture. Uncannily, they independently appeal to the phrase "the beloved community" to describe what a truly integrated America would be like. Here too, King's use of the term has a more deeply spiritual dimension; he is finally talking about the eschaton. But in both cases, their entreaties reveal that what is required is an uneasy yet charitable and deeply principled balancing act—between unity and diversity, between pluralism and consensus.

We know that in our jaded age, King's religious exhortations are cloying to many. More to the point, we have made no effort to connect these exhortations to specific policy suggestions. Many who are concerned with these issues may well fear that questions about neighborhood cohesion are nothing more than yet another elaborate strategy for maintaining segregation. These are formidable questions, and we do not want to minimize their importance, but race relations in the United States have not only reached an impasse in recent years, they have soured gravely. There is new and recurrent talk of a gigantic and insoluble fissure in the American body politic. If this is so, then perhaps it is enough to suggest that we take another look at exactly what we want to achieve. If such a reinvestigation allows us to integrate our hopes for race relations with our more general concerns about American culture, so much the better.

# CHAPTER NINE

# A Meditation on the Meaning of "Diversity" in the United States

## GERALD EARLY

"It must be remembered," James Baldwin wrote in his 1949 essay, "Everybody's Protest Novel," "that the oppressed and the oppressor are bound together within the same society; they accept the same criteria, they share the same beliefs, they both alike depend on the same reality."[1] It is perhaps the richly complex and distressingly crippling ways that both oppressor and oppressed—or blacks and whites—depend on the very reality that they co-create that makes the United States a difficult country to understand. The broad sense of freedom, the obsessive quest for freedom and for, in some telling ways, relief from the tensions of freedom, that characterizes American life is, ironically, the very complicating element in understanding how the oppressed and the oppressor relate to each other. The sense of freedom masks the complete entrapment of the relationship, although certain American writers, such as Herman Melville in "Benito Cereno," Mark Twain in *The Adventures of Huckleberry Finn* and *The Tragedy of Pudd'nhead Wilson*, W. E. B. Du Bois in *The Souls of Black Folk*, and Ralph Ellison in *Invisible Man*, have captured this irony well.

Minstrelsy in particular and American popular music in general capture another significant aspect of this relationship. Popular culture, broadly considered, is a breeding ground for a certain type of miscegenation that the country both abhors for its cheap mongrel quality (mating any two dogs seems to be no special accomplishment) and prizes for its energy and possibilities (mating any two dogs will produce an astonishing number of variations). And nothing defines America more, for good or ill, than its pervasive popular culture.

To understand diversity in America, one must begin by trying to understand the enormous proposition, the incredible gambit, embedded in the experiment of fashioning a country in which masters and slaves first tried to live together in a free society as unequals, and then, as ex-masters and ex-slaves, are trying to live together in a free society as equals. Culturally and historically, that is the root of the matter. What does it mean to be an American in an age when white male supremacy—a political convenience that attempted to become an ideology and that held the nation together for so long and so successfully but at such incredible cost—is now being so thoroughly challenged and is now slowly but surely entering a kind of twilight?

The word "diversity" threatens to become a mantra in the mouths of a good many Americans, and whether it is something Americans should want, or a condition that they are not capable of appreciating, is difficult to say. Either view is likely to seem a bit close to the argument of whether it is a premillennial or postmillennial fate that awaits us. In any case, diversity is talked about everywhere as a bromide, as salvation, as justice, as social uplift, as, well, American, but, on the other hand, it is considered social engineering, the destruction of standards and values, Balkanization, and the like. Discussion of American diversity these days is tied to affirmative action, a specific social and political policy, and to the idea of a historically inevitable and culturally determined pluralism, a deeply rooted set of attitudes about what Americans think the United States is and what being an American means.

The fervor over diversity, a remarkably insistent expression of our faith and our hypocrisy, our success and failure as a nation, is in part a threefold phenomenon: it is a rendering of old-time American pluralism; it is a reinvented populism; and it is a new version of bourgeois social reform. This idealism about the wonderful variety in America (or the mere assertion of the idea that the variety is wonderful) is rooted in all three ideas and comes close to being, to use an old-fashioned term from the "consensus" historians, a defining aspect of our national character.

The current preoccupation of Americans with diversity is often called "multiculturalism," but I refrain from using that term for several reasons. First, I am uncomfortable with the term because its meaning is too slippery. Is it meant to describe some postethnic society, to use David Hollinger's expression—that is, an interethnic society—or is it meant to describe a state of affairs that pronounces all ethnic marginalities as equal and coexistent political identities? Second, I do not like the way the term "culture" is being bandied about to signify any type of human difference or human grouping. This seems to be both a patent misuse and an overuse of the term. We live in a pluralistic society, but we do not live in a multicultural one. We have one culture built on three beliefs, the cornerstones of liberalism: (1) legalism, rights, and the court decision; (2) science, technology, empiricism, and progress through education and knowledge; (3) entrepreneurism, private ownership, competition, and making as much money as one can. Much of what American culture has produced can be explained through these prisms. This is our culture, not our romanticized, clumsy, brutal, or painful other-directed engagements with ethnic marginality.

The "diversity awareness" movement, if I might be permitted to call it something, is certainly a reworking of the old notion that we are a nation made up of immigrants. Mostly, we were told in school in the 1950s and 1960s, we are a nation of European immigrants—North European, Irish, German, Italian, Slavic, Jewish, Latin—who came here and made good. The distinct strands of these various ethnic types remained distinct, on the one hand, as a kind of local, watered-down folk culture, as a persistent ethnicity, as a persistent pluralism. The need for this belief, it seems, is virtually self-evident: Americans need a certain type of authentication— through culture and blood—of what they are. Americans also believe that Americans are blended through the alchemy of some sort of national ideal, a polis built on the creed of individual liberty and fulfillment, which helped forge the American nation. This is the tension inherent in being an American—the fear that what one is as an American is an insufficient identity, although the undeniable gift of the New World is precisely the psychic fluidity and the marketing potentiality of identity. Today that tension is exhibited, for instance, by someone like Republican presidential candidate Alan Keyes speaking at a conference at the National Civil Rights Museum, declaring that we are all American, not a bunch of different, squabbling nationalities, and that we live in a color-blind society. ("Color-blind" has become a cant word of the conservatives.) A Harvard law professor, a former clerk for Justice Blackmun, and a lawyer for the NAACP National

Defense Fund responded by saying that one of the evils of communism in Eastern Europe was its insistence that "we are all Yugoslavians together." She ended her remarks by saying that we can solve the race problem in the United States only by taking race into account. Americans believe in the myth of individual transcendence and the myth of group political identification, but in the United States these are clearly and hopelessly conflicting myths.

The elementary-school civics lesson seems to be a late-nineteenth- and twentieth-century remodeling of the eighteenth-century paradox of American identity being built on a geographical dualism: a local space *and* a national or federal abstraction. It must be remembered that even well after the American Revolution the average citizen was likely to describe himself or herself as the citizen of a state or even a region in a state before identifying himself or herself as a citizen of something called the United States. This dualism has held for how Americans see themselves, and it could hardly be otherwise in a country so self-consciously built on the energy produced by the tension of blatant ideological paradoxes, but this dualism shifted from explicit geography to implicit culture. In the twentieth century, Americans locate themselves less in geographical space than in cultural spaces, necessarily (although geographical spaces and the cultural mythologies they represent are still important in the making and the explication of the American psyche). This shift in the duality of the American identity occurred as a response to the tremendous efficiency with which the nation tended to homogenize its population. This homogenization was the result both of the advances in technology, the pervasive, relentless advance of the market and marketplace values through constant innovation in advertising, and of the intense liberal, welfare-state belief in universal education. The claims to atavistic culture origins seem to be the only way for individuals and, in recent years, for members of an oppressed group, to stop a huge assimilating juggernaut. The American developed an ideal or, more accurate, a condition of double-consciousness as a psychic gesture of resistance to his or her culture as assimilative force.

Du Bois's description of a black double-consciousness is one variant of the duality of implicit culture: "One ever feels his twoness—an American, a Negro; two souls, two thoughts, two unreconciled strivings; two warring ideals in one dark body, whose dogged strength alone keeps it from being torn asunder. The history of the American Negro is the history of this strife—this longing to attain self-conscious manhood, to merge his double self into a better and truer self." The fact that blacks today, by and large, want to be called African Americans is undoubtedly an effective expression of that "history of strife," of a sheer contradiction, of resentment toward and hope for assimilation. Built into the American's very being—historically and psychoculturally—is a sense of having a kind of divided loyalty or, in the case of the American Negro, the wish he can develop one. In part, various ethnic groups showed how Americanized they had become by demonstrating an ability to manipulate the political system in favor of their causes abroad: Germans for Germany, the Irish for Ireland, Jews for Israel or for policies in favor of free emigration from the then–Soviet Union, Cuban Americans for Cuba, Chinese Americans for China, and, to a much lesser extent because of the limitations under which they exist as Americans and because of their brutally induced sense of estrangement from their native land, African Americans for Africa.

In short, it is impossible to speak of union, more perfect or less so, outside of a dialectical construct where the possibility of union is constantly threatened, at risk. In some respects, especially when it resembles conformity or mere acquiescence to an authoritarian majority, union must be resisted. The very political and cultural ideology of romanticized rebellion in this country, from the American Revolution, to the American Adam's search for "the territory," to the confederacy's Lost Cause, to the youthful antiheroism of Rock and Roll teaches us this. The diversity awareness movement today is built on this sense of divided loyalty—that is, that one can be truly American (whatever that is) only if one is fully cognizant of being something else, and that, furthermore, one cannot be American without giving one's consent to it, for being American is a consensual relationship that thoroughly transcends blood. It is an odd aspect of being American—this quest for blood and this need to transcend it, the urge for the tribe and the desire for the nation-state that must hold many tribes together. As Lincoln suggested in his first inaugural address, the union existed before there was any formal recognition of it as a nation. Moreover, for Lincoln, this union transcended any mere idea of compact, contract, or voluntary association. It became something mystical, "our national fabric, with all its benefits, its memories, and its hopes." Mystical union and consensual citizenship are therefore hardly new. Today, however, the demand for a certain type of autonomy that is implicit in this grant of consent comes from unexpected quarters. The diversity awareness movement speaks for people of non-European origin, particularly those who were victimized by the Europeans who settled here.

Partly this is because the huge influx of non-European immigrants to the United States since the mid-1960s has changed the way many Americans see the entire Americanization process and has further intensified the sense that social groupings are built around some sense of ethnicity or nationality-cum-ethnicity. Many feel, and rightly so, that the experiences of these people have much to say about what it means to be an American. That is to say that many, including these non-European Americans themselves, are asking what it does mean to be an American, perhaps, in a new way or perhaps not. It has been reported that many recent Asian immigrants feel that they are much more American than blacks because they believe in the entrepreneurial spirit and want to get ahead in that way. They think the failure of blacks in the United States is proof that they cannot be Americans, that they are unfit for the ideological and cultural challenge of what American citizenship requires and so therefore ought to go back to Africa. On the other hand, black writers, from William Melvin Kelly to E. Franklin Frazier, from Albert Murray to Shelby Steele, have argued in varying ways that blacks certainly cannot go back to Africa because they are in effect more American than anybody else. They believe more fervently in the ideals of the nation than anyone else, and they believe more fervently in the power and promise of American citizenship than anyone else because they have seen or misperceived how this citizenship, like an economic open sesame, has worked for whites.

What does "being American" mean? In effect, the shift in thinking caused by the diversity awareness movement still leaves the idea and the ideal of American nationalism on the same ground of Emersonian tautology: that being American is a state of various forms of self-consciousness, but that this self-consciousness is virtually an awareness of being self-conscious. (A friend once put it to me that being an American was nothing more than the self-consciousness generated by thinking about what it means to be an American, or thinking about the meaning of the meaning of being American.) What strikes many now—which is why, in part, we are having a diversity awareness movement—is that the self-consciousness of the non-European stock of America is more interesting or more vital or more novel or more necessary at this moment than other forms of self-consciousness that defined earlier forms of American nationalism or American pluralism.

The current craze about diversity is a reinvention of populism, a reinvention of what constitutes "the common man," and certainly one major change has been that there can be no idea of a common man without a common woman. What is the average American experience and what is typical American life? The diversity awareness movement is changing our sense of this, although it does not question our devotion to the idea of the average, the typical, the ordinary, the common, as the personification of something truly American. In this sense, one observation about diversity awareness, taken from H. L. Mencken's view about things American generally, is that it is "a bit amateurish and childish." Indeed, at times there is something almost mawkish about the diversity awareness movement, although this is a quality more associated with its aspect as a social reform movement, which I shall discuss momentarily.

This quality of childishness, amateurishness, or mawkishness makes diversity awareness seem "sincere," and sincerity is the most important antielitist quality an American can possess.[2] Diversity awareness attacks the idea of an elite, as do all populist moods and tendencies in America. In this instance, the elite being attacked is built on being white, male, and heterosexual. This is, on the one hand, an entirely different construction from, say, C. Wright Mills's triad of "power elites" of nearly forty years ago: the military, the state, and the corporation. But on the other hand, one might say that Mills's constructions were all mere modalities of being white, male, and heterosexual.[3] The significant shift from Mills's radicalism to contemporary dissent is from a collectivist abstraction of power to something personal, a personification, from whiteness to the white male. In part, the personal nature of the new abstraction of power is an attack against an old conception of the "common man" as white, as male, as heterosexual— an attack, paradoxically, against white supremacy or superiority and white universality or commonness. In part, it is personal because, as Mencken suggested, Americans have an "unshakable belief in devils," and it is easier to attack devils when they are personifications than when they are abstract, intricate collectives of associated privilege. The diversity awareness movement is a quest for a certain type of democracy that expresses itself as an attack on privilege (and, in great measure, it sees racism as a system of privilege that must, like capitalist wealth was to the Marxists, be dismantled through redistribution). But the diversity awareness movement is also the liberal's fearful expression of the unstoppable meritocracy, the society that was spawned from liberal democracy's dream of humane technology and impersonal egalitarianism. The diversity awareness movement, deeply conflicted about the implications of a meritocratic society, wants to incorporate the "marginalized" and the oppressed into the meritocracy in order to validate the concept of liberalism itself, while using the marginalized and the oppressed to attack the very idea of a meritocracy built on "white" values, "white" standards, and so on. A great deal of the struggle over the meaning of being American is intricately tied to the meaning and nature of merit.

This leads naturally to the third observation that the diversity awareness movement is a bourgeois social reform movement resembling abolitionism in the eyes of its adherents and leftist Comstockism in the eyes of its opponents. Every self-proclaimed liberation movement in America almost invariably takes on the characteristics of exorcising devils, of prudery (despite, in this instance of the diversity awareness movement, the championing of the sexual adventurism or sexual dissent of the homosexual), of stump-thumping secular Methodism, of a philistine and unimaginative self-righteousness. For what, in the end, the advocates of the diversity awareness movement want to preach is not the goodness of diversity but the goodness in the *value* of diversity, the goodness of *believing* in diversity as an end in itself. This winds up being expressed in a number of banalities, from likening the varieties of human skin colors and types and cultures to a garden of flowers, to rainbow coalitions, to rainbows themselves, to the insipid reductionism of the profundity and complexity of what human difference truly means, to a self-righteous unending cry against white racism— as if all problems of human difference will be solved once whites undergo a mental sea change that in truth many of them could use but that, even if achieved to the most optimum effect, leaves us grappling mightily with the idea of what difference the human difference makes. As an end-of-history idea, the eradication of racism is as much an evasion as all other end-of-history solutions.

This sense of reform leads to much chatter about self-esteem and self-image, and finally to what Americans dream every reform movement should be: psychotherapy and religious conversion for the masses, or self-improvement and positive thinking. It might be that, if we read the story of the building of the Tower of Babel aright, we would discover that human homogeneity and human difference are both, in equal measure, gifts of enriching association and extraordinary problems of alienation and egotism that reach immeasurable magnitude. It has always been difficult for Americans to understand when a problem ceases to be political and becomes simply one of existence or, better put, when a problem ceases to be moral and becomes one of the general fate of the human condition. I am suggesting here, as C. Wright Mills, for instance, argues in *The Power Elite*, that the personal ought to be, in some measure, the political. Indeed, Mills is right when he writes:

> The knowledgeable man in the genuine public is able to turn his personal troubles into social issues, to see their relevance for his commu-

nity and his community's relevance for them. He understands that what he thinks and feels as personal troubles are very often not only that but problems shared by others and indeed not subject to solution by any one individual but only by modifications of the structure of the groups in which he lives and sometimes the structure of the entire society.[4]

The problem with the diversity awareness movement is that it is not interested, at least not entirely interested or completely interested, in creating a public in the sense that Mills or Dewey meant—informed and engaged.[5] The politics of the movement largely gets subsumed under a language of cure—not of psychoanalysis even but what is worse: the popularized quackery of psychoanalysis, of confessions of insult, injury, and rage, of, in truth, popularized notions of sin and redemption without the profundity of any sort of theology to buttress them. The diversity awareness movement is another substitute for religion in an age when no one can believe in a God anymore. A belief in God would temper the idea now rampant in our society that one is entitled to something simply because one has suffered. In short, the movement cannot help adopting the sentimentality of social protest, an expression of the relentless anxiety of living in "the sunlit prison of the American dream" as James Baldwin so poetically put it, and adopting as well the sentimentality of youth—the pathological fear of old age and death, which is what the American preoccupation with illness is all about. One might attribute this to American optimism, but the diversity awareness movement is built on the essential contradiction of that optimism. The diversity awareness movement wants Americans to understand the tragic nature of their history and the unrelenting destructiveness of white hatred. For the adherents of this movement, the founding of America was the despairing but cataclysmic moment when, on the North American continent, the African, the European, and the Indian met. Yet the movement itself does not want to accept conquest, tragedy, or hatred as inevitable or as human flaws, and like virtually every other American social reform movement its belief in progress is remarkably insistent. The movement sees American history not as profound tragedy but simply in the pedestrian reformer's light as a history that can be transformed by changing its present direction. Perhaps a foreign friend of mine was right when he said that while Americans are constantly trying to understand what being an American is, they have little idea of what their experience as a people actually means.

The diversity awareness movement is connected with the moral regeneration of psycho-cure because it is the result of the civil rights movement of the 1950s and 1960s. Racial integration, one of the major aims of the civil rights movement, was sustained by the idea that African Americans, maimed by the effects of a harshly segregated society that reminded them every day that they were inferior, needed integration to effect a psycho-cure, to make them whole. (The *Brown* decision of 1954 that desegregated public schools, or tried to, was based on such sociological and psychological assumptions.) Whites needed this as well to cure themselves of racism, an illness that corresponded to the various pathological illnesses of their vic-tims. The searing civil disobedience phase of the civil rights movement, with its startling violence and its burden of Christian imagery and morality, played out this aspect of the American race drama to great effect. But in the end it seemed only to emphasize, in some disturbing ways, a kind of racial co-dependency between blacks and whites, the very sort of relation-ship that is so aptly summed up in the Baldwin quotation that starts this chapter. Malcolm X and the rise of black power as an ideological alternative was a response to this idea of cure, an attempt to move African Americans into the arena of politics and economics as an aggrieved nation of exiles, not as a cohort of disaffected American citizens. The nationalists wanted to move the race struggle from its preoccupation with psychotherapy to a preoccupation with power. Of course, what the nationalists wanted was also cure, but cure unrelated to the idea of co-dependency. This too has failed and black nationalism's latest manifestation as Afrocentrism is noth-ing more than more talk about psycho-cure. In short, as a result of the civil rights movement, particularly its tremendous moments of success, the whole idea of diversity and pluralism in the United States has been inextri-cably intertwined with the idea of racial cure.

The diversity awareness movement has tried to envelop all nonwhite minorities in a relationship with whites that replicates that between blacks and whites, largely on the basis that the common thread is white racism. This is not likely to work—for a variety of reasons, all having to do with the nature of racial dynamics in American history and the fact that that history, as barbarous as it often is, cannot be read out simply as a long expression of the triumph of white racism. It may undeniably be the case that the history of America is about the long expression of the white will to power, which is an important distinction. One major expression of that will was surely racism, but it was not the sole expression of that will or the chief design of its imagination. Whites have seen dark people in similar ways, but also in quite varied ways, and in the United States the deepest and most sustained contact of whites with a dark population has been with Africans, a group that they clearly see differently from virtually any other people of color. But if it is the case that American history is the triumph of white racism merely, one must ask why white racism won, to which there seems to be at this time no adequate answer that all of us, white and "colored," could live with.

And the dependency of black on white, and of white on black, remains a relationship that in effect has no language, as it has exhausted, for both its parties, the language of psycho-cure, despite the valiant efforts of the adherents of the diversity awareness movement to keep that language alive. And it has never fully reached the language of politics and power, as neither group can fully escape the idea of dependency and the historical sentimentality of the paternalism it evokes. Perhaps neither wants to. The failure of affirmative action might be located in the fact that its language as a policy tries to accommodate both the idea of cure and the idea of power. In the end, it simply lumbers along in its crudity as yet another form of paternalism.

The only people who sound as self-righteous, as philistine, and are as deaf to the soundings of the paradox of American nationalism as those who advocate diversity awareness, are the conservatives who oppose it—or, shall I say, suspect it, speak of it as sin, as horror, as injustice, as special pleading, as wretched liberalism, and who speak of affirmative action, the prized public policy of the diversity awareness movement, as quotas, as a destruction of values and standards, as, well, a kind of miscegenated social engineering. What, indeed, is the white conservative trying to conserve?

The conservatives are right in intimating that few Americans care at all about diversity unless they can personally and crassly profit by it, and surely affirmative action is largely seen and used as a kind of patronage by the various groups who most demand it and by those who must "concede" it. For instance, the main interest of middle-class blacks is not primarily in working around whites, except perhaps for certain status reasons, but in trying to get more blacks in high-paying jobs. (The same might be said for middle-class white women, who profit more from affirmative action than any other group, but my concern here is not with gender.) On this level, diversity or human difference exists as a new form of capital, a new resource to exploit, as ethnicity, "orientation," and difference have always been exploitable resources in both perverse and creative ways in American culture. As Mencken correctly pointed out, "capitalism, in the long run, will win in the United States, if only for the reason that every American hopes to be a capitalist before he dies." Affirmative action in some measure perpetuates that very hope for a larger number of people than before by making it possible, in this country of salesmanship, for more to sell themselves by hawking their differences as a social good, as a commodity that no workplace or school or social gathering can do without. And no Americans believe in the entrepreneurial dream more than the oppressed as E. Franklin Frazier rightly pointed out in his 1957 book on the black middle class, *Black Bourgeoisie*. Black people have been entranced by the metafiction of business and entrepreneurship as the path to liberation and nationhood for the past 200 years. The criticism of some recent Asians that I mentioned earlier is thus especially misplaced. No group has ever wanted more desperately to prove its mettle through business, no group has ever more daydreamed about corporate empires, from Marcus Garvey to Louis Farrakhan (indeed, all American black nationalism of the twentieth century is a daydream about business power) from John H. Johnson to Jackie Robinson— indeed, all the aspirations of black Americans for assimilation are also a daydream about sharing the business power of the whites.

Affirmative action as an attempt to rig or engineer an atmosphere of diversity has done something clearly admirable and something unquestionably dubious. What is admirable is that it has transformed the idea of American pluralism into an ideology opposed to the idea of white nationalism. That is to say, affirmative action has created a political vision, a metahistorical myth, that several groups can use to form self-interested communities and, through a kind of energized pseudo-nationalist passion, push ahead— or let us say the middle-class elites of these various groups can push ahead. Affirmative action, coming as it has in the age of meritocracy, and standing as it does on the edge of both challenging the idea of merit while validating and fulfilling it, has also successfully created a new form of wealth divorced from old ideas of property as ownership. As Daniel Bell wrote in his summing up of *The End of Ideology*, "in a politico-technological world, property has increasingly lost its force as a determinant of power, and sometimes, even, of wealth." For affirmative action as an operative policy, these are the new modes of property as redemptive and empowered selfhood: (1) personal autonomy, (2) personal privacy, (3) mobility, (4) access, both political and technological, and (5) status, through simultaneous identification with the mainstream and with one's own social group.

The problem with affirmative action is the fact that its reality is built on the rigidity of archetypal categorization that presupposes or presumes that the difference measured by the category is the difference that matters; it is quite as likely to induce and perpetuate the role-playing politics of the various social groups that use it as it is the result of those politics. In short, affirmative action becomes, in some measure, a replication of the competitive muddle of middle-level power politics in America, a kind of wretched and overly self-conscious theater of checks and balances, where the end result of affirmative action is simply to demand more of it, because the actors hardly know what else their presence in the mainstream is supposed to signify. The affirmative action is particularly problematic for blacks, the people for whom it was mainly designed by 1960s liberals, for two huge reasons: first, blacks never come to be acknowledged as individual people but simply as representatives—even more precisely, as representations—of a social group. So the differences that matter are the differences *between* social groups, not the differences *in* them that may in fact challenge the very notions on which their unity, real and fictive, is built. In other words, the diversity awareness movement never challenges the assumptions of categorization in the United States. It simply wishes to create a self-conscious respect for them as a social necessity and to build a set of implicit political rights around an idea of patronage as a guarantee of their maintenance as viable groups.

In some sense, what affirmative action wants to achieve—the full economic and social redemption of the oppressed in the very categorization that was the source of oppression—is not to be taken lightly, although ultimately the gains made by the oppressed have been modest, just as the claims made against it in books like *The Bell Curve*, whose denouement is an astonishingly bitter and protracted denunciation of affirmative action, are overwrought. But by insisting on the reality of the sociological category as any individual's ultimate social and economic leverage, affirmative action is as likely to oppress as much as it liberates. But even more important is that blacks will never become fully a social group or a totally self-actualized category. What affirmative action has assured, in some sense, is that African Americans will continue to function as objects of fascination and annoyance, something between a fetish and a pet, a botched experiment and a curious expression of nobility. They will continue to be imprisoned by a charisma and a dread that fascinates but never fully explains. But it is this charisma and this dread that induces, evokes, provokes so much intellectual explanation. For, in the end, blacks live under the tyranny of both psychology and sociology, so-called "scientific" revelations of both their virtues and their vices, of their illness and their health.[6] On one level, all affirmative action has done is not to bring the black community to a new level of consciousness about itself, but simply to create another process by which blackness in the United States remains something foreign, in need of help and cure, that exists as a genuflection to white power and dominance.

Afrocentrism, a nationalist enterprise that has sprung up during this era of diversity awareness—specifically, in this age of wholesale challenge to the idea of white male supremacy, greatly aided in intellectual circles by the anti-Westernism of postmodernism—does not solve the problem of the split identity that is the sine qua non of being American, although its adherents believe it does. Afrocentrism simply masks black dualism under an aggressively asserted program of racial mental health based largely on the quest for an authentic idea free from the taint of whiteness and on accusations, with varying degrees of historical proof, of European thefts from darker peoples. For the Afrocentrist the division remains almost unchanged since Du Bois, rendered now in two slightly different forms of self-consciousness: a self-consciousness built on the rejection of a defiled American self centered on slavery and subordination, and a self-consciousness built on a regenerated African self built on independence and self-determination, each of which is necessary and contingent to make the other possible. This is merely an attempt to deepen the category of blackness without offering any possibility of transcending it—indeed, it considers the desire for transcendence a form of mental illness worthy only of scorn. Yet what true freedom can there be for any "person of color" unless he or she can transcend the necessity of categorization based on color? The term "African American," two huge and contradictory abstractions, is thus fraught with much that is unresolved. The question remains, especially for blacks, as the crux of the identity issue, how exactly are they a people, a social group, a set of ethnic class interests? As Lucien Goldmann observed in his famous treatise, *The Hidden God:*

> In order for a group to become a class, its interests must be directed, in the case of a "revolutionary" class, toward a complete transformation of the social structure or, if it is a "reactionary" class, toward maintaining the present social structure unchanged. Each class will then express its desire for change—or for permanence—by a complete vision both of what the man of the present day is, with his qualities and failings, and of what the man of the future ought to be, and of what relationship he should try to establish with the universe and with his fellows.[7]

It is often that I hear the comment from fellow blacks that "it is impossible to be a black conservative, for what does a black person have to conserve?"

But the very sardonic glibness of the statement merely masks a frightful anxiety. Black Americans are unable fully to understand what they should conserve from their experience as Americans. They grapple for a usable past, as they have failed to understand fully, even to this day, the meaning of their group experience or of their group reality. They have been condemned to a state of constant quandary about what they need to change and what they need to conserve in order for them to cohere and function as a group. The diversity awareness movement, in the eyes of both its proponents and its opponents, actually is a new take on an old dilemma: How do black people function as a community in the United States, and what is the significance of how their community functions or fails to function?

Richard Wright wrote in his 1945 autobiography *Black Boy:*

> After I had outlived the shocks of childhood, after the habit of reflection had been born in me, I used to mull over the strange absence of real kindness in Negroes, how unstable was our tenderness, how lacking in genuine passion we were, how void of great hope, how timid our joy, how bare our traditions, how hollow our memories, how lacking we were in those intangible sentiments that bind man to man, and how shallow was even our despair. After I had learned other ways of life I used to brood upon the unconscious irony of those who felt that Negroes led so passional an existence! I saw that what had been taken for our emotional strength was our negative confusions, our flights, our fears, our frenzy under pressure.
>
> Whenever I thought of the essential bleakness of black life in America, I knew that Negroes had never been allowed to catch the full spirit of Western civilization, that they lived somehow in it but not of it. And when I brooded upon the cultural barrenness of black life, I wondered if clean, positive tenderness, love, honor, loyalty, and the capacity to remember were native with man. I asked myself if these human qualities were not fostered, won, struggled and suffered for, preserved in ritual from one generation to another.[8]

This harsh passage—which James Baldwin and Ralph Ellison so strongly questioned—appears parenthetically in the book, almost as if it were an aside or perhaps meant to be something that could be excised from the text, or perhaps, in miniature, the author's intrusive comment on the rest of the text, a self-conscious rumination in a book that is relentlessly and ruthlessly about the creation of self-consciousness. There are many views of black community in African American literature, but Wright's is startling because—in its attack against sentimentality, against blackness as a fetish or a categorization—it asks a great deal of black people while conceding very little to them. But to be black is a way of life like any other, and after all, no matter how bereft, it did indeed produce a writer as talented as Wright. But the questions posed by Wright are: What makes black community? What do black people share, and what can they realistically be expected to share? What sort of class or group of people are black folk in America, and how has the fact that they have diversified this nation beyond all hope of homogeneity affected them? Oddly, the very questions that the diversity awareness movement should be trying to answer and, in some measure, claims it does answer, are not explored much at all. Until this exploration takes place with honesty and intelligence, Americans will never understand the nature of their experience or what it has ever meant or will ever mean to be an American.

# CHAPTER TEN

# Coda
## Three Reconstructions

## JOHN HIGHAM

The story of civil rights in the twentieth century, as followed in this book, has the shape of a great wave climbing a beach. A low swell, moving slowly, gains momentum. At a certain point it surges to a mighty crest that crashes with a roar. A wash of water flows onward, but the force is gone. The wave is receding. This is the pattern of modern racial reform: quiet, gradual improvement in the 1920s and 1930s; accelerating power after World War II; a dangerous, breath-taking climax in the 1960s; an aftermath of persistence and retreat.

At the crest of the wave in 1965, C. Vann Woodward called attention to similarities between what was happening at that moment and the dazzling enactment of racial reforms and civil rights exactly one hundred years earlier during the reconstruction of the defeated southern states. Woodward called the events occurring around him a "Second Reconstruction." He feared it might collapse as the first one had. But he hoped that this time the far greater power of African Americans would save the cause of racial justice from compromise, appeasement, and failure.[1]

Now, more than three decades later, Woodward's Second Reconstruction has completed the full cycle of the First. We have a longer time span before us, so we can extend Woodward's comparative perspective both forward and backward. From the vantage point of today, the accomplishments of the Reconstruction that followed the Civil War seem more than merely "rhetorical." Our present knowledge of what African Americans learned and did during the so-called "Tragic Era" redeems it from the dismissive judgment that historians used to pronounce.[2]

Similarly, a great advance in historical knowledge of the era of the American Revolution has shown that the "first" reconstruction of American race relations took place then, not in the 1860s, if we define "reconstruction" as a broad postwar program for reforming the social order. Moreover, this early cycle of racial reform anticipated the pattern its successors have followed: slowly rising discontent; liberation and euphoria; breakdown and retreat. Might an examination of these resemblances yield some clue to possibilities for a fourth reconstruction? I believe they do.

Each of the three cycles that punctuate the history of black-white relations in America received a powerful impetus from a major, victorious war. In each case, war expanded the choices that black people could make. Responding to offers of liberation and protection, slaves escaped to British armies during the Revolution. During the Civil War, they found an undeclared freedom behind Union lines in such numbers that people called them "contrabands"—that is, confiscated rebel property. During World War II the descendants of the slaves escaped northward from the rural South in a huge migration that opened new opportunities in factories, labor unions, and politics. In the long run, however, the immediate gains that accrued within a national struggle against an external enemy were less significant than the great upsurge of national idealism and racial hope that each war released.

By crystallizing a distinctive national ideology, the American Revolution established the enduring dynamics of racial reform. Whether an American ideology was more largely a cause or a result of the Revolution, the conflict welded together an extraordinarily durable set of ideas that came to define a national purpose. One founding principle declared that the United States exists to secure the equal, unalienable rights that individuals receive from nature. Another enshrined a broadly Christian ethic of dedication to the common good. A third offered an embracing faith in human progress, with America in the lead.[3] In the absence of a homogeneous ethnic identity, this compound of secular and religious ideas—in this amalgam of liberty, nationality, and faith—was the strongest bond of unity in the new nation.

Although flatly incompatible in all respects with slavery, what Gunnar Myrdal has called the American Creed was often construed as a future promise rather than an immediate requirement. For most Americans it was more largely a conception of capacities than a claim of achievements. But advances could not be altogether postponed. The revolutionary impulse, with its appeal to human rights as well as American rights, inspired an antislavery movement abroad and at home. Never before had so many pulpits rung with condemnations of slaveholding. Nowhere earlier had blacks petitioned for their freedom on grounds of natural rights.[4]

Why did the Civil War and World War II tap and reinforce the same strain of nationalist idealism? Surely because both conflicts lent themselves to definition in the same terms. The Civil War was understood as a struggle to preserve a union based on freedom; World War II engaged Americans in resisting a new form of slavery. In all three wars did special interests manipulate patriotism for their own ends? Of course. Did intolerance of minorities produce racial barbarities and hysterical witch-hunts? Unquestionably. But that does not negate the altruistic inducement each major war held out to Americans to locate themselves within and carry forward the Spirit of '76.

In no case did war originate the impulse it popularized. Each postwar reconstruction was continuous with a gradual, prewar buildup of moral disquiet over the state of race relations. Decades might pass before the fervent nationalism of a great war energized a long-standing moral concern, which had deeply troubled only a small minority of whites. In wartime the people as a whole were called to uphold the principles that had given the nation its identity. Only then, through an outpouring of national idealism, could a moral issue receive political expression.

For half a century before the American Revolution, individual Christians who were sensitive to the humanitarian tendencies of the eighteenth century had disavowed the buying and selling of human beings. Not until 1758, however, did the Philadelphia Yearly Meeting denounce Quakers who bought or sold Negroes. Then another seventeen years passed before Philadelphians, on the eve of the American Revolution, formed the first antislavery society in the western world.[5]

Similarly, in the nineteenth century a fragmented movement for abolishing or narrowly circumscribing slavery made headway slowly, against fierce resistance, throughout the 1830s and 1840s. Not until 1848, with the formation of the Free Soil Party, did an antislavery coalition capture 10 percent of the popular vote. In the 1850s, however, an impending breakup of the

Union connected the cause of liberty with the more immediately compelling issue of national survival.

The civil rights movement of the 1950s and 1960s was no less indebted to prewar antecedents. The power and confidence it radiated after World War II would not have existed without a slow accumulation of guilt and protest from the late 1920s through the 1930s, followed by an all-out global war that idealized American democracy. From a revulsion against southern lynchings in the late 1920s through the diffuse egalitarianism of the New Deal years, public opinion prepared the way for a communalizing experience of national dedication and sacrifice. If religion played a smaller role than in the earlier wars, a transfigured liberalism, celebrating the adhesiveness of a multiethnic people, amply took its place.[6]

Before examining these three encounters more closely, we cannot overlook a fourth great war, which fails completely to fit the general pattern. World War I—the Great Crusade, as ironic historians used to call it—made race relations worse rather than better. In this case, however, the exception helps to clarify the pattern of racial progress. American participation in World War I was relatively brief, just nineteen months in all, with only five months of intensive combat. Far more significant than the lighter burden that World War I imposed, however, was the absence of a significant prewar growth of racial reform.

Instead of the troubled national conscience that Gunnar Myrdal observed in 1944, nearly all white Americans from the 1890s to the 1920s displayed a colossal insensitivity to the hostility and abuse that rained down on racial or pseudo-racial minorities in the most advanced and highly industrialized nations of the world. Fears of impurity, pollution, corruption, and depravity coalesced. In this extravagantly racist milieu, Americans could try to address economic injustice (unsuccessfully as it turned out) but not racial oppression. When World War I ended, an unprecedented explosion of racial and ethnic strife ensued. There was much talk of "reconstruction," but only among black people did it mean a reform of race relations. Among whites, "reconstruction" suggested problems of "economic serfdom," "discipline and orderly living," and "spiritual regeneration."[7]

By crushing the hopes it raised for a new dawn of peace and freedom, World War I has diverted historians from a longer linkage in American history between major wars and advances in democracy. The dichotomy between war and racial progress has seemed plausible too because the nation's small wars, such as 1812 and Vietnam, were indeed racially regressive. Moreover, little concrete improvement in race relations took place *during* the big wars. Each cycle of racial reform began in a long preparatory phase before the war started and climaxed in a mighty surge after it ended.

In each of the three cases reviewed here, war's immediate exigencies obscured progress in race relations. The months and years of combat allowed little latitude for altering social or political life. While raising aspirations and giving demands for change a national hearing, the wars deferred the tasks of racial reform to the postwar years. That is when the big breakthroughs in race relations have occurred.

The liberating aftermath of the American Revolution was relatively modest. It simply put limits on the spread of slavery, but the limits were not inconsequential. The federal government checked the advance of slavery into the West; the states rolled it back in the Northeast. The Northwest Ordinance of 1787, which developed from an earlier proposal by Thomas Jefferson, laid down conditions for forming states north of the Ohio River. A proviso prohibiting slavery throughout the entire territory was the first national legislation that set bounds on the expansion of slavery. Meanwhile, beginning with Pennsylvania in 1780, every northern state by 1804 had adopted plans for gradual emancipation of its slaves. Two years later, federal legislation completed a similar process that banned the African slave trade from all American ports.

During the same years, antislavery sentiment persuaded state legislatures in the South to loosen existing restrictions on manumission. Especially in the Upper South, numerous slave owners freed their slaves voluntarily. In doing so they quickened a yearning for freedom among those who were left behind. Accordingly, manumission inspired a larger flight from the slave states. Nationally, the free black population rose from a mere handful— probably less than 5,000 in 1780—to 186,000 in 1810, most of whom gathered in the larger towns and cities of the mid-Atlantic region. Their communities produced such institutions as fraternities, churches, and mutual aid societies, through which freed people could manage their own affairs. The creation of autonomous black congregations from the 1780s onward, sometimes within existing denominations and sometimes entirely independently, was an important step in the building of self-sustaining African American communities.[8]

This early freedom movement was cautious and circumspect. It merely nibbled at the edges of slavery. Its Civil War counterpart was dramatic, impetuous, and visionary. Even more than during the Revolution, the main body of American Protestants was convinced that their cause was holy. In "the glory of the coming of the Lord," Julia Ward Howe wrote that she could see Him "trampling out the vintage where the grapes of wrath are stored." He was leading the Union armies to a final conquest of sin and bondage.[9] In large parts of the North the moral issue of slavery, intermixed with divine will and national destiny, was so intensely felt and widely agitated during the war that racial reform for once leaped ahead before hostilities ended. Northern black spokesmen such as Frederick Douglass were able to press for immediate emancipation while pointing proudly to the very large proportion of black males who were serving in the Union armies. Then Lincoln's Emancipation Proclamation in 1863 made inevitable the complete termination of slavery by means of the Thirteenth Amendment (1865). In states and cities influenced by southern mores, Jim Crow laws were reduced or repealed.[10]

Breathtaking advances in race relations came almost immediately after the Civil War ended, in contrast to a slower climax of reform following the Revolution and World War II. Millions of African Americans were now free to choose their own work and residence, subject only to the constraints of a general impoverishment. Their exuberant political meetings and those of their northern allies resounded with invocations of the Declaration of Independence.

Within months, white southerners set out to restore a racial oligarchy, bulwarked by the notorious "Black Codes" that were close to slavery. Crying treason, the radical leadership of the Republican party reacted by pushing beyond mere abolition. Public outrage demanded strong federal protection of freedmen's rights, and the Radicals were ready to supply it. Nothing less could ensure a "new birth of freedom" that would justify the enormous sacrifices of the war. This was the thrust of the Fourteenth Amendment.

But preserving civil rights would require a further extension of federal power, specifically to guarantee sympathetic local and state governments. In the face of insurrectionary resistance in the South and widespread disapproval in the North, Congress imposed temporary military rule in the South, created genuinely interracial governments there, and secured ratification in 1870 of a fifteenth amendment granting full voting rights to black males in North and South alike. Nowhere else in the western world was the transition from slavery to full citizenship so swift and unmediated.[11]

It was the task of the Third Reconstruction to reestablish the full panoply of political and civil rights gained in the Second Reconstruction but lost or weakened in a great reversal at the end of the nineteenth century. Beyond that, the Third Reconstruction aimed at a wider goal. It sought an equality of social respect and economic opportunity for all Americans. It reached the first goal, but only part of the second. Instead, the Third Reconstruction passed through the same changes of phase that earlier surges of racial reform had displayed. After a prewar genesis, it grew more rapidly from 1945 onward, soared from 1963 to 1968, then underwent a lingering demise. An understanding of that last phase should tell us a good deal about the vulnerabilities of progress in America.

In all three episodes the shift from commitment to retrogression was sufficiently gradual to suggest at the outset a simple waning of idealistic nationalism and moral fervor. At the very beginning of the nineteenth century the antislavery societies that had sprung up after the Revolution showed signs of enfeeblement. As the Revolution receded into the past, its broad enthusiasm for human rights dwindled into a narrower preoccupation with the right to property. Simultaneously, the migration of freed people to a few urban centers created dense neighborhoods and congested alleys where blacks were no longer under the close observation of their employers. Fears of unrest palsied reformers—especially after the turn of the century, when atrocities and racial uprisings on French islands in the Caribbean aroused lurid suspicions of black conspiracies on the American mainland. After 1800, slave codes in the South were tightened, while traditional constraints on free blacks—on their right to vote, for example, and to live where they pleased—revived. A hedge of restrictive, discriminatory legislation rose around the black communities of the North and the vast slave population of the South. Manumission was severely restricted; migration was closely controlled.[12]

The sharpening of fear and discrimination at the beginning of the nineteenth century suggests a loss of adhesiveness, a loosening of national idealism, that was more dramatically evident in the waning of the Second and Third Reconstructions. There too a fear of blacks, with accompanying deterioration of communication and concern, marked the end of racial reform.

From 1865 to 1867, and again exactly one hundred years later, a nationalizing euphoria and commitment seemed to sweep all obstacles aside. During those triumphant years bitterly racist resistance in the South only intensified the will and strength of reformers to carry through what they called "the equal rights revolution." In 1868, white southern resistance to the revolution continued unabated. In 1968 or thereabouts it was broken. Nevertheless, in the late '60s of both centuries many were tiring of strife. Ulysses S. Grant won the presidency with the slogan "Let us have peace." Richard Nixon succeeded with a similar stance. By the seventies, public interest in great moral issues was declining.[13] Liberal nationalism was running out of steam. In the midst of turmoil, locally rooted racism proved—at least in the short run—more tenacious than an inclusive, democratic spirit.

When national idealism was already on the defensive, a second factor dealt a further setback to all three reconstructions. In each case an already flagging movement for racial reform ended when the economic environment turned decisively unfavorable. This brings into sight once again the significance of the postwar moment. From the eighteenth century to the twentieth, the big advances in race relations have been borne on a flood of postwar prosperity. Twenty years after the adoption of the Constitution, twenty years after the Emancipation Proclamation, and thirty years after World War II, a long postwar boom faltered or collapsed. Each of these eras of prosperity and progress had opened space in people's lives for altruism; each had sustained a glowing vision of the nation's future. When the boom subsided, self-interest crowded to the fore, perhaps as much among blacks as whites. Indifference at the top of the social scale and bare-knuckle antagonism down below again widened the racial chasm.

In the First Reconstruction, Congress's prohibition of the African slave trade in 1808 was the last antislavery legislation of any note. A year earlier the Jeffersonian embargo, prohibiting commerce with any foreign nation, interrupted the great economic boom that followed the Revolution. A period of instability turned in 1819 into a sharp, lingering depression. In eastern cities the resulting downward pressure on the already meager wages of African Americans aroused intense hostility in the white working class. Also during this era of economic uncertainties, new ideas of irreducible inequality between races largely superseded the revolutionary generation's confidence in universal natural rights.[14]

The Second Reconstruction terminated in a similar way. In the 1850s, and especially in the years immediately following the Civil War, the North and West enjoyed dazzling economic growth with rising levels of real wages. The depression that began in 1873, however, created deep distress in the cities and reduced many farmers to tenancy. Contemporaries regarded it as the most severe depression in American history. Politicians turned their attention from moral issues to economic remedies and nostrums such as currency, tariffs, and strike-breaking. The Democratic party—the party of white supremacy—recovered from the obloquy it had suffered during the war and postwar years.[15] A century later, in 1973, the parties had reversed their positions, but the sequence of events was familiar.

The parallels between the periods of racial reform are plain to see. In all three cases dissatisfaction with the status quo had grown slowly among morally engaged minorities before intersecting with a major challenge to the nation. At that point a great surge of national idealism, abounding prosperity, a common enemy, and, it must now be added, a spirit of collaboration between whites and blacks brought the most dazzling advances of equality in American history.

So much for parallels. There is also a striking difference in the three episodes beyond their obvious contrasts of scale and aspiration. Although the First Reconstruction demonstrated a yearning for freedom among the slaves, a black elite who could play active roles in shaping events hardly existed. Moreover, virtually no whites could as yet imagine a harmonious interracial society. Black participation in making change was therefore neither expected nor sought. The First Reconstruction was in some measure *for* African Americans but not *by* them.

The Second Reconstruction brought them more fully into the historical process. William Lloyd Garrison and other nineteenth-century abolitionists had welcomed blacks as co-equal disturbers of the peace. Their eager involvement in the antislavery movement and in contests over the suffrage in northern states dramatized the meaning of freedom. Their participation in southern public life beginning in 1867 was essential, extensive, and moderately progressive. They were junior partners in Reconstruction governments, heavily obligated to white allies and not always ready for the responsibilities they held, but altogether men of varied abilities and backgrounds who gave ample proof that hundreds of former slaves could handle the business of government.[16]

The Third Reconstruction presents a major contrast in leadership. Now the initiative for and direction of change in the ascending phases was primarily in the hands of African Americans. The First Reconstruction had been the work of a governing elite of whites. The Second reflected and contributed to the democratization of American society in the mid-nineteenth century. Although it too was led by a white elite, its execution depended on broad approval in public opinion (both white and black) and on active support from the newly enfranchised black masses. In the Third Reconstruction, blacks predominated. They made the crucial decisions. They also bore the heaviest burdens. Yet the participation, validation, and power of whites remained indispensable.

How critical, then, was close, active collaboration between the races in the making of the Third Reconstruction? Earlier American history yields no precise comparison. But the trend it presents is suggestive, and the evidence of interracial cooperation in racial reform from the 1920s to the 1960s (presented in the Introduction to this book) leaves little room to doubt that the Third Reconstruction was heavily dependent on a partnership between blacks and an influential segment of the white population. I find inescapable, therefore, the conclusion that the division that opened in the civil rights movement in 1965 with the rise of black power—and the antiwhite legacy it left—was a significantly contributing cause of the movement's decline.

As we look forward to the preconditions for a fourth reconstruction in the twenty-first century, history seems to tell us that a restoration of cooperation and trust between leaders on the two sides will have to rank high. Each will need to risk unpopularity while holding firmly to a popular following. On both sides the leaders must have a flexible, loosely bounded identity, undefensive and therefore willing to incorporate something of the "other" who is different from oneself.

These qualities will not be available unless both avant gardes participate in some larger identity, some greater loyalty, that connects them without threatening their separate qualities and needs. Their wider solidarity will have to draw on the liberal nationalism that was forged in a Christianized Enlightenment and in the twentieth century renamed the American Creed. That is what has driven each of the advances toward racial equality thus far.

To recapture that spirit, will the country have to wait for another major war? What might serve as a moral equivalent? Since history may not again repeat itself, these troubling questions may not have to be faced. Some pundits tell us that racial differences are gradually losing depth and intensity as a miscegenated heterogeneity of style and appearance becomes more and more normative in American life.[17] In the quarter century since the breakdown of the civil rights movement, the reaction against it has been much shallower than the reaction against its predecessors. On the whole, the black middle class retains the great gains it made, and in many kinds of settings acceptance is coming more easily. These tendencies owe much to the globalization of communications, travel, and migration since World War II and to an accompanying recognition that no people are entirely outside our ken. In some ungraspable sense, the future must belong to the impure.

Still, Americans surely cannot rely on global forces to solve their problems. In the best as well as the worst scenarios their own history will come into play. I suggest that the prospect before us may look less bleak if the past appears less dismal. The fashionable cynicism of our time stigmatizes the entire record of American race relations. The civil rights movement of the mid-twentieth century is generally regarded as a "tragic failure," and so too its predecessors.[18] In truth, none was a failure; they were simply incomplete. For many black people, each surge reached some of their objectives, and the advances were never entirely lost in the reversals that followed.

After the First Reconstruction, some blacks in the North retained the right to vote, and some in the South preserved a substantial personal status. After the Second Reconstruction there were greater gains. Personal servitude was never reimposed, nor was the ability to move or migrate denied. Robert Wiebe has pointed out that African American rights in northern states expanded slowly in the late nineteenth century and that the notorious segregationist doctrine of "separate but equal" represented a concession to black demands for decent treatment. Moreover, blacks helped themselves. Their own mutual aid societies did much to raise blacks' per capital income, while legions of black teachers reduced illiteracy among blacks in the South from 80 percent in the 1860s to 45 percent in 1910.[19]

When the Third Reconstruction created a cornucopia of opportunities, along with bitter disappointments, it was repeating on an upward gradient the experience of its predecessors. Historians have been unable to see these events together, related within a long-term pattern, because their attention has been riveted on failure and defeat, with scant allowance for success and victory. Since the vaulting expectations of the 1960s collapsed, a "culture of defeat" has infected attitudes toward national projects among academics, much of the black middle class, and even the public at large.[20] The American Creed lives on, but only one of its three pillars—the idea of human freedom—remains essentially unchallenged. Cynicism has ravaged belief in an inclusive national community and in its reach toward a better world. Until schools and churches and other opinion-makers repair the damage to national identity and to faith in human possibility, how can race relations rise much above the level of rancorous bargaining among unequal interest groups? It is time for Americans to make richer use of their deeply divided but nonetheless inspiring heritage.

# Notes

## Chapter 1

1. August Meier and John H. Bracey Jr., "The NAACP as a Reform Movement, 1909–1965: 'To Reach the Conscience of America,'" *Journal of Southern History* 59 (1993): 4–30. See also B. Joyce Ross, *J. E. Spingarn and the Rise of the NAACP, 1911–1939* (New York: Atheneum, 1972).

2. Michael J. Klarman, "How *Brown* Changed Race Relations: The Backlash Thesis," *Journal of American History* 81 (1994): 81–118.

3. Reynolds Farley, *Growth of the Black Population: A Study of Demographic Trends* (Chicago: Markham Publishing Co., 1970); Doris Y. Wilkinson, "Gender and Social Inequality: The Prevailing Significance of Race," *Daedalus*, Winter 1995, 171; Joel Williamson, *The Crucible of Race: Black-White Relations in the American South Since Reconstruction* (New York: Oxford University Press, 1984). For comparisons with slavery, see Robert W. Fogel, *Without Consent or Contract: The Rise and Fall of American Slavery* (New York: Norton, 1989).

4. James R. Grossman, *Land of Hope: Chicago, Black Southerners, and the Great Migration* (Chicago: University of Chicago Press, 1989).

5. David Levering Lewis, *When Harlem Was in Vogue* (New York: Alfred A. Knopf, 1981), 30–33, 162–75; Lewis Erenberg, "News from the Great Wide World: Duke Ellington, Count Basie, and Black Popular Music, 1927–1943," *Prospects* 18 (1993): 483–506. See also Burton W. Peretti, *The Creation of Jazz: Music, Race, and Culture in Urban America* (Urbana: University of Illinois Press, 1992).

6. John Egerton, *Speak Now Against the Day: The Generation Before the Civil Rights Movement in the South* (New York: Alfred A. Knopf, 1994), 47–52.

7. Meier and Bracey, "NAACP as a Reform Movement," 19–20.

8. Harvey Sitkoff, *A New Deal for Blacks: The Emergence of Civil Rights as a National Issue* (New York: Oxford University Press, 1978), 169–89; August Meier and Elliott Rudwick, *Black Detroit and the Rise of the UAW* (New York: Oxford University Press, 1979); Lizabeth Cohen, *Making a New Deal: Industrial Workers in Chicago, 1919–1939* (New York: Cambridge University Press, 1990), 323–49, 361–68; Herbert Hill, "The Problem of Race in American Labor History," *Reviews in American History* 24 (1996): 189–208.

9. Robert Bone, *The Negro Novel in America*, rev. ed. (New Haven: Yale University Press, 1965), 140–60. For a remarkable earlier episode of literary collaboration, see Charles

Scruggs, *The Sage of Harlem: H. L. Mencken and the Black Writers of the 1920s* (Baltimore: Johns Hopkins University Press, 1983).

10. Sitkoff, *New Deal for Blacks*, 190–215; Walter A. Jackson, *Gunnar Myrdal and America's Conscience: Social Engineering and Racial Liberalism, 1938–1987* (Chapel Hill: University of North Carolina Press, 1990).

11. For an illuminating though severely critical account, see Stephen Steinberg, *Turning Back: The Retreat from Racial Justice in American Thought and Policy* (Boston: Beacon Press, 1995), 21-56.

12. Blacks are strikingly absent, either in uniform or as civilians, from all but a single two-page spread in *Life Goes to War: A Picture History of World War II*, ed. David E. Scherman (Boston: Little, Brown, 1977). And on that page the magazine assured its readers that blacks, although they have "never had a square deal from the U.S. white majority, . . . are glad to work and fight and die alongside their white fellow-citizens."

13. Sitkoff, *New Deal for Blacks*, 316.

14. Jackson, *Myrdal*, 273–79.

15. Taylor Branch, *Parting the Waters: America in the King Years, 1954–1963* (New York: Simon & Schuster, 1988), 124–205; Aldon D. Morris, *The Origins of the Civil Rights Movement: Black Communities Organizing for Change* (New York: The Free Press, 1984).

16. David L. Chappell, *Inside Agitators: White Southerners in the Civil Rights Movement* (Baltimore: Johns Hopkins University Press, 1994).

17. David R. Goldfield, *Black, White, and Southern: Race Relations and Southern Culture, 1940 to the Present* (Baton Rouge: Louisiana State University Press, 1990), 114.

18. Benjamin G. Rader, *American Sports: From the Age of Folk Games to the Age of Spectators* (Englewood Cliffs, N.J.: Prentice Hall, 1983), 324–29; Matthew Whitehorn, "The Baltimore Elite Giants and the Decline of Negro Baseball" (paper presented at the American History Seminar, May 5, 1981; Johns Hopkins University, Baltimore, Maryland); Frederick Lewis Allen, *The Big Change: America Transforms Itself, 1900–1950* (New York: Harper, 1952), 182.

19. Robert Coles, "Minority Dreams, American Dreams," *Daedalus*, Spring 1981, 41.

20. Howard N. Rabinowitz, *Race Relations in the Urban South, 1865–1890* (New York: Oxford University Press, 1978), 334–39. See also Robin D. G. Kelley, *Race Rebels: Culture, Politics, and the Black Working Class* (New York: The Free Press, 1994).

21. Morris, *Origins;* Goldfield, *Black, White, and Southern*, 103. See also John Dittmer, *Local People: The Struggle for Civil Rights in Mississippi* (Urbana: University of Illinois Press, 1994), and for a vividly detailed overview of the entire black movement in the 1960s and early 1970s, see Robert Weisbrot, *Freedom Bound: A History of America's Civil Rights Movement* (New York: W. W. Norton, 1990).

22. Hugh Davis Graham, *The Civil Rights Era: Origins and Development of National Policy* (New York: Oxford University Press, 1990), 27–152; *Congressional Record*, 88th Cong. 2 Sess. (June 19, 1964), 14511.

23. Graham, *Civil Rights Era*, 162–73, 346–62, 452–53; Steven F. Lawson, *In Pursuit of Power: Southern Blacks and Electoral Politics, 1965–1982* (New York: Columbia University Press, 1985).

24. Gary Orfield, "School Desegregation After Two Generations: Race, Schools, and Opportunity in Urban Society," in *Race in America: The Struggle for Equality*, ed. Herbert Hill and James E. Jones Jr. (Madison: University of Wisconsin Press, 1993), 239–240; C. Vann Woodward, "Look Away, Look Away," *Journal of Southern History* 59 (1993): 495–96; Goldfield, *Black, White, and Southern*, 228–37; *New York Times*, August 22, 1983, A22.

25. Arnold Rose quoted in Byron M. Roth's *Prescription for Failure: Race Relations in the Age of Social Science* (New Brunswick, N.J.: Transaction Publishers, 1994), 1; Louis Harris,

*The Anguish of Change* (New York: Norton, 1973), 231–35, 239; Herbert H. Hyman and Paul Sheatsley, "Attitudes Toward Desegregation," *Scientific American* 211 (July 1964): 16–23.

26. Thomas F. Pettigrew, "Actual Gains and Psychological Losses: The Negro American Protest," in *The Making of Black America: Essays in Negro Life and History,* ed. August Meier and Elliott Rudwick (New York: Atheneum, 1969), 2:321, 323–29; Pettigrew, "Race and Class in the 1980s: An Interactive View," *Daedalus,* Spring 1981, 240–41; Vincent Harding, in *America's Black Past: A Reader in Afro-American History,* ed. Eric Foner (New York: Harper & Row, 1970), 473. On the social separation of the races, see Stanley Lieberson, *Ethnic Patterns in American Cities* (New York: The Free Press, 1963).

27. Joe Klein, "The True Disadvantage," *New Republic,* October 28, 1996, 35.

28. Nicholas Lemann, *The Promised Land: The Great Black Migration and How It Changed America* (New York: Alfred A. Knopf, 1991), 3–7.

29. H. Edward Ransford, "Isolation, Powerlessness, and Violence: A Study of Attitudes and Participation in the Watts Riot," in *The Sociology of Race Relations: Reflection and Reform,* ed. Thomas F. Pettigrew (New York: The Free Press, 1980), 302–11.

30. Murray Friedman, "The White Liberal's Retreat," *Atlantic Monthly* 211 (January 1963): 43. The interaction between the southern protests and the northern riots is impressively developed in Donald L. Horowitz, "Racial Violence in the United States," in *Ethnic Pluralism and Public Policy: Achieving Equality in the United States and Britain,* ed. Nathan Glazer and Ken Young (Lexington, Mass.: Lexington Books, 1983), 186–212.

31. Hubert G. Locke, *The Detroit Riot of 1967* (Detroit: Wayne State University Press, 1969), 70–98; *New York Times,* February 26, 1978, 28. On the long history of police brutality see *New York Times,* August 20, 1995, sec. 4, 6.

32. Morris Janowitz, "Patterns of Collective Racial Violence," in *Violence in America: Historical and Comparative Perspectives,* ed. Hugh Davis Graham and Ted Robert Gurr (Washington: National Commission on the Causes and Prevention of Violence, 1969), 1:317–29; *Report of the National Advisory Commission on Civil Disorders* (Washington, D.C.: Government Printing Office, 1968), 73–75; *New York Times,* May 17, 1981, 28.

33. Sidney Fine, *Violence in the Model City: The Cavanagh Administration, Race Relations, and the Detroit Riot of 1967* (Ann Arbor: University of Michigan Press, 1989), 291–93, 325–26, 330–34, 352.

34. Edward C. Banfield, *The Unheavenly City: The Nature and Future of Our Urban Crisis* (Boston: Little, Brown, 1970), 185–209. Recent statistical studies of the history of violent crime are summarized in *New York Times,* October 23, 1994, sec. 1, 16. On the heroin epidemic of the 1960s, see Jill Jonnes, *Hep-Cats, Narcs and Pipe Dreams: A History of America's Romance with Illegal Drugs* (New York: Scribner, 1996), 250–61, 276–82. On the lure of guns, see *Baltimore Sun,* November 11, 1971, C-22, and April 28, 1974, D18.

35. Fine, *Violence,* 342–43, 347–48; Locke, *Detroit Riot,* 85-88. On other aspects of the riots, see the excellent summary in Kenneth Kusmer, "African Americans in the City Since World War II," *Journal of Urban History* 21 (1995): 466–70.

36. Locke, *Detroit Riot,* 109–22.

37. *Report of National Advisory Commission,* 218–25.

38. George Fredrickson, *Black Liberation: A Comparative History of Black Ideologies in the United States and South Africa* (New York: Oxford University Press, 1995), 286–317; William L. Van Deburg, *New Day in Babylon: The Black Power Movement and American Culture, 1965–1975* (Chicago: University of Chicago Press, 1975), 1–10.

39. Clayborne Carson, *In Struggle: SNCC and the Black Awakening of the 1960s* (Cambridge: Harvard University Press, 1981), 266–95; James F. Findlay, *Church People in the Struggle: The National Council of Churches and the Black Freedom Movement* (New York:

Oxford University Press, 1993), 201–5. See also Murray Friedman, *What Went Wrong? The Creation and Collapse of the Black-Jewish Alliance* (New York: The Free Press, 1995).

40. Van Deburg, *New Day*, 17, 294–304; W. J. Rorabaugh, "Challenging Authority, Seeking Community, and Empowerment in the New Left, Black Power, and Feminism," *Journal of Policy History* 8 (1996): 106–24.

41. See also Philip Converse, *American Social Attitudes Data Sourcebook, 1947–1978* (Cambridge: Harvard University Press, 1980), 57–75.

42. Reynolds Farley, "Racial Issues: Recent Trends in Residential Patterns and Intermarriage" (paper presented at a conference on "Common Values, Social Diversity, and Cultural Conflict," Center for Advanced Study in the Behavioral Sciences, 1996, Stanford, California), 8–12.

43. *New York Times*, January 20, 1972, 20; *Detroit Free Press*, August 7, 1970, 6A; Diane Ravitch, *The Great School Wars: New York City, 1805–1973* (New York: Basic Books, 1974), 267–398.

44. *New York Times*, November 9, 1975, E6; April 16, 1978, 24; Rand Corporation, *Student Achievement and the Changing American Family: An Executive Summary* (MR 535, Santa Monica, Calif., 1994), 11–25. The Rand study does not measure how much of the improvement may have resulted from desegregation. For evidence that "real education" can sometimes be more effective in public schools that serve only "communities of color," see *New York Times*, January 7, 1995, E18.

45. *New York Times*, November 9, 1975, E6; Howard Husock, "Boston: The Problem That Won't Go Away," *New York Times Magazine*, November 25, 1979, 32–34, 90–100.

46. James S. Liebman, "Three Strategies for Implementing *Brown* Anew," in *Race in America: The Struggle for Equality*, ed. Herbert Hill and James E. Jones Jr. (Madison: University of Wisconsin Press, 1993), 113–15; Gary Orfield, "School Desegregation," in *Race in America*, 234–46.

47. James E. Jones Jr., "The Rise and Fall of Affirmative Action," in *Race in America*, 345–69; James P. Turner, "The Fairest Cure We Have," *New York Times*, April 16, 1995, E11. See also Nicholas Lemann's somewhat different account, "Taking Affirmative Action Apart," *New York Times Magazine*, June 11, 1995, 36–43, 52–66. For constitutional background, see Robert Kagan, "Civil Rights Forged a New Legal Doctrine: Is It Fair?" *IGS Public Affairs Report* 36 (November 1995): 9–10.

48. [EDITOR'S NOTE: The absence from these pages of a more militant defense of affirmative action is not—at least not primarily—a result of editorial bias. Our roster of speakers at the symposium was intended to produce such a defense. When it did not, I was guided solely by legal scholars sympathetic to affirmative action in soliciting an additional contribution. Professor Chemerinsky's paper appears exactly as he wrote it.]

49. William Julius Wilson, *The Declining Significance of Race: Blacks and Changing American Institutions* (Chicago: University of Chicago Press, 1978).

50. Richard D. Kahlenberg, *The Remedy: Class, Race, and Affirmative Action* (New York: Basic Books, 1996), 45.

51. Katherine Tate, *From Protest to Politics: The New Black Voters in American Elections* (New York: Russell Sage Foundation, 1993), xi, 1–3, 6–7, 14–18.

52. Melvin G. Holli and Paul M. Green, *Bashing Chicago Traditions: Harold Washington's Last Campaign* (Grand Rapids, Mich.: William B. Eerdmans, 1989), 119–38.

53. Paul E. Peterson, "Introduction," *The New Urban Reality*, ed. Paul E. Peterson (Washington, D.C.: Brookings Institution, 1985), 12; *New York Times*, October 29, 1967, E9; April 4, 1972, 1. For an overall view of "profound disappointment," despair, and alienation among middle-class blacks at "the failure of the momentum of the 1960s," see *New York Times*, March 3, 1978, A26.

54. Reynolds Farley, "The Common Destiny of Blacks and Whites: Observations About the Social and Economic Status of the Races," in *Race in America*, 202; *New York Times*, March 17, 1996, 6E.

55. Orfield, "School Desegregation," 237; Charles Murray, *Losing Ground: American Social Policy, 1950–1980* (New York: Basic Books, 1984), 48–50, 67–68, 242.

56. *Work in America: Report of a Special Task Force to the Secretary of Health, Education, and Welfare* (Cambridge, Mass., 1974), 52; Terry Nichols Clark, "Fiscal Strain: How Different Are Snow Belt and Sun Belt Cities?" *New Urban Reality*, 167–73; Kusmer, "African Americans in the City," 475–79; *New York Times*, August 22, 1983, A22.

57. William Julius Wilson, "The Urban Underclass in Advanced Industrial Society," in *New Urban Reality*, 129–60; *New York Times*, September 2, 1977, D9.

58. *New York Times*, February 23, 1995, A21. The data are for 1979 and 1993.

59. Thomas J. Sugrue, "Crabgrass-Roots Politics: Race, Rights, and the Reaction Against Liberalism in the Urban North, 1940–1964," *Journal of American History* 82 (1995): 551–78; Jonathan Rieder, *Canarsie: The Jews and Italians of Brooklyn Against Liberalism* (Cambridge: Harvard University Press, 1985); John D. Kasarda, "Urban Change and Minority Opportunities," *New Urban Reality*, 43–46.

60. Thomas Byrne Edsall and Mary D. Edsall, *Chain Reaction: The Impact of Race, Rights, and Taxes on American Politics* (New York: Norton, 1991).

61. Paul M. Sniderman and Thomas Piazza, *The Scar of Race* (Cambridge, Mass.: Belknap Press, 1993); Michael Lind, *The Next American Nation: The New Nationalism and the Fourth American Revolution* (New York: The Free Press, 1995).

62. If a recent survey is to be believed, however, blacks rate unemployment as a far more important problem for them than racial discrimination. Tate, *From Protest to Politics*, 17.

63. Susan Meyers and Christopher Jencks, "War on Poverty: No Apologies, Please," *New York Times*, November 9, 1995, A29; Andrew Hacker, *Two Nations: Black and White, Separate, Hostile, Unequal* (New York: Scribner, 1992), 68, 97–102.

64. Paul Krugman, "The Wealth Gap Is Real and It's Growing," *New York Times*, August 21, 1995, A15; *New York Times*, August 13, 1995, 26.

65. James F. Simon, *The Center Holds: The Power Struggle Inside the Rehnquist Court* (New York: Simon & Schuster, 1995); Hugh D. Graham, "An Issue Transformed," *The Social Contract* 6 (1996): 271–75; *Wall Street Journal*, March 14, 1995, A16; June 13, 1995, A18; Alan Wolfe, "Affirmative Action, Inc.," *New Yorker* 72 (November 25, 1996): 106–15; Michael Lewis, "Rainbow Inc.," *New York Times Magazine*, December 8, 1996, 54.

66. On indifference (or worse) among teenagers see Jon Wiener, *Professors, Politics, and Pop* (London: Verso, 1991), 136–51; and, most poignant, the views of a high school junior from a liberal white family in H. G. Bissinger, "'We're All Racist Now,'" *New York Times Magazine*, May 29, 1994, 56. See also the statistics on Maryland teenagers reported in *Baltimore Sun*, November 11, 1982, 16, which are qualified but not, I believe, controverted by Charlotte Steeh and Howard Schuman, "Young White Adults: Did Racial Attitudes Change in the 1980s?" *American Journal of Sociology* 98 (1992): 340–67.

67. William P. O'Hare, "America's Minorities: The Demographics of Diversity," *Population Bulletin* 47, no. 4 (1992): 28–30.

# Chapter 2

1. W. E. B. Du Bois, *The Souls of Black Folk* (Greenwich, Conn.: Fawcett, 1903).

2. See George M. Fredrickson, *The Black Image in the White Mind* (New York: Norton, 1971); and Jonathan Turner and Royce Singleton, "A Theory of Ethnic Oppression: Toward

a Reintegration of Cultural and Structural Concepts in Ethnic Relations Theory," *Social Forces* 56 (1978): 1001–18.

3. For the United States, see Gerald D. Jaynes and Robin M. Williams Jr., *A Common Destiny: Blacks and American Society* (Washington, D.C.: National Academy Press, 1989). For the rest of the world, see Donald L. Horowitz, *Ethnic Groups in Conflict* (Berkeley and Los Angeles: University of California Press, 1985).

4. Gunnar Myrdal, *An American Dilemma: The Negro Problem and American Democracy* (New York: Harper, 1944).

5. See Lawrence Bobo, "Group Conflict, Prejudice, and the Paradox of Contemporary Racial Attitudes," in *Eliminating Racism: Profiles in Controversy*, ed. P. A. Katz and D. A. Taylor (New York: Plenum, 1988), 85–114.

6. Martin Luther King Jr., *Where Do We Go from Here: Chaos or Community?* (New York: Harper & Row, 1967).

7. Cornel West, *Race Matters* (Boston: Beacon Press, 1993); Douglas S. Massey and Nancy A. Denton, *American Apartheid: Segregation and the Making of the Underclass* (Cambridge: Harvard University Press, 1993); Lani Guinier, *The Tyranny of the Majority: Fundamental Fairness in Representative Democracy* (New York: The Free Press, 1994); Arthur M. Schlesinger Jr., *The Disuniting of America* (New York: Norton, 1992); and Haynes Johnson, *Divided We Fall: Gambling with History in the Nineties* (New York: Norton, 1994).

8. Andrew Hacker, *Two Nations: Black and White, Separate, Hostile, Unequal* (New York: Scribner's, 1992), 219.

9. Derrick Bell, *Faces at the Bottom of the Well: The Permanence of Racism* (New York: Basic Books, 1992), ix.

10. Ibid., 3.

11. Howard Schuman, Charlotte G. Steeh, and Lawrence Bobo, *Racial Attitudes in America: Trends and Interpretations* (Cambridge: Harvard University Press, 1985).

12. Lawrence Bobo and Ryan A. Smith, "From Jim Crow Racism to Laissez-Faire Racism: An Essay on the Transformation of Racial Attitudes in America," in *Beyond Pluralism: Essays on the Conceptions of Groups and Identities in America*, ed. W. Katkin and A. Tyree (Urbana: University of Illinois Press, in press).

13. See William Julius Wilson, *The Declining Significance of Race* (Chicago: University of Chicago Press, 1978).

14. See Jaynes and Williams, *Common Destiny*; and Lee Sigelman and Susan Welch, *Black Americans' Views of Racial Inequality: The Dream Deferred* (New York: Cambridge University Press, 1989).

15. See Ellis Cose, *The Rage of a Privileged Class* (New York: HarperCollins, 1993); and Joe R. Feagin and Melvin P. Sikes, *Living with Racism: The Black Middle Class Experience* (Boston: Beacon Press, 1994).

16. See Jonathan Rieder, *Canarsie: The Jews and Italians of Brooklyn Against Liberalism* (Cambridge: Harvard University Press, 1985); and Thomas Byrne Edsall and Mary D. Edsall, *Chain Reaction: The Impact of Race, Rights, and Taxes on American Politics* (New York: Norton, 1991).

17. Edsall and Edsall, *Chain Reaction*.

18. C. Vann Woodward, *The Strange Career of Jim Crow* (New York: Oxford University Press, 1974).

19. Schuman, Steeh, and Bobo, *Racial Attitudes*.

20. For historical research, see Fredrickson, *Black Image*; and Winthrop D. Jordan, *White over Black: American Attitudes Toward the Negro, 1550–1812* (New York: Norton, 1968). For sociological research, see Turner and Singleton, "Theory of Ethnic Oppression."

21. A. Wade Smith, "Race Tolerance as a Function of Group Position," *American Sociological Review* 46 (1981): 558–73; and A. Wade Smith, "Cohorts, Education, and the Evolution of Tolerance," *Social Science Research* 14 (1985): 205–25.

22. Schuman, Steeh, and Bobo, *Racial Attitudes*.

23. Glenn Firebaugh and Kenneth E. Davis, "Trends in Antiblack Prejudice, 1972–1984: Region and Cohort Effects," *American Journal of Sociology* 94 (1988): 251–72.

24. Charlotte Steeh and Howard Schuman, "Young White Adults: Did Racial Attitudes Change in the 1980s?" *American Journal of Sociology* 98 (1992): 340–67.

25. Schuman, Steeh, and Bobo, *Racial Attitudes*.

26. Bob Blauner, *Black Lives, White Lives: Three Decades of Race Relations in America* (Berkeley and Los Angeles: University of California Press, 1989), 317.

27. Richard G. Niemi, John Mueller, and Tom W. Smith, *Trends in Public Opinion: A Compendium of Survey Data* (New York: Greenwood Press, 1989), 168.

28. Schuman, Steeh, and Bobo, *Racial Attitudes*.

29. Howard Schuman and Lawrence Bobo, "Survey-Based Experiments on White Racial Attitudes Toward Residential Integration," *American Journal of Sociology* 76 (1988): 213–61.

30. Lawrence Bobo and Ryan A. Smith, "Antipoverty Policy, Affirmative Action, and Racial Attitudes," in *Confronting Poverty: Prescriptions for Change*, ed. S. Danziger, G. D. Sandefur, and D. H. Weinberg (Cambridge: Harvard University Press, 1994), 365–95.

31. Ibid.

32. Lawrence Bobo and James R. Kluegel, "Opposition to Race-Targeting: Self-Interest, Stratification Ideology, or Racial Attitudes?" *American Sociological Review* 58 (1993): 443–64.

33. Lawrence Bobo and James R. Kluegel, "Whites' Stereotypes, Social Distance, and Perceived Discrimination Toward Blacks, Hispanics, and Asians: Toward a Multiethnic Framework" (paper presented at the Annual Meeting of the American Sociological Association, Cincinnati, Ohio, August 1991); and Tom W. Smith, "Ethnic Images," GSS Technical Report No. 19 (Chicago: National Opinion Research Center, University of Chicago, 1991).

34. Smith, "Ethnic Images."

35. Bobo and Kluegel, "Whites' Stereotypes."

36. Reynolds Farley, Charlotte Steeh, Tara Jackson, Maria Krysan, and Keith Reeves, "Continued Racial Residential Segregation in Detroit: 'Chocolate City, Vanilla Suburbs' Revisited," *Journal of Housing Research* 4 (1993): 1–38.

37. Ibid., 18–20.

38. Lawrence Bobo, Camille L. Zubrinsky, James H. Johnson, and Melvin L. Oliver, "Public Opinion Before and After a Spring of Discontent," in *The Los Angeles Riots*, ed. Mark Baldassare (Boulder, Colo.: Westview Press, 1994), 103–34.

39. See R. A. Apostle, C. Y. Glock, T. Piazza, and M. Suelzle, *The Anatomy of Racial Attitudes* (Berkeley and Los Angeles: University of California Press, 1983); James R. Kluegel, "Trends in Whites' Explanation of the Gap in Black-White Socioeconomic Status, 1977–1989," *American Sociological Review* 55 (1990): 512–25; and Sigelman and Welch, *Black Americans' Views*.

40. Bobo and Smith, "From Jim Crow Racism to Laissez-Faire Racism."

41. James R. Kluegel and Eliot R. Smith, "Whites' Beliefs About Blacks' Opportunity," *American Sociological Review* 47 (1982): 518–32.

42. See Reynolds Farley and Walter R. Allen, *The Color Line and the Quality of Life in America* (New York: Russell Sage Foundation, 1987); and Jaynes and Williams, *Common Destiny*.

43. Karl Taeuber and Alma F. Taeuber, *Negroes in Cities: Residential Segregation and Neighborhood Change* (Chicago: Aldine, 1965).

44. T. L. Van Valey, Wade C. Roof, and J. E. Wilcox, "Trends in Residential Segregation, 1960–1970," *American Journal of Sociology* 87 (1977): 826–44.

45. Reynolds Farley, "Residential Segregation in Urbanized Areas of the United States in 1970: An Analysis of Social Class and Racial Differences," *Demography* 14 (1977): 497–518.

46. Reynolds Farley and William H. Frey, "Changes in the Segregation of Whites from Blacks During the 1980s: Small Steps Toward a More Integrated Society," *American Sociological Review* 59 (1994): 23–45.

47. Douglas S. Massey and Nancy A. Denton, "Hypersegregation in U.S. Metropolitan Areas: Black and Hispanic Segregation Along Five Dimensions," *Demography* 26 (1989): 373–92.

48. Ibid., 389.

49. Farley et al., "Continued Racial Residential Segregation."

50. William A. V. Clark, "Residential Preferences and Residential Choices in a Multiethnic Context," *Demography* 29 (1992): 451–66.

51. Reynolds Farley, Charlotte Steeh, Maria Krysan, Tara Jackson, and Keith Reeves, "Stereotypes and Segregation: Neighborhoods in the Detroit Area," *American Journal of Sociology* 100 (1994): 750–80.

52. Lawrence Bobo and Camille L. Zubrinsky, "Attitudes on Residential Integration: Perceived Status Differences, Mere In-Group Preference, or Racial Prejudice?" *Social Forces* 74 (1996): 883–909; and Camille L. Zubrinsky and Lawrence Bobo, "Prismatic Metropolis: Race and Residential Segregation in the City of Angels," *Social Science Research* 25 (1996): 335–74.

53. See Diana Pearce, "Gatekeepers and Homeseekers: Institutionalized Patterns in Racial Steering," *Social Problems* 26 (1979): 325–42; and John Yinger, "Measuring Racial Discrimination with Fair Housing Audits: Caught in the Act," *American Economic Review* 76 (1986): 881–93.

54. Wilson, *Declining Significance.*

55. William Julius Wilson, *The Truly Disadvantaged: The Inner City, the Underclass, and Public Policy* (Chicago: University of Chicago Press, 1987).

56. Richard B. Freeman and H. J. Holzer, "Young Blacks and Jobs—What We Now Know," *Public Interest* 78 (Winter 1985): 18–31.

57. Joleen Kirschenman and Kathryn M. Neckerman, "'We'd Love to Hire Them, But . . .': The Meaning of Race for Employers," in *The Urban Underclass*, ed. C. Jencks and P. E. Peterson (Washington, D.C.: Brookings Institution, 1991), 203–34.

58. Ibid., 230–31.

59. Kathryn M. Neckerman and Joleen Kirschenman, "Hiring Strategies, Racial Bias, and Inner-City Workers," *Social Problems* 38 (1991): 433–47.

60. Roger Waldinger and Tom Bailey, "The Continuing Significance of Race: Racial Conflict and Racial Discrimination in Construction," *Politics and Society* 19 (1991): 291–323.

61. Ibid., 314.

62. Margery Austin Turner, Michael Fix, and Raymond J. Struyk, *Opportunities Denied, Opportunities Diminished: Racial Discrimination in Hiring* (Washington, D.C.: Urban Institute Press, 1991).

63. Ibid., 62–63.

64. See Thomas F. Pettigrew and Joanne Martin, "Shaping the Organizational Context for Black Inclusion," *Journal of Social Issues* 43 (1986): 41–78.

65. Martin I. Pomer, "Labor Market Structure, Intergenerational Mobility and Discrimination: Black Male Advancement Out of Low-Paying Occupations," *American Sociological Review* 51 (1986): 650–59; and Ryan A. Smith, "Race, Income, and Authority at Work: A Cross-Temporal Analysis of Black and White Men, 1972–1994," *Social Problems* 44 (1997): 701–19.

66. Sharon Collins, "The Making of the Black Middle Class," *Social Problems* 30 (1983): 369–81; and Sharon Collins, "The Marginalization of Black Executives," *Social Problems* 36 (1989): 317–31.

67. See J. P. Fernandez, *Black Managers in White Corporations* (New York: Wiley, 1975); and Richard L. Zweigenhaft and G. William Domhoff, *Blacks in the White Establishment? A Study of Race and Class in America* (New Haven: Yale University Press, 1991).

68. See Melvin L. Oliver and M. Glick, "An Analysis of the New Orthodoxy on Black Mobility," *Social Problems* 29 (1982): 511–23; and Jaynes and Williams, *Common Destiny.*

69. See Cose, *Rage of a Privileged Class.*

70. See Elijah Anderson, *Streetwise: Race, Class, and Change in an Urban Community* (Chicago: University of Chicago Press, 1990).

71. Faye Crosby, Susan Bromley, and Leonard Saxe, "Recent Unobtrusive Studies of Black and White Discrimination and Prejudice: A Literature Review," *Psychological Bulletin* 87 (1980): 546–63.

72. Claire Selltiz, "The Use of Survey Methods in a Citizens Campaign Against Discrimination," *Human Organization* 14 (1955): 19–25.

73. Howard Schuman, Eleanor Singer, Rebecca Donovan, and Claire Selltiz, "Discriminatory Behavior in New York Restaurants: 1950 and 1981," *Social Indicators Research* 13 (1983): 69–83.

74. Ibid., 80 (emphasis in the original).

75. Joe R. Feagin, "The Continuing Significance of Race: Antiblack Discrimination in Public Places," *American Sociological Review* 56 (1991): 101–16.

76. Ibid., 114–15.

77. Jeffrey Prager, "American Political Culture and the Shifting Meaning of Race," *Ethnic and Racial Studies* 10 (1987): 62–81.

78. Gunnar Myrdal, *The Challenge to Affluence* (New York: Pantheon, 1963).

79. Ken Auletta, *The Underclass* (New York: Random House, 1981).

80. Wilson, *Truly Disadvantaged.*

81. Ibid., 8.

82. Ibid.

83. Ibid., 71.

84. Daniel T. Lichter, "Racial Differences in Underemployment in American Cities," *American Journal of Sociology* 93 (1988): 771–92.

85. Ibid., 788–89.

86. See Bobo and Kluegel, "Whites' Stereotypes"; and Smith, "Ethnic Images."

87. Jill Quadagno, *The Color of Welfare: How Racism Undermined the War on Poverty* (New York: Oxford University Press, 1994).

88. See Martin I. Gilens, "Racial Attitudes and Opposition to the American Welfare State" (paper presented at the Annual Conference of the American Association for Public Opinion Research, Phoenix, Arizona, May 1991); James R. Kluegel and Eliot R. Smith, *Beliefs About Inequality: Americans' Views of What Is and What Ought to Be* (New York: Aldine, 1986); and Bobo and Kluegel, "Whites' Stereotypes."

89. See Bobo and Smith, "Antipoverty Policy."

90. Shanto Iyengar, "Framing Responsibility for Political Issues: The Case of Poverty," *Political Behavior* 12 (1990): 19–40.

91. Thomas Byrne Edsall and Mary D. Edsall, "When the Official Subject Is Presidential Politics, Taxes, Welfare, Crime, Rights, or Values . . . the Real Subject Is Race," *Atlantic Monthly* 267 (1991): 77.

92. Bobo and Smith, "From Jim Crow Racism to Laissez-Faire Racism."
93. Ibid.

# Chapter 3

1. Robert Allen Rutland, *The Birth of the Bill of Rights, 1776–1791*, Bicentennial Edition (Boston: Northeastern University Press, 1991), 15.
2. Senator Doolittle's remarks are in the *Congressional Globe*, 39th Cong. 1st sess., 1866, 1010, 1011. Doolittle's view did not prevail, of course, and some members of Congress expressed extraordinary confidence in the ability of the United States to extend the franchise liberally to blacks and others. Senator Simon Cameron of Pennsylvania said he favored the amendment "because it invites into our country everybody; the Negro, the Irishman, the German, the Frenchman, the Scotchman, the Englishman, and the Chinaman" (ibid., 1036).
3. To get a detailed account of the Civil Rights Act of 1964 and the Voting Rights Act of 1965 and the various political forces and ideas behind them, see "Revolution in Civil Rights" (Washington, D.C.: Congressional Quarterly Service, 1995), 1–94. It is the best account of what is in those acts and of the intent of Congress regarding them.
4. James Farmer, Keynote Address, "Achieving Change," a report on the 1978 West Virginia Statewide Leadership Conference on Civil Rights (Washington, D.C.: U.S. Commission on Civil Rights, January 1981), 20–24.
5. Mary Frances Berry, "A Civil Rights Agenda for the 1980s" (report of the Maryland Statewide Civil Rights Leadership Conference, June 26, 1980) (Washington, D.C.: U.S. Commission on Civil Rights, May 1981), 9–11.
6. Elisa Lee, "Immigrant Rights Workers Want Language Provision in National Health Care Plan," *Asian Week*, September 2, 1994, 1, 18.
7. Quoted in A. Leon Higginbotham Jr., Gregory A. Clarick, and Marcella David, "*Shaw v. Reno:* A Mirage of Good Intentions with Devastating Racial Consequences," *Fordham Law Review* 62 (April 1994): 1595.
8. Ibid., 1645, 1644.
9. A more detailed analysis of Lani Guinier's views is in Charles Fried, "President Clinton Won't Give Me a Job Either," *Reconstruction* 2, no. 3 (1994): 127–33. Guinier responds to the points made by Professor Fried and repeated by me in ibid., 134–36. She charges Fried with failing to cite passages "from the same article in which I ultimately conclude that authenticity is at best 'a limited empowering concept.'" Guinier wants candidates "chosen by the voters" and rejects "the concept of representativeness based on physical or demographic resemblances." If that is the case, it is not clear what she means by authenticity.
10. Gerard Lim, "Lawsuit over Chinese-American High School Enrollment," *Asian Week*, August 19, 1994, 1, 21.

# Chapter 4

1. *Richmond v. J. A. Croson Co.*, 488 U.S. 469, 520 (1989) (Scalia, J., concurring in judgment).
2. 480 U.S. 92 (1987).
3. 448 U.S. 448 (1980).
4. 438 U.S. 265 (1978) (opinion of Powell, J.).

5. 497 U.S. 547 (1990).

6. In June 1995 the Supreme Court overruled *Metro Broadcasting*, although it did not focus on the issue of the value of diversity in broadcast licensing. *Metro Broadcasting* held that the appropriate constitutional standard in reviewing federal affirmative action efforts is intermediate scrutiny—whether the government's action is substantially related to an important government purpose. In *Adarand Constructors v. Pena*, 115 S.Ct. 2907 (1995), the Court held that strict scrutiny should be used in reviewing federal affirmative action efforts— whether the government's action is necessary to achieve a compelling government purpose.

7. *Miller v. Johnson*, 63 U.S.L.W. 4726, 4738 (June 29, 1995) (Ginsburg, J., dissenting).

8. Id. at 4740.

9. 113 S.Ct. 2815 (1993).

10. 63 U.S.L.W. 4726 (June 29, 1995).

11. 476 U.S. 267 (1986).

12. The State of California offered this as one of its justifications for affirmative action in *Regents of the University of California v. Bakke*, 438 U.S. 265 (1978), which concerned admissions to the University of California at Davis medical school.

13. 438 U.S. 265 (1978).

14. See, for example, *Local 28 Sheet Metal Works International Assoc. v. EEOC*, 478 U.S. 421 (1986) (considering the permissibility of goals and timetables).

15. See *University of Maryland v. Podberesky*, 38 F.3d 147 (4th Cir. 1994) (declaring unconstitutional a scholarship program for minority students).

16. 480 U.S. 92 (1987).

17. *Plessy v. Ferguson*, 163 U.S. 537 (1896) (Harlan, J. dissenting).

18. In *United States v. Hays*, 63 U.S.L.W. 4679 (June 29, 1995), the Supreme Court held that individuals do not have standing to challenge districting based on race if they are not members of the district because they have not suffered an injury. As Justice Stevens argues in dissent, it is difficult to see why the injury exists in any circumstances and why it varies depending on whether the person is inside or outside the district. Id. at 4683 (Stevens, J., dissenting).

19. See Kathleen Sullivan, "Sins of Discrimination: Last Term's Affirmative Action Cases," *Harvard Law Review* 100 (1986): 80–81.

20. *Miller v. Johnson*, 63 U.S.L.W. 4726, 4729 (June 29, 1995).

21. This argument is developed in David Straus, "The Myth of Color-Blindedness," *Supreme Court Review 1986*, 99.

# Chapter 5

1. Douglas S. Massey and Nancy A. Denton, *American Apartheid: Segregation and the Making of the Underclass* (Cambridge.: Harvard University Press, 1993), chap. 3.

2. Douglas S. Massey and Nancy A. Denton, "Hypersegregation in U.S. Metropolitan Areas: Black and Hispanic Segregation Along Five Dimensions," *Demography* 26 (1989): 373–93.

3. Douglas S. Massey and Nancy A. Denton, "Trends in the Residential Segregation of Blacks, Hispanics, and Asians," *American Sociological Review* 52 (1987): 802–25.

4. Douglas S. Massey and Andrew B. Gross, "Explaining Trends in Residential Segregation, 1970–1980," *Urban Affairs Quarterly* 27 (1991): 13–35.

5. Reynolds Farley and William H. Frey, "Changes in the Segregation of Whites from Blacks During the 1980s: Small Steps Toward a More Integrated Society," *American Sociologi-*

*cal Review* 59 (1994): 23–45; Mark Schneider and Thomas Phelan, "Black Suburbanization in the 1980s," *Demography* 30 (1993): 269–80.

6. Nancy A. Denton, "Are African Americans Still Hypersegregated in 1990?" in *Residential Apartheid: The American Legacy*, ed. Robert D. Bullard, J. Eugene Grigsby III, and Charles Lee (Los Angeles: CAAS Publications, 1994).

7. Nancy A. Denton and Douglas S. Massey, "Residential Segregation of Blacks, Hispanics, and Asians by Socioeconomic Status and Generation," *Social Science Quarterly* 69 (1988): 797–817.

8. Howard Schuman, Charlotte Steeh, and Lawrence Bobo, *Racial Attitudes in America: Trends and Interpretations* (Cambridge: Harvard University Press, 1985); Howard Schuman and Lawrence Bobo, "Survey-Based Experiments on White Racial Attitudes Toward Residential Integration," *American Journal of Sociology* 94 (1988): 273–99.

9. Reynolds Farley, Charlotte Steeh, Tara Jackson, Maria Krysan, and Keith Reeves, "Continued Racial Residential Segregation: Chocolate City, Vanilla Suburbs Revisited," *Journal of Housing Research* 4 (1993): 1–38.

10. Lawrence Bobo, Howard Schuman, and Charlotte Steeh, "Changing Racial Attitudes Toward Residential Integration," in *Housing Desegregation and Federal Policy*, ed. John M. Goering (Chapel Hill: University of North Carolina Press, 1986), 152–69.

11. Farley et al., "Causes of Continued Racial Residential Segregation."

12. Reynolds Farley, Suzanne Bianchi, and Diane Colasanto, "Barriers to the Racial Integration of Neighborhoods: The Detroit Case," *Annals of the American Academy of Political and Social Science* 441 (1979): 97–113.

13. William A. V. Clark, "Residential Preferences and Neighborhood Racial Segregation: A Test of the Schelling Segregation Model," *Demography* 28 (1991): 1–19.

14. Massey and Denton, *American Apartheid*, chap. 2.

15. John Yinger, "Measuring Racial Discrimination with Fair Housing Audits: Caught in the Act," *American Economic Review* 76 (1986): 991–93.

16. George C. Galster, "Racial Discrimination in Housing Markets During the 1980s: A Review of the Audit Evidence," *Journal of Planning Education and Research* 93 (1990): 165–75.

17. George C. Galster, "Racial Steering by Real Estate Agents: Mechanisms and Motives," *Review of Black Political Economy* 19 (1990): 39–63.

18. George C. Galster, "Racial Steering in Urban Housing Markets: A Review of the Audit Evidence," *Review of Black Political Economy* 18 (1990): 105–29.

19. John Yinger, *Housing Discrimination Study: Incidence of Discrimination and Variations in Discriminatory Behavior* (Washington, D.C.: U.S. Department of Housing and Urban Development, 1991); John Yinger, *Housing Discrimination Study: Incidence and Severity of Unfavorable Treatment* (Washington, D.C.: U.S. Department of Housing and Urban Development, 1991).

20. Ibid., table 42.

21. Ibid.

22. Ibid., table 44.

23. George C. Galster, "More Than Skin Deep: The Effect of Housing Discrimination on the Extent and Pattern of Racial Residential Segregation in the United States," in *Housing Discrimination and Federal Policy*, ed. John M. Goering (Chapel Hill: University of North Carolina Press, 1986), 119–38; George C. Galster and W. Mark Keeney, "Race, Residence, Discrimination, and Economic Opportunity: Modeling the Nexus of Urban Racial Phenomena," *Urban Affairs Quarterly* 24 (1988): 87–117.

24. George C. Galster, "The Ecology of Racial Discrimination in Housing: An Exploratory Model," *Urban Affairs Quarterly* 23 (1987): 84–107; George C. Galster, "White Flight from Racially Integrated Neighbourhoods in the 1970s: The Cleveland Experience," *Urban Studies*

27 (1990): 385–99; George C. Galster, "Neighborhood Racial Change, Segregationist Senti- ments, and Affirmative Marketing Policies," *Journal of Urban Economics* 27 (1990): 344–61.

25. Kenneth T. Jackson, *Crabgrass Frontier: The Suburbanization of the United States* (New York: Oxford University Press, 1985), chap. 11.

26. Harold A. Black and Robert L. Schweitzer, "A Canonical Analysis of Mortgage Lend- ing Terms: Testing for Lending Discrimination at a Commercial Bank," *Urban Studies* 22 (1985): 13–20.

27. Louis G. Pol, Rebecca F. Guy, and Andrew J. Bush, "Discrimination in the Home Lending Market: A Macro Perspective," *Social Science Quarterly* 63 (1982): 716–28; Gregory D. Squires, William Velez, and Karl E. Taeuber, "Insurance Redlining, Agency Location, and the Process of Urban Disinvestment," *Urban Affairs Quarterly* 26 (1991): 567–88; Harriet Tee Taggart and Kevin W. Smith, "Redlining: An Assessment of the Evidence of Disinvestment in Metropolitan Boston," *Urban Affairs Quarterly* 17 (1981): 91–107.

28. Arnold R. Hirsch, *Making the Second Ghetto: Race and Housing in Chicago, 1940– 1960* (Cambridge: Cambridge University Press, 1983); John F. Bauman, *Public Housing, Race, and Renewal: Urban Planning in Philadelphia, 1920–1974* (Philadelphia: Temple University Press, 1987); Ira Goldstein and William L. Yancey, "Public Housing Projects, Blacks, and Public Policy: The Historical Ecology of Public Housing in Philadelphia," in *Housing Deseg- regation and Federal Policy,* ed. John M. Goering (Chapel Hill: University of North Carolina Press, 1986); Douglas S. Massey and Shawn M. Kanaiaupuni, "Public Housing and the Con- centration of Poverty," *Social Science Quarterly* 74 (1993): 109–22.

29. Richard D. Alba and John R. Logan, "Variations on Two Themes: Racial and Ethnic Patterns in the Attainment of Suburban Residence," *Demography* 28 (1991): 431–53; Douglas S. Massey and Nancy A. Denton, "Spatial Assimilation as a Socioeconomic Process," *American Sociological Review* 50 (1985): 94–105; Douglas S. Massey and Eric Fong, "Segregation and Neighborhood Quality: Blacks, Hispanics, and Asians in the San Francisco Metropolitan Area," *Social Forces* 69 (1990): 15–32; Douglas S. Massey, Gretchen A. Condran, and Nancy A. Denton, "The Effect of Residential Segregation on Black Social and Economic Well-Being," *Social Forces* 66 (1987): 29–57.

30. Douglas S. Massey, "American Apartheid: Segregation and the Making of the Under- class," *American Journal of Sociology* 96 (1990): 329–58; Massey and Denton, *American Apart- heid,* chap. 5.

31. Massey and Kanaiaupuni, "Public Housing and the Concentration of Poverty."

32. Christopher Jencks and Susan E. Mayer, "The Social Consequences of Growing Up in a Poor Neighborhood," in *Inner City Poverty in the United States,* ed. Laurence E. Lynn Jr. and Michael G. H. McGeary (Washington, D.C.: National Academy Press, 1990), 111–86; Dennis P. Hogan and Evelyn M. Kitagawa, "The Impact of Social Status, Family Structure, and Neighborhood on the Fertility of Black Adolescents," *American Journal of Sociology* 90 (1985): 825–55; Frank F. Furstenburg Jr., S. Philip Morgan, Kristin A. Moore, and James Peterson, "Race Differences in the Timing of Adolescent Intercourse," *American Sociological Review* 52 (1987): 511–18; Jonathan Crane, "The Epidemic Theory of Ghettos and Neighbor- hood Effects on Dropping Out and Teenage Childbearing," *American Journal of Sociology* 96 (1991): 1226–59.

33. Douglas S. Massey, Andrew B. Gross, and Mitchell L. Eggers, "Segregation, the Con- centration of Poverty, and the Life Chances of Individuals," *Social Science Research* 20 (1991): 397–420.

34. James E. Rosenbaum and Susan J. Popkin, "Employment and Earnings of Low-Income Blacks Who Move to Middle-Class Suburbs," in *The Urban Underclass,* ed. Christopher Jencks and Paul E. Peterson (Washington, D.C.: Brookings Institution, 1991), 342–56; James E.

Rosenbaum, "Black Pioneers—Do Their Moves to the Suburbs Increase Economic Opportunity for Mothers and Children?" *Housing Policy Debate* 2 (1991): 1179–1214.

# Chapter 6

1. Since I first referred to this story in this paper, it has been reported in greater detail in two books: Todd Gitlin, *The Twilight of Common Dreams* (New York: Henry Holt, 1995), 31; and Lynne V. Cheney, *Telling the Truth* (New York: Simon & Schuster, 1995), 31. It clearly seems to be paradigmatic of the present situation.

2. Richard Bernstein, *Dictatorship of Virtue: Multiculturalism and the Battle for America's Future* (New York: Alfred A. Knopf, 1994).

3. See Jordana Hart, "Closing Cultural Gap Between Teachers, Urban Students," *Boston Globe*, August 15, 1994.

4. Consider the treatment in both *Time* and *Newsweek* of the National Standards for United States History: "History, the Sequel," *Time* (International Edition), November 7, 1994, 74; and "Red, White—and Blue," *Newsweek* (International Edition), November 7, 1994, 57. In both cases, the writers are at best bemused, and somewhat skeptical, of an approach to U.S. history that gives much more attention to minorities and women and much less to such icons in American history as Daniel Webster, the Wright brothers, and the Gettysburg Address.

5. This was my view of my own position twenty years ago in criticizing the kind of affirmative action that imposed goals or quotas. See my *Affirmative Discrimination: Ethnic Inequality and Public Policy* (New York: Basic Books, 1974; currently published by Harvard University Press). Whatever the validity of this point of view historically or constitutionally, it has not made headway against the reality of the institutionalization of these practices. But this may now change. While affirmative action has for the most part survived the assault launched against it in 1995 and 1996, it is beginning to change in some respects, after many years of impregnability, as a result of Supreme Court decisions affecting affirmative action in contracting and a Circuit Court decision affecting admissions to law school.

6. See the *Time* article, "History, the Sequel."

7. Bernstein, *Dictatorship of Virtue*, 339.

8. See Robert Lerner, Althea K. Nagai, and Stanley Rothman, "History by Quota?" *Academic Questions* 54 (Fall 1992): 69–83.

9. See Nathan Glazer, "Is Assimilation Dead?" *The Annals* 530 (November 1993), 122–36.

10. Nathan Glazer and Reed Ueda, *Ethnic Groups in History Textbooks* (Washington, D.C.: Ethics and Public Policy Center, 1983).

11. Peter Skerry, *Mexican Americans: The Ambivalent Minority* (New York: The Free Press, 1993).

12. Such proposals, incorporated into a multicultural guide for teachers in New York City, became very controversial in 1993 and led to the resignation of New York City's school chancellor.

13. For examples of the extensiveness of such criticism in the authoritative guidance teachers received, see Diane Ravitch, "Standards in U.S. History," *Education Week*, December 7, 1994, 48, 40.

14. For a discussion of the work of such a state commission and my role in it, see Nathan Glazer, "Multiculturalism and Public Policy," in Henry J. Aaron, Thomas E. Mann, and Timothy Taylor, eds., *Values and Public Policy* (Washington, D.C.: Brookings Institution,

1994) This, in revised form, is now to be found in my book *We Are All Multiculturalists Now* (Cambridge: Harvard University Press, 1997).

# Chapter 7

1. Philip Gleason, "American Identity and Americanization," *Harvard Encyclopaedia of American Ethnic Groups*, ed. Stephan Thernstrom (Cambridge: Harvard University Press, 1981), 31–58.

2. John Higham, "Ethnic Pluralism in Modern American Thought," *Send These to Me: Jews and Other Immigrants in Urban America* (New York: Atheneum, 1975), 196–230.

3. Arthur Mann, *The One and the Many* (Chicago: University of Chicago Press, 1979).

4. Milton M. Gordon, *Assimilation in American Life* (New York: Oxford University Press, 1964).

5. Lawrence H. Fuchs, *The American Kaleidoscope: Race, Ethnicity, and the Civic Culture* (Hanover, N.H.: University Press of New England, 1990).

6. Harold R. Isaacs, *Idols of the Tribe: Group Identity and Political Change* (New York: Harper & Row, 1975), 218.

7. Ibid., 2.

8. *New York Times*, August 2, 1994.

9. Horace M. Kallen, "Democracy Versus the Melting Pot: A Study of American Nationality," *The Nation*, February 1915.

10. See Gleason, "American Identity," 44–45.

11. John Higham, "Multiculturalism and Universalism: A History and Critique," *American Quarterly* 45 (June 1993): 209.

12. Ibid., 211–12.

13. Ibid., 212–13.

14. Ibid., 214.

15. Frederick Douglass, "The Future of the Colored Race," *Negro Social and Political Thought, 1850–1920*, ed. Howard Brotz (New York: Basic Books, 1966), 316.

16. Karl R. Popper, *The Open Society and Its Enemies* (London: G. Routledge, 1945), 2: 222–23.

17. Jean Johnson and John Immerwahr, *First Things First: What Americans Expect from the Public Schools* (New York: Public Agenda, 1994), 24–25, 48.

18. Richard Rorty, "The Unpatriotic Academy," *New York Times*, February 13, 1994.

19. Robert Brustein, "The Use and Abuse of Multiculturalism," *The New Republic*, September 16 and 23, 1991, 34.

20. Salmon Rushdie, "In Good Faith," *The Democracy Reader*, ed. Diane Ravitch and Abigail Thernstrom (New York: HarperCollins, 1992), 282.

21. Higham, "Multiculturalism and Universalism," 214.

22. John Dewey, "America in the World," *Essays on China, Japan, and the War*, in *The Middle Works of John Dewey, 1899–1924*, vol. 11, ed. Jo Ann Boydston (Carbondale: University of Illinois Press, 1982), 71 (first published in *The Nation* 106 [1918], from a speech delivered at Smith College, February 22, 1918).

# Chapter 8

1. We draw here on a lecture Jean Bethke Elshtain delivered in 1992 under the auspices of the Andrew Cecil Lectures for a Free Society at the University of Dallas.

2. Exclusion of African Americans in this depiction of the military melting pot was common but not complete. The movie *Bataan* (1943) is probably the most important counterexample. See Larry May, "Making the American Consensus: The Narrative of Conversion and Subversion in World War II Films," in *The War in American Culture: Society and Consciousness During World War II*, ed. Lewis A. Erenberg and Susan E. Hirsch (Chicago: University of Chicago Press, 1996), 76–77.

3. The longer story can be found in Elshtain's *Women and War* (New York: Basic Books, 1987).

4. David M. Kennedy, *Over Here: The First World War and American Society* (New York: Oxford University Press, 1980), 17.

5. Quoted in ibid., 87.

6. Quoted in ibid., 24.

7. Randolph Bourne, "Trans-national America," in *The Radical Will: Randolph Bourne, Selected Writings, 1911–1918*, ed. Christopher Lasch (New York: Urizen Books, 1977), 262.

8. Charles Taylor, *Multiculturalism and the Politics of Recognition* (Princeton: Princeton University Press, 1992), 34.

9. Alexis de Tocqueville, *Democracy in America*, trans. George Lawrence, ed. J. P. Mayer (New York: Anchor Books, 1969), esp. vol. 2.

10. Lyndon B. Johnson, "The Howard University Address," in *The American Reader*, ed. Diane Ravitch (New York: HarperCollins, 1990), 341–42.

11. Martin Luther King Jr., "An Address Before the National Press Club," in *A Testament of Hope: The Essential Writings and Speeches of Martin Luther King Jr.*, ed. James M. Washington (San Francisco: HarperCollins, 1986), 100.

12. Martin Luther King Jr., "A Public Address Before a Nashville Church Conference" (December 27, 1962), in *Testament of Hope*, 118.

13. Martin Luther King Jr., *Where Do We Go from Here: Chaos or Community?* (New York: Harper & Row, 1963), in *Testament of Hope*, 588.

# Chapter 9

1. James Baldwin, *Notes of a Native Son* (Boston: Beacon Press, 1955), 21.

2. There is an excellent section on sincerity and the American personality in David Riesman's classic sociological treatise, *The Lonely Crowd: A Study of the Changing American Character* (New Haven: Yale University Press, 1950), 219–24.

3. Herbert Aptheker accused Mills of being insufficiently aware of race and the racial struggle in his vision of the American political landscape. See Herbert Aptheker, *The World of C. Wright Mills* (New York: Marzani & Munsell, 1960).

4. C. Wright Mills, *The Power Elite* (New York: Oxford University Press, 1956), 318.

5. Walter Lippmann expressed a somewhat different idea and a different set of expectations of the public in his *The Phantom Public*. For Lippmann, there could really be no informed public on most public issues, simply ordinary people being manipulated by partisans, and there was, in truth, no public interest, as the Progressives argued, because the public the Progressives envisioned simply did not, could not, and probably should not exist. In effect, as I emphasize, the diversity awareness movement is an attempt to create a variety of publics driven by several individualized, overweening social purposes in order to make it possible to have a viable sense of the public in America. This seems an inadvertent recognition of Lippmann's observation that no truly informed broad public is possible. Therefore, the diversity awareness movement gives a set of partisan publics. But the diversity awareness movement defeats Lippmann's notion of understanding the public as a collection of self-interested individ-

uals. As I suggest in this chapter, each "ethnicity" of multiculturalism is itself a community, a nation, a collectivity, that refuses to recognize self-interested individuality within its group, that refuses to recognize its own accidental, arbitrary, tenuous nature as a public.

6. African Americans also live under the tyranny of the hard sciences, particularly biology, genetics, medicine, and statistics, all of which function to explain their intelligence, their skin color, and their pathologies. Once again, they remain the fetish of inequity and inferiority.

7. Lucien Goldmann, *The Hidden God: A Study of the Tragic Vision in the Pensées of Pascal and the Tragedies of Racine,* trans. from the French by Philip Thody (New York: Humanities Press, 1964), 17.

8. Richard Wright, *Black Boy: A Record of Childhood and Youth* (New York: Harper & Row, 1966), 45. Copyright, 1937, 1942, 1944, 1945 by Richard Wright. Copyright renewed 1973 by Ellen Wright. By permission of Harper Collins Publishers.

# Chapter 10

1. C. Vann Woodward, "From the First Reconstruction to the Second," *Harper's Magazine* 230 (April 1965): 127–33.

2. Ibid., 133; Eric Foner, "Slavery, the Civil War, and Reconstruction," in *The New American History,* ed. Eric Foner (Philadelphia: Temple University Press, 1990), 83–89. The phrase comes from the title of Claude G. Bowers' influential book *The Tragic Era: The Revolution After Lincoln* (Cambridge, Mass.: Houghton Mifflin Co., 1929).

3. Gordon Wood, *The Creation of the American Republic, 1776–1787* (Chapel Hill: University of North Carolina Press, 1969), 91–124; Ernest Lee Tuveson, *Redeemer Nation: The Idea of America's Millennial Role* (Chicago: University of Chicago Press, 1968); Ruth H. Bloch, "Religion, Literary Sentimentalism, and Popular Revolutionary Ideology," in *Religion in a Revolutionary Age,* ed. Ronald Hoffman and Peter J. Albert (Charlottesville: University Press of Virginia, 1994), 308–30.

4. David Brion Davis, "American Slavery and the American Revolution," in *Slavery and Freedom in the Age of the American Revolution,* ed. Ira Berlin and Ronald Hoffman (Charlottesville: University Press of Virginia, 1983), 276–77.

5. David Brion Davis, *The Problem of Slavery in Western Culture* (Ithaca, N.Y.: Cornell University Press, 1966), 306–32, and *The Problem of Slavery in the Age of Revolution, 1770–1823* (Ithaca, N.Y.: Cornell University Press, 1975), 213–54.

6. Gary Gerstle, "The Working Class Goes to War," in *The War in American Culture: Society and Consciousness During World War II,* ed. Lewis A. Erenberg and Susan E. Hirsch (Chicago: University of Chicago Press, 1996), 105–27, and, in the same volume, Alan Brinkley, "World War II and American Liberalism," 313–30. See also Gerstle's "The Protean Character of American Liberalism," *American Historical Review* 99 (October 1994): 1043–74.

7. David M. Kennedy, *Over Here: The First World War and American Society* (New York: Oxford University Press, 1980), 245–50. For useful suggestions on the prewar milieu, see Joel Williamson, *The Crucible of Race: Black-White Relations in the American South Since Emancipation* (New York: Oxford University Press, 1984), and Kenneth L. Kusmer's unpublished paper "Xenophobia, Violence, and Social Change in the United States and Germany, 1830–1945" (German Historical Institute, Washington, D.C., 1995).

8. Willie Lee Rose, *Slavery and Freedom* (New York: Oxford University Press, 1982), 3–17; Ira Berlin, *Slaves Without Masters: The Free Negro in the Antebellum South* (New York: Random House, 1974), 20–50; Duncan J. MacLeod, *Slavery, Race, and the American Revolution* (New York: Cambridge University Press, 1974). See also Leonard P. Curry, *The Free Black in Urban America, 1800–1850* (Chicago: University of Chicago Press, 1981), 174–215.

9. James H. Moorhead, *American Apocalypse: Yankee Protestants and the Civil War, 1860–1869* (New Haven: Yale University Press, 1978); Edmund Wilson, *Patriotic Gore: Studies in the Literature of the American Civil War* (New York: Oxford University Press, 1962), 91–98.

10. Eric Foner, *Reconstruction: America's Unfinished Revolution, 1863–1877* (New York: Harper & Row, 1988), xxiv–28.

11. Ibid., 255–79, 446–59; Larry Kincaid, "Two Steps Forward, One Step Backward," in *The Great Fear: Race in the Mind of America*, ed. Gary Nash and Richard Weiss (New York: Holt, Rinchart & Winston, 1970). See also William Gillette, *Retreat from Reconstruction, 1869–1879* (Baton Rouge: Louisiana State University Press, 1979), ix–55.

12. Winthrop D. Jordan, *White over Black: American Attitudes Toward the Negro, 1550–1812* (Chapel Hill: University of North Carolina Press, 1968), 342–426; Berlin, *Slaves Without Masters*, 79–107.

13. Foner, *Reconstruction*, 281–88, 320–21, 449, 484–510.

14. Gary B. Nash, *Forging Freedom: The Formation of Philadelphia's Black Community, 1720–1840* (Cambridge: Harvard University Press, 1988), 172–83, 212–79; Stuart Bruchey, *Enterprise: The Dynamic Economy of a Free People* (Cambridge: Harvard University Press, 1990), 144–47, 161.

15. Robert Kelley, *The Cultural Pattern in American Politics: The First Century* (New York: Alfred A. Knopf, 1979), 228–55; Foner, *Reconstruction*, 523–27. On contemporary views of depressions, see Edward C. Kirkland, *Industry Comes of Age: Business, Labor, and Public Policy, 1860–1897* (Chicago: Quadrangle Books, 1967), 7.

16. *Southern Black Leaders of the Reconstruction Era*, ed. Howard N. Rabinowitz (Urbana: University of Illinois Press, 1982); Eric Foner, *"The Tocsin of Freedom": The Black Leadership of Radical Reconstruction* (pamphlet, Gettysburg College, 1992).

17. Stanley Crouch, "Race Is Over," *New York Times Magazine*, September 29, 1996, 170–71. In a more scholarly vein, see Gary B. Nash's important essay "The Hidden History of Mestizo America," *Journal of American History* 82 (December 1995): 941–62.

18. Tom Wicker, *Tragic Failure: Racial Integration in America* (New York: William Morrow & Co., 1996).

19. Robert Wiebe, *Self-Rule: A Cultural History of American Democracy* (Chicago: University of Chicago Press, 1995), 103, 126–30; Bruchey, *Enterprise*, 279; Foner, *Reconstruction*, 587–97, 612; Robert L. Woodson, "The End of Racism?" *New York Times*, September 23, 1995, 23.

20. Tom Engelhardt, *The End of Victory Culture: Cold War America and the Disillusionment of a Generation* (New York: Basic Books, 1995). On the persistence of the "American Dream" among lower-class blacks, see Jennifer L. Hochschild, *Facing Up to the American Dream: Race, Class, and the Soul of the Nation* (Princeton: Princeton University Press, 1995).

# List of Contributors

CHRISTOPHER BEEM directs the Council on Civil Society, a project co-sponsored by the University of Chicago Divinity School and the Institute for American Values. The author of numerous scholarly and popular articles, he is currently working on a book on the history of the concept of civil society.

LAWRENCE D. BOBO is Professor of Sociology and Director of the Center for Research on Race, Politics, and Society at the University of California, Los Angeles. He is a member of the Board of Directors of the Social Science Research Council and co-author of *Racial Attitudes in America* (1988).

ERWIN CHEMERINSKY is the Legion Lex Professor of Law at the University of Southern California Law Center. He is author of *Interpreting the Constitution* (1987) and many law review articles on civil liberties and civil rights.

GERALD EARLY is the Merle Kling Professor of Modern Letters and Director of the African and Afro-American Studies Program at Washington University. His book *The Culture of Bruising: Essays on Prizefighting, Literature, and Modern American Culture* (1994) won the National Book Critics Circle Award for criticism in 1994. He has edited *Lure and Loathing: Essays on Race, Identity, and the Ambivalence of Assimilation* (1993) and in 1994 published a personal memoir, *Daughters: On Family and Fatherhood.*

JEAN BETHKE ELSHTAIN, the Laura Spelman Rockefeller Professor of Social and Political Ethics at the University of Chicago, writes on issues of public morality, including books on war and feminism. Her latest book is *Democracy on Trial* (1994).

**LAWRENCE H. FUCHS** is the Meyer and Walter Jaffe Professor of American Civilization and Politics at Brandeis University. His latest book, *The American Kaleidoscope: Race, Ethnicity, and the Civic Culture* (1990), has won three national prizes.

**NATHAN GLAZER** is professor emeritus of Education and Social Structure at Harvard University and co-editor of *The Public Interest*. His many books include *Ethnic Dilemmas, 1964–1982* (1983), *The Limits of Social Policy* (1988), and most recent, *We Are All Multiculturalists Now* (1997).

**JOHN HIGHAM**, professor of History Emeritus at The Johns Hopkins University, is a past President of the Organization of American Historians and was until recently a member of the Board of Trustees of the Balch Institute for Ethnic Studies. His writings include *Send These to Me: Immigrants in Urban America*, rev. ed. (Baltimore: Johns Hopkins University Press, 1984); *Strangers in the Land: Patterns of American Nativism, 1860–1925*, 2nd ed. (New Brunswick, N.J.: Rutgers University Press, 1988); and, most recently, "The Future of American History," *Journal of American History*, March 1994.

**DOUGLAS S. MASSEY** directs the Population Studies Center at the University of Pennsylvania. His *American Apartheid: Segregation and the Making of the Underclass* (1993), written with Nancy A. Denton, has received wide acclaim. The essay in the present volume was previously published in *Social Service Review*, 68 (December 1994): 471–87. Copyright © 1994 by the University of Chicago.

**DIANE RAVITCH**, a historian of education, is Senior Research Scholar at New York University and a nonresident Senior Scholar at the Brookings Institution. Her books include *The Great Schools Wars: New York City, 1805–1973* (1974), *The Schools We Deserve* (1985), *The Troubled Crusade: American Education, 1945–1980* (1983), *National Standards in American Education* (1995), and numerous edited works.

# Index